Why Shofars Wail in Scripture and Today

—The Exciting Stories and Miracles!

Dr. Mary A. Bruno, an ordained minister, serves with her husband, the Reverend Doctor Rocco Bruno. She is Co-founder and Vice President of Interdenominational Ministries International, and Co-founder/Vice Chancellor of IMI Bible College and Seminary in Vista, California. She has earned a Ministerial Diploma from L.I.F.E. Bible College; a Master of Theology, and Doctor of Ministry Degree from School of Bible Theology, which awarded her the Honorary Doctor of Divinity Degree. She earned a Doctor of Theology Degree, from IMI Bible College & Seminary; and Doctor of Philosophy Degree in Pastoral Christian Counseling from Evangelical Theological Seminary.

Her talks include humor, witty insights, and Scripture. She has preached in the USA and abroad. Turnouts skyrocketed when she presided over the Vista Women's Aglow. Her "Words in Season" radio broadcast aired in the 1980's and 90's over KPRZ and KCEO in San Diego County. Watch for her next book release at www.ministrylit.com. Also available at www.amazon.com.

For speaking engagements:
Visit the website: www.ministrylit.com.
Email: drmaryabruno@ministrylit.com
Or write:
Dr. Mary A. Bruno
P.O. Box 2107
Vista, CA 92085-2107 USA

Publication Date: July 2016.
Printed in the United States of America
Mary A. Bruno, Vista, California, July 2016
International Standard Book Number ISBN-13: 978-1533383020
International Standard Book Number ISBN-10: 1533383022
BISAC Category: RELO12040 Religion / Christian Life / Inspirational
Library of Congress Control Number, LCCN: 2016908503
CreateSpace Independent Publishing Platform, North Charleston, SC

Why Shofars Wail in Scripture and Today

—The Exciting Stories and Miracles!

By
Mary A. Bruno, Ph.D.

Pastor Patrick Lynch —
God has great things
ahead for your ministry!
Dare to lift up your voice
like a Shofar. Isa. 58:1

Dr. Mary A. Bruno

03/03/2017

More by Dr. Mary A. Bruno

1. *STUDY GUIDE/JOURNAL*—FOR USE WITH—*Why Shofars Wail in Scripture and Today—The Exciting Stories and Miracles!*
2. *What to Consider When Making Important Decisions (A Workbook for Making Wholesome Choices).* Coming Soon!

Watch for Dr. Bruno's new books and other ministry materials at, www.ministrylit.com and www.amazon.com.

Personal Evangelism Tracts:

Keep a stack of Dr. Bruno's uplifting tracts on hand to share. They may become God's "words in season" for a cashier, food server, person at a bus stop or waiting room. Someone may be in crisis or just need to hear an encouraging word from God.

"Is My Heart Right With God?" (How to have peace with God.)
"The Shofar Calls" (What they mean. How to have shofar impact.)
"Remember Me" (Faith strengtheners for crisis times)
"When Pressures Seem Unbearable" (Victory at a breaking point)

Contact Dr. Bruno through the website: www.ministrylit.com.
Email: drmaryabruno@ministrylit.com
Or write:

Dr. Mary A. Bruno
P.O. Box 2107
Vista, CA 92085-2107 USA

How to Order the Study Guide/Journal

Want to learn more from your shofar study?

Discover God's long-range plans for the shofar blowers and people affected by their ministry. Understand how God prepared and helped them and still helps people like you. Recognize His guidance that led to where you are today.

If new to guided study and journaling, this is a good place to start. God will remind you of places in His Word that will flood your soul with truth that begs to go in your notes. Those sacred *nuggets*/Journal entries will become your love gifts from God and a treasure of Scripture and wisdom for reflection and teaching.

God intends more for you regarding these books than a few hours of reading enjoyment. You may never be the same!

This Study Guide/Journal is Ideal for group study and/or personal spiritual enrichment! Enjoy jotting down what God teaches you—on 320 8"x10" white pages—with spacious lines that are ready to document your answers, insights, comments, lessons learned, prayer requests/potential miracles, and notes.

Order Today: *STUDY GUIDE/JOURNAL—FOR USE WITH— Why Shofars Wail in Scripture and Today—The Exciting Stories and Miracles!* ISBN: 9781535012584
www.ministrylit.com and www.amazon.com. AndE-Book/Kindle

Why Shofars Wail in Scripture and Today—   By Mary A. Bruno, Ph.D.

vi

How to Order This Book

Order *Why Shofars Wail in Scripture and Today—The Exciting Stories and Miracles!* Authored by Mary A. Bruno, Ph.D.

See Dr. Bruno's writings, at www.ministrylit.com. Her books are also available at www.amazon.com.

Or write:

Dr. Mary A. Bruno
P.O. Box 2107
Vista, CA 92085-2107 USA

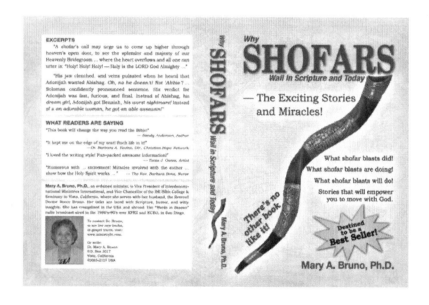

ISBN 9781533383020

Also available in LARGE PRINT (ISBN: 978-1539406891), and as E-Book/Kindle. The Audio Version is coming soon.

Why Shofars Wail in Scripture and Today—   By Mary A. Bruno, Ph.D.

Drs. Rocco and Mary A. Bruno, by the Liberty Bell in Philadelphia, Pennsylvania.

Why Shofars Wail in Scripture and Today—   By Mary A. Bruno, Ph.D.

To Father God and His dedicated kings and priests who boldly sound their shofars for His glory—within and without His sanctuaries.

Why Shofars Wail in Scripture and Today—   By Mary A. Bruno, Ph.D.

ix

**Rocco and Mary A. Bruno sounded the shofar
by The White House in Washington, D.C.**

**Color photos: Photos from this book (and more)
are viewable online at <u>www.ministrylit.com</u>.**

Why Shofars Wail in Scripture and Today—   By Mary A. Bruno, Ph.D.

Foreword

There is something very mysterious about those shofar sounds mentioned in the Bible. God longs to communicate with us and knows exactly what will get our attention quickly. He speaks to His people through His promises, which are found throughout His Word. He also gives divine illumination, encouragement, warnings, and blessings to those who search for Him. Jesus says:

"He who has My commandments and keeps them, it is he who loves Me. And he who loves Me will be loved by My Father, and I will love Him and manifest Myself to him" (John 14:21).

Have you ever heard a particular sound and wondered why you suddenly felt as if it came from heaven itself? Has a worship song ever gripped your heart to the core, and caused you to weep as the music and words pierced through your soul?

Have you ever heard a shofar's wail and wondered why you cried? It is incredible how that sound is like none other. It has a voice all of its own and seems to issue a calling that must not be ignored. Shofar cries can issue warnings, announce victory, and release heartfelt tears of praise, joy, and thanksgiving to God.

When I invited Dr. Mary A. Bruno to come with me to the Eagles' Wings event (that was alive with wailing shofars), it seemed as if God had a divine purpose for her to

Why Shofars Wail in Scripture and Today—   By Mary A. Bruno, Ph.D.

xi

be there. When she saw that beautiful shofar, I knew that she had to buy it! This was her time! This was her day to step into a fresh and glorious relationship with Jesus Christ. This was why she came! That event began a divine journey that led her to write this book.

As you explore the Old Testament and New Testament passages, I pray that you will receive God's individual healing, and anointing to appreciate the relationship He desires to enjoy with you. May the shofar's call stir your heart with a new understanding of those soul-searching cries that sound from earth to heaven, and one day soon will wail from heaven to earth.

Rev. Barbara A. Yovino, Ph.D.

www.chn.cc

Dr. Mary A. Bruno's first Yemenite shofar seemed to call to the depths of her soul.

Why Shofars Wail in Scripture and Today—   By Mary A. Bruno, Ph.D.

xii

Acknowledgements

Many thanks to God's generous people who have helped to make this book a reality; especially the Reverend Doctor Rocco Bruno, my multi-talented, tri-lingual husband, man of God, and missionary to Italy. His steady support is my treasure in his earthen vessel.

Pastor Geremia Albano, Senior Pastor of Chiesa Evangelica di Caposele, AV, Italy, and his lovely wife, Michela. Their stories are included in chapters 32 and 34.

The Reverend Shawn Brix, of ReFrame Media, a division of Back to God Ministries International, Palos Heights, Illinois, has permitted the use of his article "The Final Sacrifice" that appeared in *Today* in March/April 2011, Vol. 62.[1] His article was mentioned in chapter 28.

The Reverend Doctor Rosa L. Davis, Founder of The Gleaning Field, (homeless ministry) in Vista, California,[2] recommended the adoption of this book by Bible Colleges.

Veronica Coenraad Jenks, Director of KAIROS Resource Center at Eagles' Wings, taught me to blow a shofar. The first chapter tells how God used Veronica to affect my life.

Lorri Jennex, author, and business owner has shared writing tips, insights, and ongoing encouragement.[3]

[1] http://today.reframemedia.com/archives/the-final-sacrifice-2011-04-22. See chapter 28 of this writing entitled, Shofar Blasts Predicted – Part 1

[2] www.gleaningfield.com

[3] lorri@lorrijennex.com

Why Shofars Wail in Scripture and Today—   By Mary A. Bruno, Ph.D.

xiii

Kim Kinman, Owner of KK Grafix, in Fallbrook, California, took my basic ideas and a shofar photo, and then applied her design skills and talents to transform them into the book cover.

The Reverends Michael and Michelle Lucas, of Web Options, LLC,[4] Oceanside, California, designed the website.[5]

Carmine and Antonietta Merola, of Caposele, Italy. Carmine was our photographer/videographer during church services. Antonietta experienced a startling miracle from God in our kitchen, as told in chapter 32.

Pastor Michael Nasrallah, of Unconditional Love Ministries, Jerusalem, Israel, and Carrollton, Texas,[6] surprised all at the conference dining table when he confirmed God's will to write this book. Moments after we had met at Eagles' Wings, he looked at me and prophesied, "You are going to write a book. You already have the outline, title, and publisher." Those words encouraged me to complete the assignment that God started at one Eagles' Wings event and confirmed 19 months later at another. The account of his prophecy is in the first chapter.

Bishop Robert Stearns, Founder and Executive Director of Eagles' Wings, in Clarence, New York,[7] may not have known that his tremendously anointed ministry would stir my heart to move with God and a wailing shofar.

---

[4] www.weboptionsllc.com, mlucas@weboptions.net, michellelucas@weboptions.net
[5] www.ministrylit.com
[6] www.unconditionalloveministries.com
[7] www.eagleswings.to

Why Shofars Wail in Scripture and Today—   By Mary A. Bruno, Ph.D.

xiv

Pastors Matthew Stoehr, D.D., and Amy Stoehr have been faithful encouragers. They shepherd The River Family Church, 390 Mimosa Avenue, Vista, California.[8]

The Reverend John Welch, retired Baptist minister (with John Welch Ministries), gave a timely comment that prodded me into a life-changing, shofar-blowing, ministry adventure with Rocco, my husband. See chapter 31 for how the Lord used John's *word in season* to motivate me into a new ministry adventure with God and Rocco.

The Reverend Barbara Anne Yovino, Ph.D., has enriched this effort with her prayers and encouragement. She serves as Vice Pres. and Dir. of the Christian Hope Network, in Brooklyn, New York,[9] which has partnered with John Ramirez Ministries,[10] and Matt Sorger Ministries.[11] She is an Assoc. Pastor at Gateway City Church, in Brooklyn;[12] New York State Coordinator for the Day to Pray for the Peace of Jerusalem; New York Dir. of God.tv Prayer Line;[13] and advisor for IMI Bible College & Seminary. She was right there in chapter one when this story began.

San Diego Christian Writers Guild (SDCWG). The critique groups of Escondido, Oceanside, National City, and San Marcos, have given valuable help and suggestions.[14]

Others who have shared editorial comments and counsel: Miranda Bellman; the Rev. Barbara L. Bone; the late, Al Collins; Cindy Collins; Doris Corie, former President

---

[8] www.theriverfamilychurchnc.org
[9] www.chn.cc
[10] www.johnramirez.org
[11] www.mattsorger.com
[12] www.gatewaycitychurch.net
[13] www.god.tv
[14] http://sandiegocwg.com.

Why Shofars Wail in Scripture and Today—   By Mary A. Bruno, Ph.D.

xv

of the San Diego Aglow; Miryam Evans; Tonia J. Garza; the Rev. Doctor Deone Gushwa; the Rev. Phadrae T. Halfacre; the Rev. Daralene Hardrick; Glen D. Hayden; The Rev. Amy Hoover; the Rev. Duane Hoover; Pascal John Imperato, Author[15]; Nancy C. Karvonen, Author; the Rev. Carol Kasberger; Beth Lucas; Ret. SgtMaj. James Lucas; Diana Mamary; Pastor Arthur Montgomery,[16] the Rev. Mary Anne Moyer; Ben Pedersen; Justeen E. Pedersen; Mary Quatrone; Evelyn C. Rubidoux; the Rev. Carrie M. Smith; the Rev. Faith E. Volkerts.

Other Writers—Blessings to the many gifted writers whose books and websites (listed in the bibliography) have enhanced the research phase of this book. Any errors or omissions were purely unintentional.

May God reward each person's labor for His glory.

Mary A. Bruno, Ph.D.

---

[15] JohnPascal.com
[16] www.fbichrist.com

Why Shofars Wail in Scripture and Today—   By Mary A. Bruno, Ph.D.

xvi

Contents

Why Shofars Wail in Scripture and Today—   By Mary A. Bruno, Ph.D.

xvii

Why Shofars Wail in Scripture and Today—   By Mary A. Bruno, Ph.D.

xviii

Why Shofars Wail in Scripture and Today—   By Mary A. Bruno, Ph.D.

xix

Why Shofars Wail in Scripture and Today—   By Mary A. Bruno, Ph.D.

xx

Why Shofars Wail in Scripture and Today—   By Mary A. Bruno, Ph.D.

xxi

Why Shofars Wail in Scripture and Today—   By Mary A. Bruno, Ph.D.

xxii

Why Shofars Wail in Scripture and Today—   By Mary A. Bruno, Ph.D.

xxiii

Why Shofars Wail in Scripture and Today—   By Mary A. Bruno, Ph.D.

xxiv

Why Shofars Wail in Scripture and Today—   By Mary A. Bruno, Ph.D.

xxv

Why Shofars Wail in Scripture and Today—   By Mary A. Bruno, Ph.D.

xxvi

Preface

This book addresses every shofar mention in Scripture (72 in 63 verses) and God's involvement in events that led to the shofar blasts, the miracles that followed, and what can happen for those who dare to blow a shofar. Chapter one tells of how God used a shofar and a prophet to urge this writing that took eight years to finish.

Events that led to the shofar blasts appear in standard biblical sequence. In some chapters, it seemed fitting to backtrack enough to show mindsets and events that preceded the shofar incidents. *Poetic license* has helped to flesh out feelings and bring scenes to life.

Hebrew purists may know the plural form of the *shofar* can be *shofrot, shofroth or shophroth*. Because *The Complete Jewish Bible* used "shofars" to indicate the plural, I have chosen to do the same.

While reading this book (and working through the Study Guide/Journal if you have it), God will be near to you and unveil spiritual truths. "Ah, ha!" illumination will delight your soul as He reveals His handiwork for the Bible characters, and in your life. You may think of those precious moments as being in your secret place of the Most High.

If we had known that the last four chapters would be about our shofar blowing ministry adventure (with photos), we might have dressed better and upgraded the camera.

The *New King James Version* (NKJV) is the primary source of Scripture unless otherwise shown.

Why Shofars Wail in Scripture and Today—   By Mary A. Bruno, Ph.D.

Other translations that were cited as they were used:

New *American Standard Bible* (NASB). Scripture taken from the New American Standard Bible © Copyright 1960, 1962, 1963, 1968, 1971, 1972, 1973, 1975, 1977, 1995 by the Lockman Foundation. Used by permission.

New Revised Standard Version Bible: Catholic Edition (NRSVCE) New Revised Standard Version Bible: Catholic Edition, copyright © 1989, 1993 the Division of Christian Education of the National Council of the Churches of Christ in the United States of America. Used by permission. All rights reserved.

Amplified Bible, Classic Edition (AMPC) Copyright © 1954, 1958, 1962, 1964, 1965, 1987 by The Lockman Foundation.

The Amplified Bible. Scripture quotations marked (AMP) are taken from The Amplified Bible, Old Testament. Copyright © 1965, 1987 by Zondervan Corporation. Used by permission. All rights reserved. Scripture quotations marked (AMP) are also taken from The Amplified Bible, New Testament. Copyright © 1954, 1958, 1987, by The Lockman Foundation. Used by permission.

Complete Jewish Bible. Scriptures marked (CJB) are taken from the Complete Jewish Bible by David H. Stern. Copyright © 1998. All rights reserved. Used by permission of Messianic Jewish Publishers, 6120 Day Long Lane, Clarksville, MD 21029. www.messianicjewish.net.

The King James Version (KJV). Word studies were from the *Holy Bible, King James Version* in *Strong's Exhaustive Concordance of the Bible* at the Blue Letter Bible: http://www.blbclassic.org/index. cfm.

The Orthodox Jewish Bible. Scripture marked (OJB) taken from The Orthodox Jewish Bible. Copyright © 2011 by AFI International. All rights reserved.

Why Shofars Wail in Scripture and Today—   By Mary A. Bruno, Ph.D.

xxviii

Bible Book Abbreviations

Old Testament:

Genesis	Gen.
Exodus	Ex.
Leviticus	Lev.
Numbers	Num.
Deuteronomy	Deut.
Joshua	Josh.
Judges	Judg.
Ruth	Ruth
1 Samuel	1 Sam.
2 Samuel	2 Sam.
1 Kings	1 Kings
2 Kings	2 Kings
1 Chronicles	1 Chron.
2 Chronicles	2 Chron.
Ezra	Ezra
Nehemiah	Neh.
Esther	Est.
Job	Job
Psalm(s)	Ps.
Proverbs	Prov.
Ecclesiastes	Eccl.
Song of Solomon	Song.
Isaiah	Isa.

Jeremiah	Jer.
Lamentations	Lam.
Ezekiel	Ezek.
Daniel	Dan
Hosea	Hos.
Joel	Joel
Amos	Amos
Obadiah	Obad.
Jonah	Jonah
Micah	Mic.
Nahum	Nah.
Habakkuk	Hab.
Zephaniah	Zeph.
Haggai	Hag.
Zechariah	Zech.
Malachi	Mal.

New Testament:

Matthew	Matt.
Mark	Mark
Luke	Luke
John	John
Acts	Acts
Romans	Rom.
1 Corinthians	1 Cor.

Why Shofars Wail in Scripture and Today—   By Mary A. Bruno, Ph.D.

xxix

2 Corinthians	2 Cor.
Galatians	Gal.
Ephesians	Eph.
Philippians	Phil.
Colossians	Col.
1 Thessalonians	1 Thess.
2 Thessalonians	2 Thess.
1 Timothy	1 Tim.
2 Timothy	2 Tim.
Titus	Titus
Philemon	Philem.
Hebrews	Heb.
James	James
1 Peter	1 Peter
2 Peter	2 Peter
1 John	1 John
2 John	2 John
3 John	3 John
Jude	Jude
Revelation	Rev.

Why Shofars Wail in Scripture and Today—   By Mary A. Bruno, Ph.D.

30

Chapter 1
The Call

It was doubtful that Mary A. Bruno, D.Min., Th.D., Ph.D.(PCC), D.D., (an ordained minister) could release a powerful shofar blast that could rattle a soul. However, a chorus of shofars at an Eagles' Wings conference in July 2008 ignited her intense attraction for a stunning shofar.

The Reverend Doctor Barbara A. Yovino, Mary's close friend, had invited her to the event. On God's cutting edge in ministry, Barbara served as Vice President of the Christian Hope Network (CHN),[17] United States Coordinator for the Day to Pray for the Peace of Jerusalem, Associate Pastor at Gateway City Church, in Brooklyn, and Advisor for the IMI Bible College and Seminary. She would serve later as the New York Director for the God.tv Prayer Line. CHN has also partnered with Evangelist John Ramirez Ministries,[18] and with Matt Sorger Ministries.[19]

God had arranged events eight years earlier to free Mary for the Eagles' Wings meeting. He had led to suspend

---

[17] www.chn.cc
[18] www.johnramirez.org
[19] www.mattsorger.com

Why Shofars Wail in Scripture and Today—   By Mary A. Bruno, Ph.D.

31

enrollment for the IMI Bible College and Seminary that she and the Reverend Doctor Rocco Bruno, her husband, had co-founded. Rocco ran their secular business, and she oversaw the school until all of the students were graduated. Then God led her to help Rocco in their business until they sold it six years later in 2008. As calves released from a stall, they longed to feast and frolic in God's green pastures.

Rocco wanted to visit his family in Italy, where preaching opportunities awaited. Mary spoke very little Italian, and being unable to communicate for three months was not her idea of a good time. He had her blessing to stay with Concetta, his sweet sister, and enjoy her pampering.

Eagles' Wings Conference—Maryland
Exhausted and spiritually dry as a twig, Mary joined Barbara for the Eagles' Wings event in Fort Washington, Maryland. Songs of praise, joyful shouts and wailing shofars filled the church. Sometimes the shofars sounded in spontaneous unison from various parts of the congregation.

Something about those shofars caused Mary's tears to flow. God was using them to release floods of refreshing upon her spiritually dry ground. Could He have led her to travel over 3,000 miles to experience their spiritual impact?

The Reverend Doctor Robert Stearns (later Bishop Stearns), with Stephen Jenks and others on the Eagles' Wings worship team, led the audience in glorious worship to God. Shofar calls opened Mary's spirit as she raised her hands and wept in humble adoration before the Lord.

One of the conference speakers elaborated about the shofar's supernatural impact upon human hearts and events. He said the shofar's sound waves never stop, but they keep flowing upward, and through the heavens.

Why Shofars Wail in Scripture and Today—   By Mary A. Bruno, Ph.D.

32

Rodlyn Park, Global Coordinator for the Day to Pray for the Peace of Jerusalem, taught on the surprising effects that spoken words have on water (and plants?). Mary wondered if the shofar had a similar impact on humans.

People danced freely, as King David had done, while others waved colorful banners to exalt the LORD Most High. They sang and celebrated God's incredible Presence as believers knelt or surrendered themselves at the altar when the Holy Spirit moved upon the congregation.

Books, banners, and ministry tools graced colorful display tables in the foyer. One presentation offered something that seemed to call to the depths of Mary's being.

Jumbo Shofar

It was like a precious jumbo–jewel, amid dozens of common shofars. That huge brown animal horn was no ordinary Jumbo-Shofar. It measured 44 inches around the three twisted brown arcs that formed its body. Streaks of dark maroon encompassed its almond-shaped mouthpiece. Its dark colors gradually faded to various shades of brown keratin that formed its length. Telltale places inside the bell end must have escaped the cleansing process. The horn's supernatural attraction tugged relentlessly at Mary's spirit.

"This is a Yemenite Shofar, from an African Kudu's horn," petite and perky Veronica Coenraad (Now Mrs. Stephen Jenks) proclaimed. "The oval mouthpiece will make it easier to blow because your lips can nestle right into it." Her eyes flashed with holy enthusiasm as her radiant smile and swishing dark hair emphasized every word.

Sensing God's involvement, Barbara raised a curious eyebrow and flashed a delighted smile.

Why Shofars Wail in Scripture and Today—   By Mary A. Bruno, Ph.D.

33

Mary lifted and stroked the polished shofar. It had perfect balance in her hands, as though it belonged there. Excitement rippled through her being. She knew people who had purchased shofars but could not blow a note. Sadly, their beautiful horns had become mute objects of art. Mary placed the glistening horn back on the table, sighed, turned, and walked away. But that remarkable shofar kept tugging at her heartstrings. Whenever they neared the display, her eyes locked on the horn as her spirit responded to its pull. She longed to put it to her lips but left without it.

Barbara knew that God was doing something special. She observed Mary as Mary observed the shofar, and God probably smiled and observed them both.

Dare she attempt the lofty goal of launching a shofar blast when respected others had tried, but could not produce a sound? The dreaded fear of failure had reared its mocking head. The meeting would end the next day. Mary had to settle her struggle with that shofar. God would hear about her intense attraction to that handsome horn.

"Lord, do You want me to buy that[20] thing? If so, would you, please, confirm it by helping me to blow a long and recognizable blast on it tomorrow?" she prayed.

God was silent that night as Mary wrestled with thoughts of the shofar and risk of public humiliation. When morning came, she and Barbara almost ran to the display. The shofar was still there. Whew! Mustering all courage, her voice almost quivered as she asked, "May I try to blow this?"

"Sure!" Veronica smiled while sanitizing the tip with

---

20 Jonah 1 Unwelcome Assignments By Kent Crockett www ..,
http://storage.cloversites.com/makinglifecountministriesinc/documents/Jonah%201-
(accessed April 12, 2016).

Why Shofars Wail in Scripture and Today—   By Mary A. Bruno, Ph.D.

a disposable wipe. "The secret is to buzz your lips. It is not about how hard you force air through, but the soft and gentle vibration. Moisten your lips and make a *very* tiny sliver of an opening so air can *barely* escape. Then, *buzz* your lips and let the air out *very* slowly and gently." Her Christ-like eyes emphasized every word as though they were prophecies from God's Holy Throne.

Mary's heart was beating like a frenzied drummer. She raised the instrument to her lips. Onlooker's stares sent stun gun tingles through her back. She took a deep breath and tried to buzz[21] a note. A feeble wail squeaked out. She could build on that. Confidence swelled with a slightly louder blast. A third attempt sent a strong 15-second blast, that drew approving glances.

"I'll take it!"

Veronica's eyes beamed brightly. Her student had passed the buzz test, and she had made a sale. As far as they knew, that was the end of it. Mary would go home, display the horn, and blow it occasionally.

"I knew God was leading you to buy that shofar," Barbara whispered. "You could not tear your eyes from it![22] This was way out of your element." Mary nodded; unaware that God's plan was already in motion.

Veronica probably had no hint of how her *words in season* would affect Mary's life. That was no mere sales transaction—*God was involved!* If Veronica had not given her time and tips, this book might not be in print.

---

[21] mirror match - @arcaneadagio, http://arcaneadagio.tumblr.com/ (accessed April 12, 2016).

[22] This Is The Way We End (Or Begin Again) - Chapter 1 .., http://archiveofourown.org/chapters/14524063?add_comment_reply_id=56002849& s (accessed April 12, 2016).

Why Shofars Wail in Scripture and Today—   By Mary A. Bruno, Ph.D.

35

Research

God said nothing about why He led Mary to buy that particular shofar. Savage hunger to learn more launched exciting research in the Bible, which brought understanding. That was so like God! When He wants to teach someone something, He usually takes them straight to His Word and then breathes upon it and them.

The word "shofar" was not in the main concordance of *Strong's Exhaustive Concordance of the Bible*[23] (*Strong's*). It had to be in there somewhere! People blew them in Bible times. Translators may have called it something else, but what? She finally found it in Exodus 19:16.

A column to the right of each Bible reference gave a Hebrew Dictionary number for every word that translated as "trumpet." The Hebrew word 7782 *showphar* (or *shofar*) practically grinned, kicked its syllables, and waved hello from its place on the list. "Cornet" and "trumpet" were also translations of *showphar.* Their translated forms would make it easy to find all of the *shofar* references in Scripture.

While Rocco was in Italy, shofar research took most of Mary's waking hours at their home in Vista, California. Internet searches yielded helpful websites, such as BibleGateway.com. Yet, the blueletterbible.org website was a terrific study tool for the word *showphar, which* was there in black and white with a few splashes of bright blue. All 72 mentions of *shofar* were nestled within 63 Bible verses, just a keystroke away. What a gold mine! And it was free! May God reward His servants for helping people everywhere to mine the deeper riches of His Word!

---

[23] Strong, James, LL.D., S.T.D.
The New Strong's Exhaustive Concordance of the Bible
Nashville, Thomas Nelson Publishers, 1990

Why Shofars Wail in Scripture and Today—   By Mary A. Bruno, Ph.D.

36

Eagles' Wings Conference—Pennsylvania

Nineteen months later, while packing for another Eagles' Wings event, Mary flipped past her binder of shofar notes and whispered, "Lord, I wonder if anything will ever become of that," as she selected a book to read on her flight.

The conference took place in the heart of Amish country during the "Snowstorm of the Century." The anniversary of Mary's spiritual birthday would be the day after the event. She wondered if God might have a little something special for her as He often did on those days.

Prophecies

The blizzard forced road closures; therefore, everyone had to stay an extra night. Strangers dined with strangers and watched the falling snow. Barbara and Mary had barely started to eat, when Pastor Michael Nasrallah, of Unconditional Love Ministries;[24] whom, they had met moments earlier, glanced at Barbara and began to speak in a conversational tone. He commended what God was doing through Barbara and in her ministry—The Christian Hope Network (CHN),[25] and her support of other ministries. The shocker was when he said that God would be giving Barbara, her own facility for CHN, (which happened a year or so later, as he had spoken). The ladies quickly understood that a prophet of God was speaking to them.

Pastor Nasrallah turned to Mary and said, "You are going to write a book. You already have the title, outline, and publisher." He added that she would be traveling and speaking and that God would take care of her husband and children's needs. Mary's hair nearly stood on end, and her

---

[24] Jerusalem, Israel, and Carrolton, Texas, www.undonditionalloveministries.com
[25] www.chn.cc

Why Shofars Wail in Scripture and Today—   By Mary A. Bruno, Ph.D.

37

eyes were wide with wonder. God had sent His servant, (who had just arrived from Jerusalem), with the answer to her pre-flight question about whether anything would ever come from her research for a book about the shofar.

What God began at one Eagles' Wings Leadership Conference in July 2008, He confirmed at another Eagles' Wings Conference in February 2010. According to that prophetic word (eight years from when Mary bought her first shofar, and six years from Pastor Nasrallah's prophetic word); *Why Shofars Wail in Scripture and Today —The Exciting Stories and Miracles!,* was finally published in July 2016, and its *Study Guide/Journal,* in the following month.

God's supernatural help followed that prophecy. There would be no more questions about "if" Mary would write the book. Her commission from God verified that she would see it through. His dynamic life in Pastor Nasrallah's prophetic words confirmed His enabling power, purpose, and provision to finish her divinely assigned project.

What role did God play or will He play in the Holy Scriptures regarding *shofars?* Does He have a shofar? Who blew them—when, where, why, how, and what happened afterward? What will happen when shofars sound in the Last Days? Why would anyone want to blow one today?

Trace God's handiwork in what led to the shofar's cries thru the living pages of His Holy Word. Discover what God did when Rocco and Mary blew their shofar during a seven-week ministry trip across the United States of America, and in Canada, and Italy, and what happened after they returned home.

* * *

Why Shofars Wail in Scripture and Today—   By Mary A. Bruno, Ph.D.

38

Chapter 2
Transformation

A horn from a kosher animal was okay to make a shofar. Those from a cow or bull were ineligible because of their ties with heathen worship. A horn destined to be a shofar would need a lot of work to make room for a new owner's message. It had to stop relying on its animal instincts, and become a yielded and separated instrument with new desires. The shofar's change brought to mind transitions in one's walk with God.

Some have claimed that a good way for a horn to reach a turning point and break away from its former head was to let them spend ample time together in a heated setting, such as staying in hot water. Others have noted that staying just under the boiling point, and stewing in one's juices tends to promote separation.

The separation process may have been challenging, but it could happen quickly. As the connection deteriorated, the horn could break free of its old source of life. That sounded hopeful, but how did the horn demonstrate that it was liberated and ready to move on with the new master?

Why Shofars Wail in Scripture and Today—   By Mary A. Bruno, Ph.D.

39

A freedom test was involved. The new master helped the horn to reach a turning point, where it was ready to turn and leave the old head. When the horn broke free and yielded itself to the new master's hands, it was useful for a higher purpose. That new placement would be far greater than what the horn could have experienced while still bound to the old head. The separation had to happen first.

A liberated horn had to be open on the inside before it could convey anyone's message. It had to yield to the new owner's cleansing process and make room for his unobstructed breath (spirit life) to flow in purity, with power to proclaim a better message and higher calling.

The new master brought out his trusty flesh-probers to dig, pry, poke, prod and release things from the past that were out of harmony with his plans. He knew how to find the horn's old power point—the willful place that brought pain and damage, where it used to bully whatever got in the way. He had to sever that part and pierce an opening straight through the core of where it was attached. The former instrument of pride, pain, and stress would become a proclaimer of peace, purpose, and provision.

Cleansing

The new owner used his sharpest tools for the core-piercing pressure test that readied the horn to express his love and mercy. After a deep cleansing, the horn had to pass the artisan's whiff test to prove it had a sweet aroma.

Blood or cartilage (flesh?) left on the inner walls would stink. Some folks advised to rinse it with bleach water. Others vowed alcohol or Witch Hazel was a sure cure. Purists held out for dry bicarbonate of soda. One said to shake dry rice or tiny fish tank pebbles inside the shofar

Why Shofars Wail in Scripture and Today—   By Mary A. Bruno, Ph.D.

40

to loosen debris, yet others objected.

Many methods failed for *Shofie*, a beautiful but nasty-smelling shofar that Mary had purchased. Shofie's ripe stench might have gagged a maggot! As a last resort, Mary plugged the small end with wax earplugs and wondered what might rid the vile odor that not even myrrh could tame. *Ah-ha!* It summoned, like a red beacon from her white washing machine—Tide liquid laundry detergent! The label claimed to deodorize laundry.

Ignoring warnings that soaking a horn might cause it to crack, Mary was ready to try anything. Shofie held up well when filled with warm water and a few glugs of Tide. The beautiful horn smelled better after the bubbles burst.

Repeated shakeups and refills released more of the deep down stinky stuff. The clean, refilled and propped up horn stayed upright in an umbrella urn and marinated in silence while Liquid Tide worked its wonders. The next morning, flakes of what looked like jerky floated out with the murky gray liquid. Water from a garden hose shocked off the rest. Shofie's aroma sweetened as warm sunshine, and heavenly breezes carried away the residue of her past.

Separation from her old head was necessary, but that was not good enough for Shofie's high calling. Getting rid of the flesh and that disgusting odor was vital, but not enough to prepare for her new purpose. As it was with most shofars, Shofie needed more than separation, deep cleansing, tempering, and anointing. She needed polishing.

Polishing

A smear of oil was the usual way to launch a polishing and seasoning process. After its gentle anointing, a carefully chosen buffer rubbed the horn the wrong way

Why Shofars Wail in Scripture and Today—   By Mary A. Bruno, Ph.D.

41

until it heated up, but stayed yielded. Buffing produced a lovely radiance. A polished horn that reflected an artisan's image was sure to pass his buff test. Of course, someone said to skip the polishing and keep the rough edges from the old life, as reminders of its former head.

When buying a shofar, if possible, examine it carefully, inside and out, and then try it out to hear how it sounds. Rub your fingers over decorative stickers and check for rough spots, which could hide flaws.

One of the Brunos' costly shofars sported a gleaming gold seal that boasted, "Made in Jerusalem." All went well until one day while rinsing it with a hose . . . A cleansing stream lifted its golden sticker and exposed a botched repair job from when an artisan's drill had pushed too far. An ugly wound in the first curve had left a pencil-wide hole, nearly an inch long. Someone had plugged it with a hard charcoal-gray substance. The golden cover-up had worked well—until a water *pressure test* exposed the flaw that needed a serious clean out and skillful repair. When restored, the horn sounded sweet and sent a clear message.

Spiritual pressure tests can reveal ineffective cover-ups or hidden areas that need God's cleansing and healing touch. It is best to deal with them quickly while one can do so privately. Who wants to risk having a matter exposed publicly? Unwise choices could go viral in seconds!

King David experienced something similar when the prophet Nathan came to him privately and addressed his "secret" relationship with Bathsheba. If David had assumed nobody knew about their sin, he was mistaken.

The phrase, *we should keep this between us,"* should set off screaming sirens and flashing lights in one's spirit.

Why Shofars Wail in Scripture and Today—   By Mary A. Bruno, Ph.D.

42

Those nine words should shout—*Warning! Warning! Warning!—you are on a collision course with disaster!*

God knows what goes on in one's private life, and grants time, mercy, and grace to repent. However, as a skilled surgeon exposes and cuts out deadly cancer, to save a life, the Great Physician may reveal a hidden matter to break its power and protect a soul.

When approved for the new master's use, it was time to stop nursing old wounds, and time to honor the new master. Instead of repeating the same old tale of woe, it was time to focus on and proclaim a new message—His message of peace, life, hope, and joy.

* * *

Why Shofars Wail in Scripture and Today—   By Mary A. Bruno, Ph.D.

43

Rocco taught a Bible Study after dinner in Caposele.

They blew the shofar, pulled down strongholds and asked God to pour out His Spirit on Caposele, Italy.

Why Shofars Wail in Scripture and Today—   By Mary A. Bruno, Ph.D.

44

Chapter 3
The Message

Prayer, diligence, and a little knowledge can help to coax pleasing sounds from a shofar. Shofie sounded best when aimed about two-thirds of the way toward heaven. An internet search revealed that positioning the lips to pronounce the letter "P" before blowing a shofar could help to produce suitable sounds.

During its old life, a horn had enforced its former head's will and battled every opponent. However, belonging to a new master involved separation and cleansing, which changed everything and made all things new.

A cleansed, seasoned and yielded shofar could become a choice tool in its new master's hand. His life-breath and message of hope could flow powerfully through His new creation and stir hearers to action.

A shofar could issue a call to worship, declare God's Presence, and summon to battle. It could sound an alarm, announce a new king, and proclaim a fast, a feast, or freedom. The wordless commands or warnings delivered invitations to come up higher and closer to God.

Why Shofars Wail in Scripture and Today—   By Mary A. Bruno, Ph.D.

45

Blasts differed in sound but were all of the same length or duration. A very long single blast was equal in length to various combinations of the others.

Blood

The shofar was comprised of keratin, which was similar to fingernails or animal hooves. Blood, however, circulated at the large end where a horn attached to the head. Thus, a soul-piercing shofar cry—through the blood—may bring to mind God's calls to humankind down through the ages. His calls began in Genesis 3:9 when He called to Adam and said, "Where art thou?" (KJV). God knew where Adam and Eve were but wanted them to acknowledge the naked mess into which they had gotten themselves.

God lovingly draped Adam and Eve with new garments that He had made of animal skins (which involved bloodshed) and then unveiled His rescue plan in Genesis 3:15. He still loved them, and wanted them near; yet, sin as a wedge had driven them apart. God had a plan and made a way to lead them back home and back into His loving arms.

His plan would unfold through the *woman's seed*. Even though Eve had sinned, and Adam had willingly chosen to participate with her in that sin; Yeshua, the Messiah—God's Antidote for sin's curse—would come from *Eve's* offspring.

This time, God would not *create*, but would *Father* the only Son that He would ever *generate*—with human flesh. The Holy Spirit (Ruach Kodesh) with God's DNA would cause Mary (Eve's seed) to become pregnant so that God's only *begotten* Son could have, both, God's DNA and human flesh.

Why Shofars Wail in Scripture and Today—   By Mary A. Bruno, Ph.D.

46

Scarlet Thread

That promise became the *scarlet thread* of hope that wove throughout the Scriptures. It pointed by faith to Jesus Christ (Yeshua, the Messiah)—the Lamb of God. He would come and shed His Holy Blood on Mount Calvary.

By Genesis 4:1–5, sin had manifested as a deadly disease in Adam and Eve's family. Cain knew all about God's blood sacrifice requirement; however, he ignored God's instructions and proudly spread out his gorgeous produce before Him. Cain's bright cherries, pomegranates, beets, watermelons, and pumpkins, or whatever, were beautiful— but bloodless. That was not his most brilliant idea. God accepted Abel's obedient offering, (which God's fire from on high must have consumed). Cain was furious because the LORD had rejected his offering of imperfectly good works that shrunk and withered on God's altar when no fire fell.

Burning with resentment, Cain's sin-crazed mind may have reasoned that if God wanted a blood sacrifice, He could have one—with Abel's innocent blood! Blinded by jealousy and seething with rage, Cain killed his brother. He showed no regret as Abel's blood soaked into the soil. Cain's crime that grieved his parents also divided the family. God confronted Cain and held him accountable—for murder.

> And He said, "What have you done? The voice of your brother's blood cries out to Me from the ground."
> —Gen. 4:10

Flashbacks

Thoughts of Eden shot through the First Humans as they stared at Abel's cold and lifeless body. They remembered when they had entertained the charming

Why Shofars Wail in Scripture and Today—   By Mary A. Bruno, Ph.D.

47

serpent in the garden and had playfully toyed with his lies, and experimented with the forbidden fruit. Sadly, during the excitement of temptation's thrill, they had forgotten God's clear warning of sin's deadly consequence.

Grieving over their godly son's death, Adam, Eve, (and possibly Cain?) clung by faith to God's promise of the Redeemer. He would conquer the lying serpent, and crush sin's power.

The writer of *Hebrews* shows how the Old and New Testaments embrace God's promise. They give a clear picture of Christ's fulfillment and redemption.

> But you have come to Mount Zion and to the city of the living God, the heavenly Jerusalem, and to myriads of angels, to the general assembly and church of the firstborn who are enrolled in heaven, and to God, the Judge of all, and to the spirits of *the* righteous made perfect, and to Jesus, the mediator of a new covenant, and to the sprinkled blood, which speaks better than *the blood* of Abel.
>
> —Heb. 12:22–24 NASB

Angels would shudder when hammers pounded sharp spikes through Jesus' yielded hands and feet, and fastened Him to a God-forsaken cross. Nobody would take His life. Jesus—the Holy Lamb of God—*the Messiah*—would willingly *lay down* His life when He redeemed humankind.

Mercy

God's scarlet thread of promise would come—it would be Jesus' sacred blood!—the Only acceptable sacrifice that could take away sin. His *holy blood* drops would hit the soil, as great boulders of mercy that would crush sin's curse, overthrow death's power, and set us free. Jesus

Why Shofars Wail in Scripture and Today—   By Mary A. Bruno, Ph.D.

48

Christ—Yeshua, the Messiah—God's only begotten Son—would (and did) rise from the dead and lives forever!

> Therefore He is able also to save forever those who draw near to God through Him, since He always lives to make intercession for them.
>
> —Heb. 7:25 NASB

Father God still hears Jesus' blood that, as a Great Shofar, proclaims forgiveness from Heaven's Mercy Seat, and calls us to come up higher.

Five Shofar Blasts

There are at least five shofar blasts, possibly more.

The Tekiah sound is one long blast. In Deuteronomy 6:4–5 the tekiah's singleness, power, and duration remind listeners that the LORD God is one God.

The Shevarim blast produces a wailing sound that repeats three times. The combined length of the three wails equals that of a Tekiah. Many have claimed that this sound was reminiscent of Sisera's mother sobbing when he failed to return from battle. Others have likened it to a sad heart that longs to reunite with God.

The Teruah has nine rapid short blasts in groups of three (*ta, ta, ta—ta, ta, ta—ta, ta, ta*). When combined they equal the length of the Tekiah or Shevarim. The Teruah sends an alarm or wake-up call. In Leviticus 25:9–10, it also announces God's great Jubilee blessings and joy.

The Shevarim Teruah launches three wailing blasts followed by nine staccato blasts. Some have said this blast could open the heavens. (It may also open hearts to God.)

Why Shofars Wail in Scripture and Today—   By Mary A. Bruno, Ph.D.

49

The Tekiah Gedolah, the *Great Blast* or Great Tekiah, is one very long continuous blast that sounds for as long as possible. It urges the people to rejoice, praise, and welcome the Great Creator as it announces His presence or coming.

Shofars also called to anoint a new king, to call people to repentance, to sound an alarm, or to call troops to battle. They called to set captives free, to proclaim victory, to announce the day of Jubilee, and to announce a Sabbath or New Moon. Shofars alerted people to hear God's Word and to praise and worship Him.

Shofar blasts also brought big shakeups on Mount Sinai when they called God's people to hear His Word.

The shofar blasts were ready to sound.

Dr. Rocco Bruno read God's Word, declared God's promises and prayed for revival in his hometown.

Why Shofars Wail in Scripture and Today—   By Mary A. Bruno, Ph.D.

50

Chapter 4

Religious Error

T he Book of Exodus tells of the first shofar blasts in Scripture. They were God's love calls for His people to hear and obey His message and to recognize His anointed leader. In Exodus 19:5–10 and 20:2–5, the shofar called to leave false religious worship, to make God King, and to enter the safety of His protection and provision.

We shall review some of the happenings that led to when the first shofar wailed in Scripture. God's people had suffered under Egypt's bonds of slavery. He knew they were familiar with her idol worship—which may have explained why He addressed other gods and idols when He wrote the Ten Commandments. He had answered the Israelites' prayers for freedom, by a show of power with signs, wonders, and miracles and then, led them to where powerful shofar blasts would stir their hearts.

God may have used plagues and miracles to expose flaws in Egypt's false gods and to show the Egyptians and Israelites that He is the Living God. He also used them to

Why Shofars Wail in Scripture and Today—   By Mary A. Bruno, Ph.D.

51

sway Pharaoh to release those whom he thought were *his* slaves—who were, in fact, *God's* chosen people.

Hapil

The *Plague of Blood* came in Exodus 7:14–25 when God turned the Nile River to blood. It proved that Hapil, Egypt's river god, could give no clean water. Egyptians needed to learn that God could satisfy their thirsts.

> Jesus stood and cried out, saying, "If anyone is thirsty, let him come to Me and drink. He who believes in Me, as the Scripture said, 'From his innermost being will flow rivers of living water.'"
> —John 7:37b–38 NASB

Heket

The *Plague of Frogs*, from Exodus 8:1–15, exposed their misguided worship of the Nile—a breeding place for frogs, and a reminder of the goddess Heket. Her image had a frog's head and woman's body. Pregnant women mistakenly relied on her for relief during childbirth. They needed to call on the Living God, Who made humankind and frogs.

> For *in* six days the LORD made the heavens and the earth, the sea, and all that *is* in them, and rested the seventh day.
> —Ex. 20:11a

> God *is* our refuge and strength,
> A very present help in trouble.
> —Ps. 46:1

Osiris, Min, and Sopdet

The *Plague of Lice* (Some translations say *gnats*.),

Why Shofars Wail in Scripture and Today—   By Mary A. Bruno, Ph.D.

52

happened in Exodus 8:16–19 when the tiny insects sprang up from Egypt's beloved soil. (The fruit of the Egyptian's misguided worship had risen up to bite them.) They shuddered while rubbing the biting vermin from their scalp and hair. Their hope in Osiris, Min, and Sopdet, their false gods associated with soil and fertility, brought no relief. The next plague involved a slightly larger insect.

Super Fly

The *Plague of Flies* came in Exodus 8:20–32. Stinging flies swarmed people and animals that could not escape the scary drone of their wings. Tent-wives plucked them from food and fanned them away. The fly that symbolized Egypt's military power (Isa. 7:18)—their "Hero Fly" (Whose outstretched wings resembled a hero's cape.) had attacked when it should have assisted. They could have relied on the Living God and enjoyed His Presence and His help.

> For the LORD God *is* a sun and shield;
> The LORD will give grace and glory;
> No good *thing* will He withhold
> From those who walk uprightly.
>
> —Ps. 84:11

Nevis

The *Plague on Cattle* came in Exodus 9:1–7 as animals dropped dead and crashed Egypt's *stock market.* Horses (vehicles of war), donkeys (pickups), camels (limos/SUVS), and cattle, sheep, and goats (diversified investments) had collapsed without warning. Pricey reserves fell in a day and sent panic throughout the land! Puzzled Egyptians stared at their fallen livelihood and ruined retirement plans. They had trusted in lifeless idols,

Why Shofars Wail in Scripture and Today—   By Mary A. Bruno, Ph.D.

53

unaware that the Living God could have prospered all of their business ventures.

> And keep the charge of the LORD your God: to walk in His ways, to keep His statutes, His commandments, His judgments, and His testimonies, as it is written in the Law of Moses, that you may prosper in all that you do and wherever you turn.
> —1 Kings 2:3

Nevis, their sacred bull god, could not revive their bloated livestock that went belly-up in the field. However, Egypt had other big idols in her arsenal. It was time for Sekhmet to turn up the heat.

Sekhmet

The *Plague of Boils and Blains* erupted in Exodus 9:8–12, and created significant problems from within. God told Moses to take handfuls of soot from a furnace (brick kiln)[26] that signified Israel's cruel slavery, and sprinkle it toward heaven (right in front of Pharaoh). Ugly throbbing-hot boils cropped up on Pharaoh and everyone else, including the animals. It was not pretty.

They wondered where Sekhmet, Egypt's lion-headed goddess, was during all of this. She was supposed to deliver from plagues and cure diseases. An image of burning heat from their hot desert sun was her symbol. Yet, she could not stop the hot festering boils. Hope in Sekhmet cooled as the burning boils ached and drained. The Egyptians could have

---

[26] Va'eira - Wikipedia, the free encyclopedia, https://en.wikipedia.org/wiki/Va%27eira (accessed April 12, 2016).

Why Shofars Wail in Scripture and Today—   By Mary A. Bruno, Ph.D.

54

called upon the Living God—The Lion of Judah—and received His miraculous healing.

> Bless the LORD, O my soul,
> And forget not all His benefits:
> Who forgives all your iniquities,
> Who heals all your diseases.
>
> —Ps. 103:2–3

Geb

The *Plague of Hail* that slammed down with lightning in Exodus 9:18–34, topped all storms in Egypt's history. Huge hailstones killed farmhands and animals in open fields. Lightning bolts zapped laborers and scorched livestock. Fire devoured the ripened harvest and sent profits up in smoke.

Hope in Geb, their god of the earth, wilted. He was supposed to have helped their crops. If the Egyptians had trusted in the Living God, Who made the earth, they could have enjoyed productive seasons of prosperity.

> He shall be like a tree
>   Planted by the rivers of water,
>   That brings forth its fruit in its season,
>   Whose leaf also shall not wither;
> And whatever he does shall prosper.
>
> —Ps. 1:3

The death of their expensive slaves and animals drained Egypt's remaining finances. Her ripe and profitable crops lay buried under a cold slab of hail. Would or could Anubis—their esteemed jackal-headed god (Jackels look like wild dogs.), run to their rescue?

Why Shofars Wail in Scripture and Today—   By Mary A. Bruno, Ph.D.

55

Anubis and Serapis

The *Plague of Locusts* swarmed in like uninvited guests in Exodus 10:1–20. Chomping freeloaders devoured any surviving crops that had escaped the hail. Egyptians took hard hits in their money pouches because their stubborn ruler would not obey God. It was similar to when one refused to tithe (to give God 10 percent of his increase) and then wondered why there were financial problems.

Lifeless objects of worship, including Anubis, god of the fields, and Serapis, protector from locusts, could not prevail against the Living God. The Lord God Most High would have rescued the Egyptians if they had relied on Him.

> Because you have made the LORD, *who is* my refuge,
> *Even* the Most High, your dwelling place,
> No evil shall befall you,
> Nor shall any plague come near your dwelling;
> For He shall give His angels charge over you,
> To keep you in all your ways.
> —Ps. 91:9–11

By then, the Egyptians may have wondered if Ra, their sun god, could put a damper on the disasters.

Ra

The *Plague of Darkness* overshadowed the Egyptians in Exodus 10:21–23. Thick darkness covered Egypt with gloom for three days. The luster of their most important god, Ra, their flashy sun god, faded when God put out Ra's lights. The people needed to know Jesus—(Yeshua) the Messiah. He could have brightened their lives.

Why Shofars Wail in Scripture and Today—   By Mary A. Bruno, Ph.D.

56

> Then Jesus spoke to them again, saying, "I am the light of the world. He who follows Me shall not walk in darkness, but have the light of life."
>
> —John 8:12

Confused Egyptians stumbled in thick darkness, and pondered the Living God, who had exposed their fake deities' weaknesses. They scratched their vermin-infested heads, squeezed painful boils, mourned fallen gods, longed for light, and wondered how they would pay their bills. Their faith in Pharaoh and his son was another mistake.

False god-king

The *Plague of Death on the Firstborn,* the final plague, brought great anguish in Exodus 11:4–7 and 12:17–30. Pharaoh and his eldest child claimed to be god-kings. Sadly, Pharaoh could save neither his son nor any of Egypt's firstborn, who died that dreadful night. Egyptians needed to know the True and Living God, Who loved them.

> For God so loved the world that He gave His only begotten Son, that whoever believes in Him should not perish but have everlasting life. For God did not send His Son into the world to condemn the world, but that the world through Him might be saved.
>
> —John 3:16, 17

Egyptians learned the hard way that people or things (idols) became very repulsive when they occupied God's place in someone's heart.

Big changes came after Egypt's firstborn died. God led His people out of captivity. However, they still had to pass through the place of hopelessness before they could reach the other side—where the shofar called.

Why Shofars Wail in Scripture and Today—   By Mary A. Bruno, Ph.D.

57

* * *

**Shofie rode up front after belting out
her finest blasts at Mesquite, Nevada.**

"Let everything that has **breath praise the LORD.
Praise the LORD!**" (Psalm 150:6)

Why Shofars Wail in Scripture and Today—   By Mary A. Bruno, Ph.D.

Chapter 5
Impossibilities

Israelites stood nervously at the Red Sea's edge—with Pharaoh's army closing in. Water blocked their way of escape. God was there to help. Moses obeyed God and stretched his rod over the waters; and when he did, God congealed the Red Sea and made way for His amazed people to hurry across on dry ground. The travelers may have pushed against walls of water to watch them shake.

> And with the blast of Your nostrils
> The waters were gathered together;
> The floods stood upright like a heap;
> The depths congealed in the heart of the sea.
> —Ex. 15:8

They had made a swift exit from Egypt—with no time to bake their bread. Tent-wives had grabbed their bread pans, dough and all, and fled. Israelites hurried past the walls of stacked up water. Aroma of rising bread dough tantalized appetites. They would eat when they reached the other side, and sample their first taste of freedom. It was right there, just a little farther.

Why Shofars Wail in Scripture and Today—   By Mary A. Bruno, Ph.D.

The last of the Israeli camels peeked over his shoulder, grunted farewell to the charging army, and then loped to the other side—seconds before the water splashed back down and God drowned Pharaoh's army.

Celebration

Hebrew freedom shouts rose up as their pursuers went under. Victory chants echoed over the army's watery tomb and paralyzed enemy stragglers with fear.

> Then Miriam the prophetess, the sister of Aaron, took the timbrel in her hand; and all the women went out after her with timbrels and with dances.
> —Ex. 15:20

Miriam, believed to be about 85 years old then, grabbed her tambourine, took off leaping and dancing, and broke loose in a soul-stirring prophetic song of praise that exalted the living God of their salvation.

As she sang her victory song, "*all* of the women" joined in with shaking tambourines and joyous dancing. They may have numbered in the hundreds of thousands. Miriam's song sent contagious waves of delight rippling through the camp as exhilarated former slaves shouted praises and danced freely before the Living God.

He probably smiled, swooped into their praises, tapped His foot, and harmonized with them. One day we will get to hear God's perfect voice—in perfect pitch and full range—singing joyfully throughout the heavens, possibly at the Marriage Supper of the Lamb. The Father, Son, and Holy Spirit—The Three in One (The Author and Creator of music)—may even sing a love song to the Bride of Christ, as

Why Shofars Wail in Scripture and Today—   By Mary A. Bruno, Ph.D.

60

the voice of The Redeemed echoes back in sweet refrain. Selah. (Pause and think about that.)

> The LORD thy God in the midst of thee is mighty; he will save, he will rejoice over thee with joy; he will rest in his love, he will joy over thee with singing.
> —Zeph. 3:17 KJV

Israelites enjoyed their new independence. They gladly moved with God and pitched camp in the wilderness near the base of Mount Sinai. Barren desert stretched for as far as they could see, with a lofty mountain before them.

Rules

The honeymoon was over. God knew His people needed some new rules. Unlike the One Commandment in Eden, this time, there would be Ten—engraved in stone.

God calling—trip one. The new campsite spanned nearly two miles of flatland surrounded with high sloping walls. The natural amphitheater offered plenty of room for the two million or so Hebrews.

Sound waves bounced off the basin's walls. What an ideal place for Moses to address the people. Jesus (Yeshua), Master Designer of the universe, must have planned for this event when He formed the earth.

> He is the image of the invisible God, the firstborn over all creation. For by Him all things were created that are in heaven and that are on earth, visible and invisible, whether thrones or dominions or principalities or powers. All things were created through Him and for Him. And He is before all things, and in Him all things consist.
> —Col. 1:15–17

Why Shofars Wail in Scripture and Today—   By Mary A. Bruno, Ph.D.

61

A divine appointment was coming with scads of special effects. A God tug drew Moses, their God-appointed leader, who recognized God's explicit call. Moses knew he had to get alone with God, and hiked up the rugged mountain. Adonai was waiting for him and told him exactly what to say to the Israelites. God's covenant message was:

> 'You have seen what I did to the Egyptians, and *how* I bore you on eagles' wings and brought you to Myself. Now therefore, **if** you will indeed obey My voice and keep My covenant, then you shall be a special treasure to Me above all people; for all the earth *is* Mine. And you shall be to Me a kingdom of priests and a holy nation.'
>
> — Ex. 19:4–6a, emphasis added

In essence, God had shared His heart's desires and reminded folks that they had seen Him wipe out their captors and deliver them from slavery. He had caused them to soar with Him in heavenly places, to see what others had missed, and had brought them close to His loving heart. He loved His people and wanted them close by His side.

Ifs

God gave them these (summarized) *if* promises:

If—you choose wisely and "obey My voice;

I*f*—you will pay attention, listen, and do what I ask;

I*f*—you will "keep My covenant"; and

I*f*—you will obey My instructions. . .

God's promise that went with the *"Ifs"* meant they would be His. Their *obedience* would show they were reserved for Him and were His personal treasure.

Why Shofars Wail in Scripture and Today—   By Mary A. Bruno, Ph.D.

62

God reminded them of His faithfulness and promised to take care of their needs. He even proved His ability to do so by disclosing His assets—ownership of Earth and all within, including them. He promised to claim them as His own and then unveiled His wonderful plan. They would become His holy nation of priests, reserved for Him. It was easy enough. What could go wrong?

Unity

Moses returned to camp, called an elders meeting, and related God's offer. Everyone agreed to God's terms.

Encouraged by the show of unity, Moses' next climb up Mount Sinai went a little easier as he hurried to deliver his report. Before he uttered a word, God explained His plan to give him credibility with the people and to help them keep their commitment. He explained how it would unfold:

> And the LORD said to Moses, "Behold, I come to you in the thick cloud, that the people may hear when I speak with you, and believe you forever."
>
> —Ex. 19:9a

The Egyptians had seen the *thick darkness* that showed they had trusted in false gods and had followed the wrong leader. However, the Israelites saw a *thick cloud* that confirmed the True and Living God was with them and that they were following God's appointed leader—Moses. The cloud was impressive. Everyone could see it and would hear God speak to Moses. God's faith-builder sounded terrific. The people would remain steadfast, which was encouraging.

At that point, Moses joyfully told God his good news, which was that God's people had agreed to His commands. The LORD already knew about Moses's message; however,

Why Shofars Wail in Scripture and Today—   By Mary A. Bruno, Ph.D.

63

He let him experience the joy of bringing a good report. Could it be that good reports would become a rarity?

Shofar

God sent Moses back with a new set of instructions. (*Trumpet* in verse 13 is *yowbel, a* ram's horn shofar.)

> Then the LORD said to Moses, "Go to the people and consecrate them today and tomorrow, and let them wash their clothes. And let them be ready for the third day. For on the third day the LORD will come down upon Mount Sinai in the sight of all the people. You shall set bounds for the people all around, saying, 'Take heed to yourselves *that* you do *not* go up to the mountain or touch its base. Whoever touches the mountain shall surely be put to death. Not a hand shall touch him, but he shall surely be stoned or shot *with an arrow;* whether man or beast, he shall not live.' When the **trumpet** sounds long, they shall come near the mountain."
>
> —Ex. 19:10–13, emphasis added

After his God conference, Moses practiced the most important points for his speech regarding separation to God. They had three days to prepare themselves. The order included abstinence from physical intimacy, and taking care of their dirty laundry (Exodus 19:14–15). All went well, and he consecrated everyone to God.

A powerful shofar was ready to sound.

* * *

Why Shofars Wail in Scripture and Today—   By Mary A. Bruno, Ph.D.

64

Chapter 6
What a Blast!

Just before dawn on the third day of camp by Mount Sinai, Israelites were still nestled under their warm sheepskins. Rolling thunder rumbled against the mountain and interrupted closing strains of their "Moonlight Snore-adas." Lightning forked through the sky and lit their tents as bright as day. Glorious shofar sound waves bounced off the mountain and multiplied in the wilderness amphitheater. Camp dwellers trembled in their sandals as God roused everyone for His news.

Who blew that shofar? What lungs! What breath control! The Scripture mentions nobody on Mount Sinai except God. Now, where would God get a shofar? We shall backtrack for a moment and ponder some possibilities.

Could the clothes that God made for Adam and Eve have come from animals with horns? One may wonder how those creatures died, and if God had plans for their horns. He may have been the first to shed an animal's blood to cover nudity and sin, and first to convert a horn to a shofar.

Traditionalists have pondered the ram's horns that

Why Shofars Wail in Scripture and Today—   By Mary A. Bruno, Ph.D.

65

caught in a bush in Genesis 22:14 (KJV) when Abraham was ready to sacrifice Isaac. Jewish custom held that God, *Jehovahjireh (KJV spelling)* kept one of the ram's horns. (This name for God, *Jehovahjireh (Jehovah Jireh)*, means, "Jehovah sees" (sees to it). In the NKJV it is "The-LORD-Will-Provide.") This is the only place that the Bible mentions *Jehovahjireh.* God chose that instance to reveal this aspect of His character to Abraham and Isaac. From then on, they knew they could rely on Adonai to provide for all of their needs.

Isaac, Abraham's yielded son of promise, had followed his father up the mountain, willing to lay down his life in faith, knowing that, God[27] could raise him up and fulfill His promise to build a great nation through him. In faith, Abraham and Isaac had both embraced God's promise, had both received God's provision, and had both, returned in greater faith from the mountain.

Jewish tradition also suggests that God made one of the ram's horns into a shofar to blow on Mount Sinai when giving the Ten Commandments. And that He saved the other horn to blow when Jesus Christ, His only begotten Son— (Yeshua), the Messiah—(Who willingly laid down His life as a Holy Sacrifice) returns from heaven to earth.

Holy Terror

Some folks have embraced the idea that Satan probably shudders in fear every time he hears a shofar blast because he thinks it announces Christ's (Yeshua's) second coming and that his (Satan's) time on earth is over, and he must face his doom and serve his sentence.

Jewish tradition also holds that God's life-charged

---

[27] Truth Seekers Ministries - The Potter's House: A lesson on ..,
http://www.truthseekersministries.org/index.php/8-general-articles/49-the-potter (accessed April 12, 2016).

Why Shofars Wail in Scripture and Today—   By Mary A. Bruno, Ph.D.

66

breath flowed through His shofar on Mount Sinai and awakened the camp. There was no mention of anyone else up there when the blasts sounded. What must it have been like to experience shofar blasts of God's breath flowing from that holy mountain? Those power-charged sound waves bounced in all directions and grew louder, and louder, and louder. Israelites quivered as Divine breaths buzzed from that sanctified instrument and stirred their souls. God's wake-up call shook the camp with holy terror!

Louder

> And Moses brought the people out of the camp to meet with God, and they stood at the foot of the mountain. Now Mount Sinai *was* completely in smoke, because the LORD descended upon it in fire. Its smoke ascended like the smoke of a furnace, and the whole mountain quaked greatly.
>
> —Ex. 19:17, 18

Moses led God's people to the foot of Mount Sinai and waited for His next move. Hot, intimidating smoke blanketed the mountain. God Almighty was up there! Smoke billowed up as if from an enormous furnace. An earthquake jerked the mountain. Rocks tumbled, and dust flew, as tents and toes quivered in the valley. Continuous, ear-piercing, and soul-shaking shofar blasts grew louder and louder.

God called to Moses from the mountain peak, to come on up. This was no time for a lukewarm response. Moses had to go all the way with God. In Exodus 19:19, he rushed over rugged terrain to answer God's call. Adonai answered with a voice so everyone would know and remember that Moses was His man of the hour. The Israelites must have

Why Shofars Wail in Scripture and Today—   By Mary A. Bruno, Ph.D.

67

been relieved to know their leader was hearing from God. Moses' workouts from dashing up and down the mountain kept him in good physical condition for leadership.

To save lives, God sent Moses to warn the curious not to press through to see what was happening up there. If they did, many would perish (Ex. 19:21-25).

Moses instructed the priests who would come near to the Lord, to sanctify themselves lest the Lord should break forth against them. If priests needed reminders to stay pure unto the Lord—so must the rest of us.

Four chapters later in Exodus 24:14, Aaron, the priest, remained in the valley with the people, while Joshua accompanied Moses back to the mountain.

A camp crier may have yelled, "Now hear this!" Sources saw Moses and Joshua going up to Mount Sinai shortly before dawn under the cover of thunder and lightning. An informant said Moses was going to a closed tent-flap meeting with God at His Sinai conference center.

Wait! This is just in! Sources close to Moses say Jehovah God will set His Ten Commandments in stone today. When that occurs, spiritual matters as we have known them will change. We will all be more accountable to God, and will not be able to plead ignorance of His Law. Those days will be gone forever!

Engraved in Stone

God wrote (engraved) His Commandments, as told in Exodus 20:1–17, on two sides of stone tablets at Mount Sinai. To clarify any misunderstandings, God added the following in His closing remarks:

Why Shofars Wail in Scripture and Today—   By Mary A. Bruno, Ph.D.

68

"You shall not make *anything to be* with Me—gods of silver or gods of gold you shall not make for yourselves."

—Ex. 20:23

That command was hard to misunderstand. The ban on idolatry included silver or gold religious medals with images of people or things—living or dead—as objects of prayer or worship. God insisted on being His people's One and Only when they offered worship. He forbade them to trust in any religious images for help, (regardless of how expensive, or how beautiful, or how spiritual they looked, or who had blessed, kissed, or given them). The Israelites knew their Egyptian captors had trusted in idols; however, they also knew that the living God (not idols) had brought them *out* of bondage. They were free at last. It was time to go all out for God and trust in Him alone with—*no idols*—no other gods, and not even one favorite statue or medal.

"In every place where I record My name I will come to you, and I will bless you."

—Ex. 20:25b

God lovingly committed Himself to take care of His Israelites and provide for all their needs. He even promised to bless them wherever He recorded and remembered His name. He still honors that commitment today whenever we gather to exalt His name, whether at church, synagogue, temple, home, Bible studies, or other places.

God gave His people a calming visual to show that He was with them. They already had His fire by night and cloud by day to confirm His Presence, provision, and protection. He was ready to give them a lovely reminder of His Presence, salvation, and mercy—the Ark of the Covenant.

Why Shofars Wail in Scripture and Today—   By Mary A. Bruno, Ph.D.

69

* * *

**The Brunos declared God's blessings
and ownership of the land.**

Why Shofars Wail in Scripture and Today—   By Mary A. Bruno, Ph.D.

70

Chapter 7
The Ark of God's Covenant

There seems to be a connection between Moses'
rescue at birth, his tiny ark, the Ark of the Covenant,
the veil of the temple, and why shofars wailed.
Pharoah had ordered the midwives to kill all male Hebrew
babies at birth (perform full-term abortions). However,
Jochebed hid her adorable bundle of joy, Moses, as
documented in Exodus chapter two.

The Hebrew word *tebah*, used for Noah's Ark, also
indicated the tiny ark that Jochebed made. She
waterproofed it, made it soft and cozy, placed her smiling
infant son inside his ark of safety, and hid him among reeds
in the water. (One might wonder if those reeds hinted of the
rod that Moses would use to rescue Israel.) From shore, big
sister, Miriam, faithfully guarded her baby brother.

Jochebed, Miriam, and Aaron (about three years old
then) knew not that in due time, God would groom Moses to
lead Israel, with Aaron and Miriam at his side.

Moses' survival through that water hinted of God's
rescue plan for him to lead the Israelites through a larger

Why Shofars Wail in Scripture and Today—   By Mary A. Bruno, Ph.D.

71

body of water—the Red Sea. God looked forward to when His former little ark-dweller could receive and understand His building plans for another Ark—the Ark of the Covenant. One day King David would escort it with hundreds of worshipers, trumpets, and blaring shofars.

Building Plans

Exodus 25:10–16, tells of when, Moses as an adult, had stationed the camp at the base of Mt. Sinai. God, during their private 40-day, conference, had told him to build a sanctuary. He also provided detailed plans to construct the Ark of the Covenant, and mercy seat, and then engraved the Ten Commandments. God, being Himself, always had a plan and knew the best person for a job. While He was engraving His Holy Word on the mountain above, Aaron (the Priest) was using his God-given talents and position to engrave a beautiful, but unholy idol (a golden calf) in the valley below.

The Ark of the Covenant was a striking visual of God's abiding Presence, Law, and Mercy. In Exodus chapter 24, He gave Moses the specifics of its design, materials, and construction. It would have a pure gold covering on all sides, and on the carrying poles. Shofars would sound on the Ark's moving day (addressed in Chapter 19).

Cherubim

God tempered justice with mercy and told Moses to build a mercy seat. It would rest *above* the Ark containing His covenant. He would speak *intimately* from *above* the mercy seat, between cherubim's wings.

Sweet cherub faces seen adorning Valentine cards were very different from cherubim (plural of cherub) of the Bible. Those hefty angelic beings were *powerful guards* in God's kingdom. In Genesis 3:24, God posted them and a

Why Shofars Wail in Scripture and Today—   By Mary A. Bruno, Ph.D.

72

flaming sword to guard the tree of life in Eden. Cherubim are also beside God's throne. It is unlikely that they would be running around half-naked and clad in loincloths.

Symbols

Later, the shofar would sound again to announce the Ark of the Covenant as it traveled under its sacred covering—the veil of the temple. Shofar blasts would also announce God's Presence and all that the Ark and veil represented. As He did for Noah's Ark and the Ark of the Covenant, God gave specifics for the mercy seat that rested on top. The Ark symbolized Jesus Christ (Yeshua), God's promised Redeemer—the Messiah. He would reconcile fallen humanity to Father God. In Exodus 25:17–22, details had to be per God's exact instructions.

The mercy seat rested beyond the beautiful thick veil in the tabernacle, within the *holy of holies.* The dense hanging softened sounds and gave privacy for all who entered into the secret place of the Most High.

> "You shall make a veil woven of blue, purple, and scarlet *thread,* and fine woven linen. It shall be woven with an artistic design of cherubim. You shall hang it upon the four pillars of acacia *wood* overlaid with gold. Their hooks *shall be* gold, upon four sockets of silver."
> —Ex. 26:31–32

The veil hung from four metal clasps, affixed to acacia wood. It was a type of Christ's (Yeshua's) body nailed to the cross by metal spikes driven through His hands and feet while He hung suspended between heaven and earth, paid the price with His life, and redeemed fallen humanity.

Why Shofars Wail in Scripture and Today—   By Mary A. Bruno, Ph.D.

73

Colors

Colors woven into the veil pointed to Christ's ministry. *Blue*, a heavenly color, indicated Jesus Christ—the Eternal One who would come down from heaven, lay down His life, and bear sin's penalty. He would break death's power, rise from the dead, and resume His rightful place at Father God's right hand. There, as our Great High Priest, He would intercede for[28] believers and proclaim that His blood has cleansed their sin; His wounds have provided their healing; and that He has baptized (saturated) them with the Holy Spirit (Ruach Kodesh) and fire. See: Isa. 53:5, Luke 3:16, Acts 2:32–33, Heb. 7:24–25, and 1 Peter 2:24.

Purple in the veil, the color of royalty, signified *Jesus Christ, the Creator, Word of God, Risen Son of the Living God, King of Kings, and Lord of lords.*

> In the beginning was the Word, and the Word was with God, and the Word was God. He was in the beginning with God. All things came into being through Him, and apart from Him nothing came into being that has come into being.
> —John 1:1–3 NASB

> "And on His robe and on His thigh He has a name written, "KING OF KINGS, AND LORD OF LORDS."
> —Rev. 19:16 NASB

Scarlet suggested that Jesus Christ's (Yeshua's) shed blood on the cross, as a great shofar, would (and does) cry out for forgiveness, cleansing, and restoration.

---

[28] PRAYERS FOR THE LORD'S MERCY - ISC Netherlands, http://www.iscnetherlands.nl/downloads/prayer.doc (accessed April 12, 2016).

Why Shofars Wail in Scripture and Today—   By Mary A. Bruno, Ph.D.

Linen

Fine twined linen symbolized Christ's righteousness that would (and does) clothe believers. This new covering would be (and is) superior to the one that sin had stripped away. *Father God sees believers as clothed in Christ's righteous*—with no sin. Consider what God did for the following list of sinners. "Cleansed, set apart, and counted as righteous," sounds very good for that group. God is merciful.

> Don't you know that unrighteous people will have no share in the Kingdom of God? Don't delude yourselves—people who engage in sex before marriage, who worship idols, who engage in sex after marriage with someone other than their spouse, who engage in active or passive homosexuality, who steal, who are greedy, who get drunk, who assail people with contemptuous language, who rob—none of them will share in the Kingdom of God. *Some of you used to do these things.* But you have cleansed yourselves, you have been set apart for God, you have come to be *counted righteous* through the power of the Lord Yeshua the Messiah and the Spirit of our God.
> —1 Cor. 6:9–11 CJB, emphasis added

Old Testament priests had to pass by the veil to enter into the Holy of Holies where they could commune with God. Believers now enter in through faith in Jesus Christ.

> But you are a chosen generation, a royal priesthood, a holy nation, His own special people, that you may proclaim the praises of Him who called you out of darkness into His marvelous light.
> —1 Peter 2:9

Why Shofars Wail in Scripture and Today—   By Mary A. Bruno, Ph.D.

75

Revelation 1:5–6 assures that believers cleansed through Christ's blood are already kings and priests to God.

Veil

The temple's veil was not a lightweight mesh curtain. It was a heavy drape made of strong embroidered linen and was dense like a thick rug.

In L. Thomas Holdcroft's book *The Pentateuch*,[29] he wrote, "According to tradition, the inner veil in Herod's temple that stood in Christ's time, was four inches thick."

> And Jesus cried out again with a loud voice, and yielded up His spirit. And behold, the veil of the temple was torn in two from top to bottom; and the earth shook and the rocks were split.
> —Matt. 27:50–51 NASB

When Jesus cried out, *"It is finished!"* in John 19:30, and gave His life on the Cross, someone or something *ripped that veil* of the temple in two—*from the top* to the bottom. Revelation 1:15 tells of a sharp two-edged sword that proceeds from Jesus' mouth. His cry of "It is finished" may have torn, split, or severed the thick veil. Others have speculated that Father God might have done the tearing.

A shofar would call again for consecration and commitment when its blasts rang out on moving day. Shofars were ready to wail.

* * *

---

[29] Holdcroft, L. Thomas. *The Pentateuch.* Oakland: Western Book Company, 1966.

Why Shofars Wail in Scripture and Today—   By Mary A. Bruno, Ph.D.

76

Chapter 8
Moving With God—Part 1

Aaron's sons Nadab and Abihu violated authority and offered strange (unholy) fire before God in Leviticus 10:1–3. One can imagine what God felt when they put their unholy fire—*on His Holy Altar!*

So they wanted to play with fire, did they? God knew all about fire. Before they could hurry to snuff it out, fire came out from before God and snuffed them out as two flickering candles in the wind.

Dealing with the Ark involved respect for spiritual matters. God went through His chain of command and told Moses in Leviticus 16:2–4 to tell Aaron how he could safely access the Ark, and come back out alive. He would need to address his sin, before entering God's Holy Presence.

When God's appointed and anointed leaders give warnings for protection that agree with His written Word, hearers should comply. Not just anyone could tend to the Ark. In Numbers 3:29–32, God put Kohathites in charge of it and the utensils. Eleazar, another of Aaron's sons, supervised the Levites and Kohathites.

Why Shofars Wail in Scripture and Today—   By Mary A. Bruno, Ph.D.

77

Cloud and Fire

Israelites constructed the tabernacle (dwelling place) according to God's instructions, which may have led to the term "House of the Lord." After its completion, God confirmed His Presence by manifesting a comforting cloud by day and a reassuring pillar of fire at night that spread a calming warm glow over the camp.

Like a two-edged sword, God's fire burned in two ways. In Numbers chapter 11, complainers learned about that the hard way. Fire from God flared out during their gripe fest and burned them crisp at the outskirts of the camp. Those who followed God's lead kept calm when things heated up around them. The Holy fire warmed yielded hearts while others grew cold.

> Now on the day that the tabernacle was raised up, the cloud covered the tabernacle, the tent of the Testimony; from evening until morning it was above the tabernacle like the appearance of fire.
>
> —Num. 9:15

God led His people by a cloud and the[30] appearance of fire. When they moved, the believers followed.

> So it was always: the cloud covered it *by day,* and the appearance of fire by night. Whenever the cloud was taken up from above the tabernacle, after that the children of Israel would journey; and in the place where the cloud settled, there the children of Israel would pitch their tents.
>
> —Num. 9:16–17

---

[30] Seeing God's Glory sermon page 2, Seeing God's Glory .., http://www.sermoncentral.com/sermons/seeing-gods-glory-david-elvery-sermon-on-go (accessed April 12, 2016).

Why Shofars Wail in Scripture and Today—   By Mary A. Bruno, Ph.D.

78

When God stopped, everyone stopped. The people had no Bibles, except for God's Ten Commandments. God led them by two miraculous signs of His Presence—the cloud and appearance of fire (and Moses). Moving with God in our time involves two things—obeying *His written Word* (Holy Bible), and following *His Holy Spirit's leading. God's* anointed pastors will feed His flock with knowledge and understanding per His promise in Jeremiah 3:15. Israelites were safe when they followed God's presence and timing.

> *Whether it was* two days, a month, or a year that the cloud remained above the tabernacle, the children of Israel would remain encamped and not journey; but when it was taken up, they would journey.
>
> —Num. 9:22

Silver Trumpets

Silver trumpets signaled it was time to go.

> And the LORD spoke to Moses, saying: "Make two silver trumpets for yourself; you shall make them of hammered work; you shall use them for calling the congregation and for directing the movement of the camps."
>
> —Num. 10:1–2

Those metal horns (from the Hebrew word *chatso-tsĕrah*) *were* long straight horns made of silver, with a bell end. Hammered silver pictured our redemption through Christ's (Yeshua's) pierced and beaten body as He endured the horror of crucifixion, which paid for our sins, and

Why Shofars Wail in Scripture and Today—   By Mary A. Bruno, Ph.D.

79

provided our healing (Isa. 53:5).[31] The horns that wailed during His crucifixion were shofars. (See chapter 28.)

The two silver trumpets also exemplified the Old and New Testaments. They called in harmony for God's people to come closer to Him, to His house, to other believers, and to follow Him to the Promised Land.[32]

> When they blow both of them, all the congregation shall gather before you at the door of the tabernacle of meeting.
>
> —Num. 10:3

Two trumpet blasts called everyone to hurry to the tent (place of worship). They called to hear God's message and follow His leading. The tent door was a type of Christ.

> "I am the door. If anyone enters by Me, he will be saved, and will go in and out and find pasture."
>
> —John 10:9

Leaders knew a single blast meant to meet with other frontrunners. Gatherings that were important to God were imperative for those who guarded His flock.

> But if they blow *only* one, then the leaders, the heads of the divisions of Israel, shall gather to you.
>
> —Num. 10:4

---

[31] Those who dont believe in God? | Yahoo Answers, https://answers.yahoo.com/question/index?qid=20080903210724AAqpe5b (accessed April 12, 2016).

[32] Those who dont believe in God? | Yahoo Answers, https://answers.yahoo.com/question/index?qid=20080903210724AAqpe5b (accessed April 12, 2016).

Why Shofars Wail in Scripture and Today—   By Mary A. Bruno, Ph.D.

80

In Numbers 10:5-6, various trumpet blasts told tribes when it was their turn to move out.

> And when the assembly is to be gathered together, you shall blow, but not sound the advance.
>
> —Num. 10:7

Priests

Israel's kind Shepherd gently leads His flock in paths of peace. Trumpet blowers had to be priests.

> The sons of Aaron, the priests, shall blow the trumpets; and these shall be to you as an ordinance forever throughout your generations.
>
> —Num. 10:8

Some may have longed to release silver trumpet blasts, but; by not being priests, they lacked lip to silver horn privilege. However, New Testament believers are neither male nor female in Christ. They are all kings and priests to God—with trumpet and shofar privilege.

> There is neither Jew nor Greek, there is neither slave nor free, there is neither male nor female; for you are all one in Christ Jesus.
>
> Gal. 3:28

> But you *are* a chosen generation, a royal priesthood, a holy nation, His own special people, that you may proclaim the praises of Him who called you out of darkness into His marvelous light.
>
> —1 Peter 2:9

Why Shofars Wail in Scripture and Today—   By Mary A. Bruno, Ph.D.

Victory

Trumpet alarms before battle did not sound to scare enemies. Still, as some have said, if adversaries had known why they sounded, they may have fled in fear.

> When you go to war in your land against the enemy who oppresses you, then you shall sound an alarm with the trumpets, and you will be remembered before the Lord your God, and you will be saved from your enemies.
> —Num. 10:9

When addressing an attacking enemy, sounding the alarm (*ta ta, ta . . .*) caught God's attention. He had promised to save from opponents—*if* they sounded the alarm—*before* confronting an enemy. New Testament believers may sound their spiritual trumpets (clap, sing, and shout praises to God) *prior to* facing an opponent (See chapter 25 for how to make sounds that have shofar effect). In Numbers 10:10, God ordered to blow the trumpets on other times.

He might like to hear horns on our days of gladness (worship celebrations). Blowing them on the first day of the month is in His Book. Did He ever say to stop?

Since trumpets sounded over offerings, one might wonder why our offerings are so quiet. Trumpet blasts at feasts and offerings reminded God of His people, and the people of when God had supplied their needs and brought victory, which inspired shouts of praise and thanksgiving.

Excitement filled the camp. All eyes followed God's cloud that had lifted and was moving forward. Households packed up as tribal banners showed the way. Yes, it was time to move with God. More shofars were ready to wail.

* * *

Why Shofars Wail in Scripture and Today—   By Mary A. Bruno, Ph.D.

82

Chapter 9
Moving With God—Part 2

The moving cloud meant it was time to pick up, pack up, and move on. Obeying God's instructions about how to prepare the Ark for travel was a matter of life or death. They had to do it His way to reach the place where the shofar would proclaim its joyful sound.

> When the camp prepares to journey, Aaron and his sons shall come, and they shall take down the covering veil and cover the ark of the Testimony with it. Then they shall put on it a covering of badger skins, and spread over *that* a cloth entirely of blue; and they shall insert its poles.
>
> —Num. 4:5–6

Kohathites cared for the Ark and furnishings for the sanctuary, and carefully observed God's instructions on moving day. They did not merely barge in, pack things up, throw them over a camel's hump, and leave. They waited for Aaron and his sons to ready the Ark for travel.

The thick veil went on first to cover the Ark. Then waterproof badger skin (some translations say *porpoise*

Why Shofars Wail in Scripture and Today—   By Mary A. Bruno, Ph.D.

83

skin) protected the veil. A heavenly blue colored cloth covered it all. When all were in place, with gold overlaid poles in the rings, the Ark of the Covenant was ready to go.

> And when Aaron and his sons have finished covering the sanctuary and all the furnishings of the sanctuary, when the camp is set to go, then the sons of Kohath shall come to carry *them;* but they shall not touch any holy thing, lest they die.
> —Num. 4:15a

It was not the time for hastiness. Kohathites waited for Aaron to release them to carry the Ark on their shoulders. Although this was their job, they still had to wait until the priest told them it was their time to serve. The Kohathites were very careful not to touch or peek at any of the holiest things. Their survival hinged on obedience. When God says "No," it may be because He wants to protect someone and save a life, as in Numbers 4:17–20).

God made sure that Levites protected the Kohathites for work of the ministry. It was a great privilege to carry God's Ark of the Covenant. Yet, great opportunity brought high accountability—and great blessings for that bloodline. Those who were ordained to minister had to submit to instruction, training, and timing—and do things God's way.

Moving Day

The camp buzzed with excitement. Happy children chattered and asked how they could help pack. Meanwhile, dads fed the camels, inspected their humps and hooves, and then gave them as much fresh water as they could hold. A desert camel could guzzle thirty-five to fifty gallons—in about eighteen minutes (nearly 3 gallons a minute). That

Why Shofars Wail in Scripture and Today—   By Mary A. Bruno, Ph.D.

84

was about what seven to ten five-gallon containers might hold. Dads dodged swift kicks, licking, and flying spit while adjusting harnesses and load straps.

Whole families pitched in, pulled up stakes and folded their tents. To stay blessed, they had to follow the Ark, find out where they were supposed to fit in, and then stick with that group. Tribe hopping was not an option.

How like God to send Judah's division (worship leaders) first in Numbers 10:14–16, with the armies and military banners. God loves to inhabit His people's praises. To attract His attention, just sing, clap, shout, magnify His name, and, of course, release a few shofar blasts.

Israelites numbered in the millions. Families settled in behind the standard-bearers for their tribes. Flags helped everyone to find their place and to stay in divine order. Colorful banners pointed upward to God in the lead, as the tribes obeyed His marching instructions.

Gershon and Merari's sons used great care to take down the tabernacle and position it safely between the armies. Faithful Kohathites followed in Numbers 10:17–20, bearing the sacred objects from the tabernacle.

Rear Guard

Numbers 10:21–28 tells of Dan's tribe and the *rear guard* armies, which provided security for the camps that went before them. Being part of the rear guard implied respect. The diligent protectors warded off enemies and gathered stragglers. It was a dirty job, but one of honor. God gave some glorious *rearguard* promises for all who fast and pray to set the captives free.

Why Shofars Wail in Scripture and Today—   By Mary A. Bruno, Ph.D.

85

Then your light shall break forth like the morning,
Your healing shall spring forth speedily,
And your righteousness shall go before you;
The glory of the LORD shall be your rear guard.
Then you shall call, and the LORD will answer;
You shall cry, and He will say, 'Here I *am.*'

"If you take away the yoke from your midst,
The pointing of the finger, and speaking wickedness,
If you extend your soul to the hungry
And satisfy the afflicted soul,
Then your light shall dawn in the darkness,
And your darkness shall *be* as the noonday.
The LORD will guide you continually,
And satisfy your soul in drought,
And strengthen your bones;
You shall be like a watered garden,
And like a spring of water, whose waters do not fail.
Those from among you
Shall build the old waste places;
You shall raise up the foundations of many generations;
And you shall be called the Repairer of the Breach,
The Restorer of Streets to Dwell In.
                            —Isa. 58:8–12, emphasis added

Let us consider the Hebrew word for God's "glory." His *glory* will follow those who fast and pray to set captives free. Glory is from *kabowd*[33], which means: glory, honor, glorious, abundance, riches, splendor, dignity, reputation, and reverence. When God says, "I've got your back," He backs an intercessor (one who prays for others) with all of the above. What a glorious way to go through life! That verse is loaded with promise.

---

[33] "H3519 - kabowd - Strong's Hebrew Lexicon (KJV)." Blue Letter Bible. Accessed 4 Jun, 2016.
https://www.blueletterbible.org//lang/Lexicon/Lexicon.cfm?Strongs=H3519&t=KJV

Why Shofars Wail in Scripture and Today—   By Mary A. Bruno, Ph.D.

86

An intercessor's light would break through like the dawn to end a night season, with a new vision for a new day, and a new beginning. None could stop the morning. Recovery would come forth quickly. This meant unstoppable healing and recovery from whatever had depleted strength and resources or dimmed one's vision.

A situation may have hurt for a while, but God promised swift recovery. An intercessor's righteousness (right standing with God) paved the way to wherever one needed to go. God's glory guarded the back and protected from blind spots and sneak attacks. This may be why no spiritual armor is given for the back in Ephesians 6. *God's glory* protects the intercessor's/warrior's back and makes up the rearguard—which is more than enough for anything or anyone that attacks from behind, including one's past.

That is how our LORD watches over His prayer warriors. Intercessors may hear Him whisper; *Fear not, I have your back,* as they recall his written promise, from Isaiah 58:8, "The glory of the LORD shall be your rear guard." When all was in order, the Israelites followed God and the sacred Ark of the Covenant.

> So they departed from the mountain of the LORD on a journey of three days; and the ark of the covenant of the LORD went before them for the three days' journey, to search out a resting place for them. And the cloud of the LORD *was* above them by day when they went out from the camp.
>
> —Num. 10:33–34

Tender Care

Father God had lovingly provided an ideal resting place for His flock. He knew the trip could be a challenge **for**

Why Shofars Wail in Scripture and Today—   By Mary A. Bruno, Ph.D.

87

the young and elderly although none was feeble among them (Ps. 105:37). His mobile air conditioning unit (cloud) kept them comfortable. Heavenly breezes probably refreshed people and animals.

Moses' heart overflowed with praise and rejoicing as the Ark moved out. Blessed beyond measure, he probably threw up both arms—right in front of everybody—and praised the LORD in his loudest voice.

> So it was, whenever the ark set out, that Moses said:
>
> "Rise up, O LORD!
> Let Your enemies be scattered,
> And let those who hate You flee before You."
>
> And when it rested, he said:
>
> "Return, O LORD,
> *To* the many thousands of Israel."
>
> —Num. 10:35–36

After three days of traveling, Moses rejoiced over their progress and delighted in God's Presence as the Ark came to rest. He invited God to return to His flock that had overcome obstacles. The people were ready to embrace the warmth of God's fiery presence. They relaxed in sweet peace as echoes of trumpet calls resonated in their hearts.

Israelites would soon hear the shofar again and would rejoice in its joyful sound. God was getting ready to unveil His generous new love token, *The Day of Jubilee!* On that great day, shofar blasts would ring throughout the land to announce release, restoration, and reconciliation with loved ones. God had already scheduled that exciting appointment on His calendar.

* * *

Why Shofars Wail in Scripture and Today—   By Mary A. Bruno, Ph.D.

88

Chapter 10
Jubilee

Adonai and Moses met again on Mount Sinai. Israel's Shepherd was ready to bestow His love token that would delight His kingdom of priests and their land.

As told in Leviticus 25:9–10, God established the Day of Atonement (Yom Kippur) and declared the trumpet (*shofar*) of the Jubilee would sound on the tenth day of the seventh month (Tishri on the Jewish calendar), which was in late September or early October.

Shofar blasts rang out on the Day of Jubilee to proclaim liberty to those who were in bondage, and to *consecrate* the fiftieth year. It was cause for great celebration. The trumpet[34] of the Jubilee was a ram's horn (a shofar).

The word *Jubile (Jubilee)* was from two Hebrew words. Verse 9 used *Teruw'ah,*[35] which referred to a shofar

---

[34] "H7782 - showphar - Strong's Hebrew Lexicon (KJV)." Blue Letter Bible. Accessed 4 Jun, 2016.
https://www.blueletterbible.org//lang/Lexicon/Lexicon.cfm?Strongs=H7782&t=KJV
[35] "H8643 - tĕruw`ah - Strong's Hebrew Lexicon (KJV)." Blue Letter Bible. Accessed 4 Jun, 2016.
https://www.blueletterbible.org//lang/Lexicon/Lexicon.cfm?Strongs=H8643&t=KJV

Why Shofars Wail in Scripture and Today—   By Mary A. Bruno, Ph.D.

89

blast, or could mean "an alarm, a signal, a shout, blast of war, or a cry of joy." However, verse 10 used, *yowbel*,[36] which meant "a ram, ram's horn (*shofar*), trumpet, cornet, or jubilee year."

The shofar's sound waves sent powerful flashes of hope, joy, and thanksgiving as they proclaimed God's Jubilee freedom. Those in bondage were free to return home to their loved ones' tender embraces, to reap their labors' rewards, and reclaim their belongings.

Trumpet blasts announced the Jubilee order to restore houses and lands to rightful heirs. Possessions were not lost forever, only until God's Day of Jubilee. God's Jubilee blessings showed His love and mercies for His people.

Israelites knew that shofars called to come closer to God. It was time to enter His Presence, to hear His voice, and to receive His love and gifts. God is the Great Gift Giver!

The shofar called to let God heal old and new hurts and to make life better. It called to repent of all that was not pleasing to Him. It called to put away idols and sever all fellowship with sin. It called to enter into God's rest, refreshing, and favor, and to drench in His love.

Jesus

Jesus, Lamb of God, Savior, and Redeemer may have been thinking of the Jubilee when He stood in a synagogue one Sabbath, unrolled the scroll, and read,

> The Spirit of the Lord GOD is upon me,
> Because the LORD has anointed me

---

[36] "H3104 - yowbel - Strong's Hebrew Lexicon (KJV)." Blue Letter Bible. Accessed 4 Jun, 2016.
https://www.blueletterbible.org//lang/Lexicon/Lexicon.cfm?Strongs=H3104&t=KJV

Why Shofars Wail in Scripture and Today—   By Mary A. Bruno, Ph.D.

90

To bring good news to the afflicted;
He has sent me to bind up the brokenhearted,
To proclaim liberty to captives
And freedom to prisoners;
To proclaim the favorable year of the LORD
And the day of vengeance of our God;
To comfort all who mourn.

—Isaiah 61:1–2 NASB

Jesus lifted up His voice *like a shofar* as He altered some of the wording and declared the acceptable day of the LORD. His words blazed like a holy fire that kindled hope of restoration and forgiveness, with God's grace to forgive one's self and others, "And recovering of sight to the blind."

"The Spirit of the LORD *is* upon Me,
Because He has anointed Me
To preach the gospel to *the* poor;
He has sent Me to heal the brokenhearted,
To proclaim liberty to *the* captives
And recovery of sight to *the* blind,
To set at liberty those who are oppressed;
To proclaim the acceptable year of the LORD."

—Luke 4:18–19 emphasis added

His voice—holy breath that flowed from Jesus Christ—the Lamb of God—The Living Word and the Messiah—rang out like a heavenly shofar that proclaimed the New Testament Jubilee. The synagogue throbbed with His Heavenly Presence. His voice echoed against the cold walls of stone, etched His words on yielded human hearts and drew the people closer to their Creator. God's Only-begotten Son, Yeshua, the Messiah, stood before them—clothed with God's DNA in human flesh.

Why Shofars Wail in Scripture and Today—   By Mary A. Bruno, Ph.D.

91

In the beginning was the Word, and the Word was with God, and the Word was God. He was in the beginning with God. All things were made through Him, and without Him nothing was made that was made. In Him was life, and the life was the light of men.

—John 1:1–4

As promised, Jesus, God's only begotten Son, had come through the woman's seed. Jesus (Yeshua, the Messiah) was ready to lay down His life to redeem fallen humankind. His voice had resonated in human hearts on another occasion, when—as a Divine Shofar—He boldly proclaimed,

"It is the Spirit who gives life; the flesh profits nothing. The words that I speak to you are spirit, and *they* are life."

—John 6:63

Some in the synagogue may have gasped as every eye fastened on Him when He announced,

"Today this Scripture is fulfilled in your hearing."

—Luke 4:21

The dynamic shofar power and impact of His words infused each heart with surging life that raised gooseflesh, sent hearts pounding, and intellects reeling. They wondered if Jesus was *more* than a carpenter's son.

The locals knew that Joseph and Mary had, at least, seven children, and mentioned most of them by name. They included Jesus, and his half-brothers and sisters: James, Joseph, Simon, and Judas, plus two (or more) half-sisters. (If there were only two sisters, translators would have used the word "both" instead of "all" in the following passage.)

Why Shofars Wail in Scripture and Today—   By Mary A. Bruno, Ph.D.

92

He came to his hometown and began to teach the people in their synagogue, so that they were astounded and said, "Where did this man get this wisdom and these deeds of power? Is not this the carpenter's son? Is not his mother called Mary? And are not his brothers James and Joseph and Simon and Judas? And are not **all his sisters** with us? Where then did this man get all this?"

—Matt. 13:54-56, emphasis added
—New Revised Standard Version Catholic Edition
(NRSVCE)

Leviticus 25:1–9 tells of when God established the Year of Jubilee. As indicated earlier, Jubilee,[37] *Teruw'ah*, in verse nine, held exciting meanings. The nine or more rapid shofar blasts in groups of three, sounded alarms, wake-up calls, and Jubilee blessings.

All references to *Jubilee* from Leviticus 25:10 to the end of that chapter were from *yowbel*[38] (ram's horn). For additional Jubilee references, see Leviticus 25:9–54, 27:17–24, and Numbers 36:4. The Jubilee message still resounds today: "Proclaim liberty throughout the land unto all the inhabitants thereof" (Lev. 25:10 KJV).

Liberty Bell

That same verse (Leviticus 25:10) is at the Liberty Bell Center's website.[39] It shows a photo of the Liberty Bell hanging near a glass wall at Liberty Center in Philadelphia, Pennsylvania, bearing the following inscription: "*Proclaim*

---

[37] "H8643 - těruw`ah - Strong's Hebrew Lexicon (KJV)." Blue Letter Bible. Accessed 4 Jun, 2016.
https://www.blueletterbible.org//lang/Lexicon/Lexicon.cfm?Strongs=H8643&t=KJV
[38] "H3104 - yowbel - Strong's Hebrew Lexicon (KJV)." Blue Letter Bible. Accessed 4 Jun, 2016.
https://www.blueletterbible.org//lang/Lexicon/Lexicon.cfm?Strongs=H3104&t=KJV
[39] http://www.nps.gov/inde/liberty-bellcenter.htm.

Why Shofars Wail in Scripture and Today—   By Mary A. Bruno, Ph.D.

93

LIBERTY throughout all the Land unto all the Inhabitants thereof Lev. XXV X . . . "

Another website also has a photo of the Liberty Bell's inscription from Leviticus 25:10.[40]

The United States of America displays this beautiful passage from God's Holy Word on the Liberty Bell! God's Word goes wherever the bell goes.

Wikipedia's website indicates a replica of the Liberty Bell is in each state, in the District of Columbia, and near many state capitol buildings.[41]

The Liberty Bell's image is on a United States Postal Service's Forever Stamp. Just think about it for a moment. God's Word goes wherever that stamp goes—in homes and offices, governmental buildings, through the air, over the land, and by sea, which may cause some powers and principalities to tremble.

In chapter 33, read about the excitement that broke loose when the Brunos visited the Liberty Bell.

However, some other shofar blasts were coming to shake things up in the physical realm, with some timely shouting—at Jericho.

* * *

---

[40] http://www.visitphilly.com/history/philadelphia/the-liberty-bell-center/.
[41] See: http://upload.wikimedia.org/wikipedia/commons/0/08/Liberty_Bell_2008.jpg.

Why Shofars Wail in Scripture and Today—   By Mary A. Bruno, Ph.D.

94

Chapter 11
Jericho—Part 1: Groomed

Joshua's name, *Yĕhowshuwa,*[42] meant "Jehovah is salvation." He is called *Oshea*[43] in Numbers 13:8, 16, and *Hoshea* in Deuteronomy 32:44, both of which were from the word, *Howshea*—that meant "salvation." Joshua was *one of Moses' young men.*

> Y'hoshua, the son of Nun, who from his youth up had been Moshe's assistant.
> — Num. 11:28 CJB

Nun chose well when he bestowed the righteous name of *Joshua*—and raised his son to trust in God. No wonder Joshua loved hearing about God's promises and great victories. That was how Nun had bent his little *"twig."* Neither of them knew that God would provide experiences

---

[42] "H3091 - Yĕhowshuwa` - Strong's Hebrew Lexicon (KJV)." Blue Letter Bible. Accessed 4 Jun, 2016.
https://www.blueletterbible.org//lang/Lexicon/Lexicon.cfm?Strongs=H3091&t=KJV
[43] "H1954 - Howshea` - Strong's Hebrew Lexicon (KJV)." Blue Letter Bible. Accessed 4 Jun, 2016.
https://www.blueletterbible.org//lang/Lexicon/Lexicon.cfm?Strongs=H1954&t=KJV

Why Shofars Wail in Scripture and Today—   By Mary A. Bruno, Ph.D.

95

through Joshua's youthful bond with Moses that would help him to lead Israel. Moses groomed Joshua to serve God, and God groomed Joshua to serve Moses. Joshua became Moses' minister at some point between Exodus chapters 17–24.

> So Moses arose with his assistant Joshua, and Moses went up to the mountain of God.
>
> —Ex. 24:13

Joshua

The Bible first mentions Joshua in Exodus 17:9–14,[44] when a battle with Amalek brewed at Rephidim. Moses told Joshua to choose men to fight Amalek.[45] By then, Joshua could make strategic decisions. He and his warriors stretched out their strong hands with clashing swords against Amalek in the valley below while Moses stretched out his veteran hands with his sturdy shepherd's rod (that brought miracles), on the hill above, and God stretched out His mighty hand of victory over all of them.

Aaron and Hur stood beside Moses and raised his[46] hands toward heaven when he was too tired to do so himself. In Exodus 17:12, they also improvised a makeshift seat (a rock) for him to rest. Bless God for those who know how to undergird His ministers during times of crisis.

---

[44] JOSHUA Joshua's life Before the Conquest - lbctruthforlife.org, http://www.lbctruthforlife.org/wp-content/uploads/2015/06/TRUTH-FOR-LIFE-Joshua- (accessed April 12, 2016).

[44] when Joshua was first mentioned in Bible « THE CHURCH OF ..., https://churchofphiladelphia.wordpress.com/tag/when-joshua-was-first-mentioned-i (accessed April 12, 2016).

[45] when Joshua was first mentioned in Bible « THE CHURCH OF .., https://churchofphiladelphia.wordpress.com/tag/when-joshua-was-first-mentioned-i (accessed April 12, 2016).

[46] Aaron & Hur sermon, Aaron & Hur sermon by Robert Leroe .., http://www.sermoncentral.com/sermons/aaron--hur-robert-leroe-sermon-on-encourage (accessed April 12, 2016).

Why Shofars Wail in Scripture and Today—   By Mary A. Bruno, Ph.D.

96

> Joshua *discomfited* Amalek and his people with the edge of the sword.
>
> —Ex. 17:13 KJV, italics added

The word discomfited,[47] *chalash,* means, "to be weak, be prostrate, or disabled." It is a good word to pray when asking God to stop enemy power. He will work wonders for those who trust in[48] Him to *discomfit* their enemies.

Handbook

Book learning was part of Joshua's training to serve as general over the Israeli Army. Not just any book would do. Joshua cut his "military teeth" on what we shall think of as, *God's Military Handbook for Up and Coming Conquerors* (aka the Bible, or the part that was written then). When God gave Moses something in print, the Ten Commandments, etc., it was for teaching purposes. Moses not only handed Joshua the book—he instructed him in its use.

> Then the LORD said to Moses, "Write this *for* a memorial in the book and recount *it* in the hearing of Joshua, that I will utterly blot out the remembrance of Amalek from under heaven." And Moses built an altar and called its name, The-LORD-Is-My-Banner; for he said, "Because the LORD has sworn: the LORD *will have* war with Amalek from generation to generation."
>
> —Ex. 17:14–16

---

47 "H2522 - chalash - Strong's Hebrew Lexicon (KJV)." Blue Letter Bible. Accessed 4 Jun, 2016.
https://www.blueletterbible.org//lang/Lexicon/Lexicon.cfm?Strongs=H2522&t=KJV
48 Patriarchs and Prophets - White ® Estate,
http://www.whiteestate.org/books/pp/pp45.html (accessed April 12, 2016).

Why Shofars Wail in Scripture and Today—   By Mary A. Bruno, Ph.D.

97

That was a promise of what to expect regarding the Amalekites. Their victory songs and dances were over. This is the only mention of Jehovah Nissi (Jehovah is my Banner) in Scripture. God wanted Moses and Joshua to remember what actually happened on that day of great conquest.

Joshua and his chosen men bravely wielded sharp swords in bloody combat against Amalek in the valley. They knew that *Jehovah Nissi's* unseen Presence—their real Victory Banner—was waving over them and enabling them to triumph. God was preparing Joshua for a promotion and higher calling. God still calls leaders to equip themselves with His Word. One may wonder how many will obey.

> Study to shew thyself approved unto God, a workman that needeth not to be ashamed, rightly dividing the word of truth.
> —2 Tim. 2:15 KJV

> And that servant who knew his master's will, and did not prepare *himself* or do according to his will, shall be beaten, **with many *stripes*.**
> —Luke 12:47, emphasis added

Woe to those who have based their ministries on spiritual gifts; instead of applying themselves to training so that they could rightly divide the Word of Truth, and build their ministries on the solid foundation of God's Word.

Joshua's hunger for God and loyalty to Moses set him apart from others. There was no mention of his appearance; however, bulging muscles and battle scars may have borne silent witness to his conquests. Joshua and Caleb had

Why Shofars Wail in Scripture and Today—   By Mary A. Bruno, Ph.D.

98

brought a good report in Numbers 14:6–10[49] after spying out the Promised Land. Sure, giants were there, but Joshua knew Jehovah Nissi was bigger and better than any giant.

Other spies had whined to return to Egypt. They wanted to elect a new leader (a Chief Executive Officer (CEO) of Bondage?) to lead them back to slavery—after having tasted God's sweet freedom. Joshua and Caleb tried to sway them from rebellion and assured God would give them the land. However, instead of giving their godly leaders a big round of applause, the people wanted to hurl big round stones—at them!

However, God swooped in to rescue them and manifested His glory in the tabernacle. Everybody knew that when His glory was there, it was time to stop everything—even the stoning of His servants—and head for the tent (go to church, synagogue or temple). Adonai had to keep Joshua alive for an exciting adventure that would involve the power of obedience, with shofar blasts and shouting.

Promotion

When God told Moses that his days on earth were almost over, Moses asked Him to set a new man over the people, one who would be able to guide them. God told him how to assemble everyone and anoint Joshua as the leader.

Deuteronomy 20:24–29 shows Aaron's son Eleazar was the priest then. Anointing for leadership involved God's Spirit and the laying on of hands. After decades of backing Moses, it was Joshua's time for promotion. God gave Moses explicit instructions on how to go about it.

---

[49] The Word Made Flesh: Real Life Meets Real Truth | Just ..., https://twmf.wordpress.com/ (accessed April 12, 2016).

Why Shofars Wail in Scripture and Today—   By Mary A. Bruno, Ph.D.

99

> And the LORD said to Moses: "Take Joshua the son of
> Nun with you, *a man in whom is the Spirit,* and lay your
> hand on him; set him before Eleazar the priest and
> before all the congregation, and inaugurate him in their
> sight. And you shall give *some* of your authority to him,
> that all the congregation of the children of Israel may be
> obedient.
>
> —Num. 27:18–20, italics added

Joshua, *the man in whom was God's Spirit,* met God's qualification for leadership. Moses took him before all the people—including the *stone-throwers*. He laid his hands on Joshua, transferred the leadership and charged him to lead *them,* including the ones who had tried to stone (kill) him.

The book of Acts gives that kind of standard for those involved in the food ministry. How many priests, pastors, rabbis, and godly leaders will uphold God's minimum standard for leadership—before appointing someone to serve His flock?

> Then the twelve summoned the multitude of the
> disciples and said, "It is not desirable that we should
> leave the word of God and **serve tables**. Therefore,
> brethren, seek out from among you seven men
> of *good* **reputation, full of the Holy Spirit and
> wisdom,** whom we may appoint over this business; but
> we will give ourselves continually to prayer and to the
> ministry of the word."
>
> And the saying pleased the whole multitude. And they
> chose Stephen, a man **full of faith and the Holy Spirit**,
> and Philip, Prochorus, Nicanor, Timon, Parmenas, and
> Nicolas, a proselyte from Antioch, whom they set before
> the apostles; and when they had prayed, they laid hands
> on them.
>
> —Acts 6:1-6, emphasis added

Why Shofars Wail in Scripture and Today—   By Mary A. Bruno, Ph.D.

100

God's four-point basic requirement for those who are eligible to serve His flock is to be: of good reputation, full of the Holy Spirit, full of wisdom, and full of faith.

A reasonable person might realize that this is also God's *minimum standard* for others who minister to His flock, including the worship leaders, preachers, teachers, pastors, evangelists, elders, deacons, treasurers, ushers, administrators, board members, youth leaders; council members, sound technicians, supervisors, and those who teach and tend to children, visit the sick, or fill any other position in the church. Should they not also meet *God's minimum standard for serving food to His flock*? Secular skills, and natural talents, abilities, can never replace the fullness of God's Holy Spirit and wisdom in His servants.

One might wonder how many pastors or Christian leaders will humble themselves, trust God, and honor His Word when appointing men and women to serve His flock.

Finish Strong

During their trips up and down Mount Sinai, Joshua's muscular arms might have reached out to steady a lesser man—but not Moses! Even with 120 birthdays under his sash, Moses could have read the fine print on the bottom of a scroll. One could almost envision him with his robe hiked up, racing back to camp as he glanced over his muscular shoulder, flashed a bearded grin, and yelled to the man four decades his junior, "Come on 'Josh'—Hurry up!"

> Moses *was* one hundred and twenty years old when he died. His eyes were not dim nor his natural vigor diminished.
>
> —Deut. 34:7

Why Shofars Wail in Scripture and Today—   By Mary A. Bruno, Ph.D.

101

Since he was in such good health, one might wonder how Moses died. His earthly time clock may have simply stopped ticking when he finished *Project Israel*. After Moses' friend, Adonai, held his private funeral, he would go with Him to Paradise—where there would be no more gut-wrenching complaints or rebellion. However, wait! God just might have wrapped up some unfinished business ...

Moses had asked previously to see God's glory, which He had refused because the results would have been fatal (Ex. 33:18, 20). Moses had to stay alive to lead the Israelites and train Joshua, which he had done.

However, after Moses had finished his final assignment, God may have let him have a peek at His smiling face and behold His great glory. If that happened, it might have become Moses' checkout key from Planet Earth. (Because no one can see God's face and live.) Moses could have left this world in a great blaze of God's glory. The Scripture does not say that He did; however, God does like to take care of details and grant hearts' desires.

Moses was ready to unwind from decades of hearing Israel's grievances. A long soak in one of God's bubbling hot springs and an extended vacation would be welcome. His inner shofar whispered to come up higher. He was relieved that his role in *Project Israel* was finished. Deuteronomy 34:5–7 tells of when God lovingly buried Moses in a valley of Moab, near Beth-Peor.

It was time for Joshua to lead Israel. She would do well with his lead. He would guide her to victory in the upcoming Jericho campaign.

Shofars would help to bring down barriers.

* * *

Why Shofars Wail in Scripture and Today—   By Mary A. Bruno, Ph.D.

102

Chapter 12
Jericho—Part 2: Preliminaries

The Jericho encounter was fast approaching. God spoke reassuring words and sprinkled spectacular confidence builders along the way that enabled Joshua and his men to march into the miraculous.

General Joshua needed assurance that he had heard from the LORD. God understood and issued an excellent command, "Be strong and of good courage." Those six words (almost exactly) came up repeatedly in Deuteronomy 31:6,23, Joshua 1:1–9,18, 10:25; 1 Chronicles 22:13, 28:20, 2 Chronicles 32:7, and in Isaiah 41:10. The heart of the message was to be strong, not because of human ability, but because God Almighty was with him. God's strength was more than enough for whatever Joshua would encounter.

Impartation

When the LORD said, "Be strong . . ." *He was imparting* His supernatural strength into Joshua. It was more than a command—it was an *impartation,* similar to when Jesus said, *"Be healed,"* and the person received healing.

Why Shofars Wail in Scripture and Today—   By Mary A. Bruno, Ph.D.

103

Jesus also told His followers, "I will never leave thee nor forsake thee" (Heb. 13:5b KJV).

He did not need to tell them to be strong or of good courage because He was sending the Holy Spirit, Who would give[50] them all of the holy power and holy confidence they would ever need. Jesus' last words to His followers (right before a cloud received Him out of their sight) were:

> "But you will *receive power* when the Holy Spirit has come upon you; and you shall be My witnesses both in Jerusalem, and in all Judea and Samaria, and even to the remotest part of the earth."
> And after He had said these things, He was lifted up while they were looking on, and *a cloud received* Him out of their sight.
> —Acts 1:8–9 NASB, italics added

Father God seemed to enjoy leading by cloud and by fire, and manifesting His Presence in a glory cloud that filled the temple. Therefore, one may wonder if He might have been in that cloud, giving Jesus hugs and pats on the back, as *Heaven's elevator* received Jesus back into Heaven.

Receive

Before we examine the word "power," it seems logical to consider the word *receive*, which as noted above, came right before it in Acts 1:8. In this passage and others, Jesus gave believers the *same* Holy Spirit (Ruach Kodesh) with the *same* dynamic power that enabled Him to preach God's Word, perform signs and wonders, raise the dead, and deal with difficult people. The Holy Spirit Who strengthened

---

[50] Why the Cross? | Dead Heroes Don't Save, http://deadheroesdontsave.com/2013/03/27/why-the-cross/ (accessed April 12, 2016).

Why Shofars Wail in Scripture and Today—   By Mary A. Bruno, Ph.D.

104

Jesus to accomplish His Father's will on earth would also empower believers to continue His ministry.

You shall receive, meant believers *would* (Not *might*, but *would*) reach out, take hold of God's precious gift, and not undertake their God-given mission without it.

The word, *receive*,[51] in Acts 1:8 was from *lambano*. It means: *to take with the hand, lay hold of any person or thing to use it; to take in order to carry away;*[52] *to take what is one's own, to make one's own; and to associate with one's self as a companion.* It also means *to take a thing due, to receive a person, give him access to one's self, and receive (as a gift).*

A study of *lambano* brought a good idea of exactly what Jesus meant when He used the word *receive*. He indicated believers would reach out, embrace His promised Holy Spirit, and leave with His enabling Presence and Power to serve God. It was the same word used for *received* when a person received Jesus Christ (Yeshua, the Messiah), the Lamb of God, and was born again.

> But as many as received him, to them gave he power to become the sons of God, even to them that believe on his name.
>
> —John 1:12 KJV

If you have never told God's Son, Yeshua, the Lord Jesus Christ—the Messiah—that you are receiving Him as

---

[51] "G2983 - lambanō - Strong's Greek Lexicon (KJV)." Blue Letter Bible. Accessed 4 Jun, 2016.
https://www.blueletterbible.org//lang/Lexicon/Lexicon.cfm?Strongs=G2983&t=KJV
[52] The Perfect Day: Alignment, Part 1 of 6: Face To Dirt,
http://ldsperfectday.blogspot.com/2015/09/alignment-part-1-of-3-face-to-dirt.htm (accessed April 12, 2016).

Why Shofars Wail in Scripture and Today—   By Mary A. Bruno, Ph.D.

105

your Savior, wisdom will encourage you to pause and do so right now. He may have been waiting a long time to hear those precious words from your faithful lips.

Paul used that same word for *receiving* the Holy Spirit after some men at Ephesus had become believers.

> He said to them, "Did you receive the Holy Spirit when you believed?" And they said to him, "No, we have not even heard whether there is a Holy Spirit."
> —Acts 19:2 NASB

> And when Paul had laid his hands upon them, the Holy Spirit came on them, and they *began* speaking with tongues and prophesying.
> —Acts 19:6

Power

In Acts 1:8, Jesus spoke of receiving God's enabling *power* for Christian ministry. Let us consider some exciting implications regarding the word *power*. *Power* is the same word translated as *virtue* in Mark 5:30, concerning the woman with the issue of blood. When she reached out and touched the hem of Jesus' garment, it was as if she had touched a live wire of healing. *Virtue* flowed out instantly from Jesus and into her. His virtue stopped the unhealthy flow from her body. The faith-filled tassel-toucher received *immediate* healing—and an amazing testimony that she would share for the rest of her life.

Numbers 15:37–41 indicates that it was common knowledge in that region, that a border with corner tassels on the hem of an Israelite's garment (some say it was a prayer shawl) was a reminder to obey God's Law and to claim His miraculous *fringe benefits*.

Why Shofars Wail in Scripture and Today—   By Mary A. Bruno, Ph.D.

106

And Jesus immediately knowing in himself that *virtue* had gone out of him, turned him about in the press, and said who touched my clothes?

—Mark 5:30 KJV, italics added

Virtue

The word for virtue,[53] *dynamis* (pronounced du-na-mes), was from the same word used for God's *dynamic power* in Acts 1:8. Its meanings included: "strength, power, ability; power for performing miracles; power and influence, which belong to riches and wealth; and power consisting in or resting upon armies, forces, and hosts." That tremendous *dynamis* power—Holy Spirit enablement—flowed from Jesus Christ directly into the woman's flesh as she dared to reach out and *receive* (take hold of) and leave with her life-changing fringe-benefit miracle.

In the meantime, back at Joshua's pre-Jericho pep talk, he perked up after hearing from God through Moses and receiving other encouragement directly from the Lord. In Joshua 1:1–9, when God told Joshua to be strong, and of good courage, He was building him up for something big. Those encouraging words hinted that a battle was coming—which, of course, implied victory.

Joshua was experienced in espionage and knew the importance of protecting military secrets. He kept the upcoming Jericho mission quiet and dispatched two under-cover agents to spy out the city and size up their opposition.

Severed

Joshua may not have known that a great shofar-

---

[53] "G1411 - dynamis - Strong's Greek Lexicon (KJV)." Blue Letter Bible. Accessed 4 Jun, 2016.
https://www.blueletterbible.org//lang/Lexicon/Lexicon.cfm?Strongs=G1411&t=KJV

Why Shofars Wail in Scripture and Today—   By Mary A. Bruno, Ph.D.

107

blowing victory was coming, or why he felt compelled to reinstitute the covenant of circumcision. However, he did know that the people could not claim God's covenant promise without practicing that rite.

How will we respond when God says it is time to sever a personal matter with someone or something? Will we cut it off and obey Him, or stay attached to whatever He says must go, and forfeit His blessing?

Joshua would have his own holy ground encounter when he came face-to-face with the Captain of the armies of heaven. The event was part of his preparation for when he and his men would blow their shofars at the right time, in the right place, in the right way, and have the right results.

If Joshua had gone in prematurely, his shofar blasts might have brought an undesirable end.

* * *

Why Shofars Wail in Scripture and Today—   By Mary A. Bruno, Ph.D.

108

Chapter 13
Jericho—Part 3: Holy Ground

Joshua's holy ground moment happened when he met the Captain of the armies of heaven—with His sword drawn! That must have been a heart-pounder. Joshua had heard about Moses' holy ground encounter with God at the burning bush, and had seen the other miracles. He often recalled them to encourage himself in the LORD.

Shoes

In Exodus 3:3–17 Joshua was close to Moses's age at the time of his holy ground/burning bush incident. Moses' old shoes had been adequate to go on the run from a murder rap in Egypt, and to lead Jethro's bleating flock through the back of the desert to Mount Sinai. Nevertheless, when he saw the bush that was burning but not consumed by God's fire from on high, it was time to step out of his old shoes and stand in God's Presence—on holy ground.

New Calling

God gave Moses a new calling, a new commission, and a new anointing to lead a new flock—God's flock. His new mission and commission came with God's miraculous

Why Shofars Wail in Scripture and Today—   By Mary A. Bruno, Ph.D.

109

equipping power. It was Moses' time to walk in his new spiritual shoes of God-given position, God-given power, God-given authority, and God-given miracles.

That passage ended when God gave Moses a sign. Part one, of the sign, was that God would be with him. Part two, was that when Moses had brought the people out of Egypt, he would worship God again on that mountain.

What began for Moses as a routine shepherd's job to feed his father-in-law's bleating sheep had led him to a holy ground encounter with God—Israel's Shepherd. Moses faithfully led God's flock during *Project Israel,* and enjoyed some fiery times with Him at Mount Sinai.

Personal Encounter
However, Joshua was by Jericho, perhaps walking it out and wondering how to take that city for God. He looked up and saw a man standing near him[54] (Josh. 5:13–15)— with a drawn sword in his hand! A shy man might have cringed, and hid; but Joshua went right up to him and asked, "Are you for us, or for our[55] adversaries?"

When the man identified himself as the prince of the LORD's host, humble Joshua fell on his face and worshiped. The prince of God's host received Joshua's worship, which showed the armed man was divine. (Theologians call an Old Testament visitation of Christ, such as this, a *Christophany.*)

During his God encounter, Joshua asked the armed man what he had to say to him. (Joshua wanted a word from the LORD.) He would cherish that day. No longer would he

---

54 NLV - Joshua 5:13 - When Joshua was by Jericho, he looked ..,
https://www.studylight.org/bible/nlv/joshua/5-13.html (accessed April 12, 2016).

55 Joshua 5:13-15, New International Version (NIV) Now when ...,
https://www.bible.com/bible/111/jos.5.13-15.niv#! (accessed April 12, 2016).

Why Shofars Wail in Scripture and Today—   By Mary A. Bruno, Ph.D.

110

need to dwell on his leader's accounts of God encounters. He was having his own holy ground moment—with God!

> Then the Commander of the LORD's army said to Joshua, "Take your sandal off your foot, for the place where you stand *is* holy." And Joshua did so.
>
> —Josh. 5:15

Joshua knew what that meant. Something good was coming! (Yes, God, go on . . .) God continued with a promise of what He had already done. He indicated it was a done deal; however, Joshua still had to battle it out on Earth.

> Now Jericho was securely shut up because of the children of Israel; none went out, and none came in. And the LORD said to Joshua: "See! I have given Jericho into your hand, its king, *and* the mighty men of valor."
>
> —Josh. 6:1–2

What a nice gift!

Joshua had crossed a victory threshold with God. It was time for him to trade in his apprentice sandals for general's shoes. Confident that the captain of the Lord's host would lead him, Joshua would dare to lead God's people forward to conquer and possess the Promised Land.

Sure, Jericho, laced up tight as a drum, had high, thick walls with homes built into them (and laundry drying on balconies). However, God knows how to turn barriers into victory paths with stepping-stones. The mighty men of valor inside that fortress were good, but they were no match for Israel's Mighty God of Miracles.

Why Shofars Wail in Scripture and Today—   By Mary A. Bruno, Ph.D.

111

Details

God showed Joshua how to take the city, right down to the smallest details. They included one scarlet cord, seven wailing shofars, the Ark of the Covenant, quiet times, the line-up, marching, lots of shouting, and obedience.

> "You shall march around the city, all *you* men of war; you shall go all around the city once. This you shall do six days. And seven priests shall bear seven trumpets of rams' horns before the ark. But the seventh day you shall march around the city seven times, and the priests shall blow the trumpets. It shall come to pass, when they make **a long *blast*** with the ram's horn, *and* when you hear the sound of the trumpet, that all the people shall shout with a great shout; then the wall of the city will fall down flat. And the people shall go up every man straight before him."
>
> —Josh. 6:3–5, emphasis added

Long Blast

That long blast was likely the Tekiah Gedolah. It was nice that God took care of the king and his mighty men for Joshua. We have heard a lot about how Jericho's wall flattened, but not much about the armed men of courage who stayed on high alert behind that barrier. *Jericho's finest* were ready to deal with intruders if and when, anyone reached the top of their massive wall. However, God had other plans for what happened on and to that wall.

Expert fighting men (Green Turbans?) may have been Jericho's equivalent of Green Berets. They had heard that God fought for Israel—with miracles! Jericho's finest knew they were no match for the Living God, Who was a *mighty mobile wall of protection* around Israel's army.

Why Shofars Wail in Scripture and Today—   By Mary A. Bruno, Ph.D.

112

Word was out on the cobblestones that two Israeli spies were already *inside* Jericho! Jericho's mighty men may have suspected that defeat was inevitable, which could have sapped their strength and courage.

Rahab

Rahab, a prostitute, had heard about the miracles of Egypt and reports of when God opened the Red Sea for His people. She feared God[56] and flirted with a charge of treason when she honored Him and hid the two spies in her home. It is doubtful that she would have done so if they had acted like any other traveling adulterer or fornicator who had tied his camel by her private entrance.

These godly men were very different. They were on a special assignment for God. Rahab threw her faith into action and hid them on her roof—*not in her bedroom*—where she covered them with stalks of flax—not bedding. They, in turn, covered her with God's grace. The men gave her a scarlet cord to fasten to her window and promised to spare her and her family—if they stayed inside, embraced the promise that went with the scarlet cord, and did not tell anyone about their mission.

Until then Rahab may have kept a scarlet light in her window to attract customers to her door. However, she had believed the true report and received the scarlet cord with the promise of salvation for herself and her family. From then on, that scarlet cord of hope that she boldly displayed in her window of faith, (as a great shofar) would boldly proclaim that her former house of sin and shame had become a house of salvation.

---

[56] Life After Miracles | Our Daily Bread, http://odb.org/2003/02/20/life-after-miracles/ (accessed April 12, 2016).

Why Shofars Wail in Scripture and Today—   By Mary A. Bruno, Ph.D.

Transformed

Something very wonderful happened when Rahab honored God and His servants and relied on their promised salvation. She gave them the straw and chaff (waste) of her broken life, and they gave her peace and protection, with the promise of safety for herself and her family, and a blessed new life with God's people.

One can almost see her fastening that scarlet cord to her window. She probably grasped it with both hands, braced a bare foot against her windowsill and relied on God's strength to pull the knot tight. That scarlet cord was going nowhere! Their lives depended on it.

Rahab would never again sell herself for a coin. She would gladly leave the dregs of her old life behind when God rescued her and destroyed her customer base. Rahab embraced God's free salvation with her whole heart, for herself and her family, and instantly, became a courageous woman of faith.

God likes it when people trust in Him and believe His Word. He was so impressed with how Rahab relied on Him, that He put her in His Book—right next to the great heroes of the faith. Matthew 1:5 cites Rahab as Boaz's mother—in the genealogy of Jesus Christ, which means that God claimed her as part of His family. In Hebrews 11:30, 31, Joshua's name is not in the Jericho account; however, God made sure that Rahab's name got in, and even commented on her faith. He must have been extremely pleased with her.

Because Rahab stood firm and trusted God, her home would stand firm as a tower of faith amid disaster's rubble when God worked His wonders at Jericho.

* * *

Why Shofars Wail in Scripture and Today—   By Mary A. Bruno, Ph.D.

114

Chapter 14
Jericho—Part 4: The Blasts

Joshua's courage soared after his God encounter. His men had healed after circumcision. The sweet smell of victory was in the air. In Joshua 6:8–9, he told the priests how to order the lineup. One might imagine what it was like for Jerichonians inside their proud and lofty wall when the daily shofar blasts began to wail. The unnerving scene could have unfolded as follows.

Day One—Joshua made sure everyone knew the drill. He put armed men in front. Seven priests with seven shofars came next, then the Ark of the Covenant (symbol of God's Presence). God wanted the army to see the Ark, which would confirm that He was right there to help and was in the battle with them. Others formed the rearguard.

The procession marched around the city once, with the seven priests blowing seven shofars. They may have begun with a wailing *Shevarim* to call Jerichonians to repentance. The Bible does not specify which blasts sounded, but a *Shevarim* might have been timely.

Why Shofars Wail in Scripture and Today—   By Mary A. Bruno, Ph.D.

115

> Now Joshua had commanded the people, saying, "You shall not shout or make any noise with your voice, nor shall a word proceed out of your mouth, until the day I say to you, 'Shout!' Then you shall shout." So he had the ark of the LORD circle the city, going around *it* once. Then they came into the camp and lodged in the camp.
>
> —Josh. 6:10–11

It was lip-zip time—with no chance to gripe, offer suggestions, or share opinions. There must have been a lot of pointing and gesturing going on during that week because the only voices heard were those of the seven wailing shofars that sent a clear message from God.

> And Joshua rose early in the morning, and the priests took up the ark of the LORD. Then seven priests bearing **seven trumpets of rams' horns** before the ark of the LORD went on continually and blew with the trumpets. And the armed men went before them. But the rear guard came after the ark of the LORD, while *the priests* continued blowing the **trumpets**. And the second day they marched around the city once and returned to the camp. So they did six days.
>
> —Josh. 6:12–14, emphasis added

Sandals on the Ground

Jerichonian men of valor peeked through windows. Uneasiness troubled brave hearts. Homes on the wall would take the first hits in an attack. The rhythmic *thump-thump, thump-thump* of Hebrew sandals was orderly, but no weapons rattled. Joshua's steel-eyed soldiers marched in silence before and after the priests with blaring shofars.

Jerichonians wondered why the men carried that box-like object (the Ark) by golden poles. They looked more like a parade than a war party. The army marched around

Why Shofars Wail in Scripture and Today—   By Mary A. Bruno, Ph.D.

116

Jericho once, which historians say took less than an hour, and then returned to camp, which puzzled the Jerichonians.

Day Two—Joshua's men were up early, but nothing appeared to have changed. Soul-piercing shofar blasts and thumping sandals announced their presence. They marched around Jericho once and then returned to camp in time for lunch. Jericonians stared, sipped their beverages and wondered what was going on with those Israelites.

Day Three—Joshua's soldiers woke early and obeyed orders again, even though everything *looked* unchanged. God seemed to be in no hurry as they took another lap around Jericho with shofars blaring. The men had obeyed God's instructions and had marched once around the city for three consecutive days. Victory seemed no closer than when they had begun—but they kept on marching.

Day Four—Shofar blasts may have repeated the wailing three-blast Shevarim, to call Jerichonians to humble their hearts before the Living God. Israeli sandals kept on thumping on Jericho's hard ground.

A Jerichonian husband probably whispered, "Relax, honey. They should be on their way soon."

"I hope so. Those shofar blasts bring me to tears."

The men repeated the same routine daily and had the same results. But they kept on marching.

Day Five—Joshua's muted army continued to obey God's marching orders. *Blast!-blast!-blast! Thump!-thump! Thump!-thump!* Unaware that Jerichonian nerves were ready to snap, the men of faith kept on marching.

Day Six—Joshua's loyal soldiers obeyed God's orders again, even though their efforts appeared to be futile. Un-

Why Shofars Wail in Scripture and Today—   By Mary A. Bruno, Ph.D.

117

easiness filled Jericho. Peacocks may have screeched and fanned their feathers as dogs bristled, cats hissed, and hairline cracks shot through floors and walls. The wall *looked* as intimidating as ever—but they kept on marching.

Joshua's men relaxed in silence by their campfires that night and pondered God's Presence, power, and promises. Soldiers may have sensed a new closeness to God, and to each other, as invisible barriers and conflicts dissolved. They must have savored the sweet exhilaration that comes from knowing when one is doing something very right and very good, even though the results are not yet visible.

> But it came to pass on the seventh day that they rose early, about the dawning of the day, and marched around the city seven times in the same manner. On that day only they marched around the city seven times. And the seventh time it happened, when the priests blew the trumpets, that Joshua said to the people: "Shout, for the LORD has given you the city! Now the city shall be doomed by the LORD to destruction, it and all who *are* in it. Only Rahab the harlot shall live, she and all who *are* with her in the house, because she hid the messengers that we sent.
>
> —Josh. 6:15–17

Wailing Shofars

Day Seven—Shofars rang out early. The procession did not stop after the first lap. Priests kept on blowing their shofars as the men kept on marching, and marching, and marching. *B-l-a-s-t! B-l-a-s-t! B-l-a-s-t! Thump!-Thump! Thump!-Thump!* Uneasy wall-dwellers sensed something had changed. The army was on lap three and still marching with purpose. Priests with wailing shofars blasted on, and on, and on, through laps four, and five and six.

Why Shofars Wail in Scripture and Today—   By Mary A. Bruno, Ph.D.

Rounds one thru six—Feeling safe within their trusted stronghold, a Jerichonian husband may have asked, "Why are you weeping, honey? Come and stand by me. They will be gone soon. Whoa! What was that?"

Round seven—Joshua's men listened for his command. The final shofar cries could have started with a nine-blast Teruah to sound the alarm. The seven priests probably switched to the Tekiah Gedolah to praise God, and announce His coming. Joshua's men waited for the signal—when the seven priests would blow their seven shofars for the seventh time around Jericho.

Then Joshua ordered the men to "Shout, for the LORD has given you the city!" (Josh. 6:16).

The word *shout,*[57] *ruwa,* in Joshua 6:16 translates in Scripture as: "To shout, raise a sound, cry out, give a blast; to shout a war cry[58] alarm of battle; to sound a signal for war or to march; shout in triumph (over enemies), and to shout in applause." The men's mighty shout(s) had the effect of enormous shofar blasts.

Terrified Jericonians clung to swaying doorways as shofar blasts, victory shouts, and God's unseen Presence crumbled mortar, dislodged bricks, wilted their fortress, flattened their wall, and exposed them to Joshua's men—who kept on marching.

---

[57] "H7321 - ruwa` - Strong's Hebrew Lexicon (KJV)." Blue Letter Bible. Accessed 4 Jun, 2016.
https://www.blueletterbible.org//lang/Lexicon/Lexicon.cfm?Strongs=H7321&t=KJV
[58] Praise Him, Praise Him - SERMON OUTLINES,
http://www.sermonoutlines.org/Owen%20Sermons/Psalms/(OT%2019)%20Psalm%20100%20-% (accessed April 12, 2016).

Why Shofars Wail in Scripture and Today—   By Mary A. Bruno, Ph.D.

119

So the people shouted when *the priests* blew the trumpets. And it happened when the people heard the sound of the trumpet, and the people shouted with a great shout, that the wall fell down flat. Then the people went up into the city, every man straight before him, and they took the city. And they utterly destroyed all that *was* in the city, both man and woman, young and old, ox and sheep and donkey, with the edge of the sword . . . . And Joshua spared Rahab the harlot, her father's household, and all that she had. So she dwells in Israel to this day, because she hid the messengers whom Joshua sent to spy out Jericho.

—Josh. 6:20–21, 25

Victory shouts (*ruwa*) that shot up before God and echoed into the heavens were like powerful shofar blasts that humbled Jericho's high and mighty wall down to the ground. The shouting Israelis kept on marching and marching, and marching—every man straight before him, over mounds of rubble that (before their shouting) had looked like an impassable fortress.

Pillar of Faith

Rahab, a new woman of faith, and her family of new believers survived because they had believed and received the salvation message. They stayed by the scarlet cord, which had become their new window of hope in her house of salvation that towered over Jericho's fallen fortress.

Rahab, a social misfit, would have a place with Israel's godly women as they welcomed her and helped her to grow in God's grace. She would have been delighted to know that in God's appointed time when His good plans had unfolded for her, that she would be laughing while bouncing little Boaz on her knees, and that she would also become Jesus' great, great, great, great . . . grandma (Matt. 1:5).

Why Shofars Wail in Scripture and Today—   By Mary A. Bruno, Ph.D.

120

Joshua's army was glad they had gotten up early and obeyed God one more time, because, on that time—the last time—everything changed.

In contrast to Rahab's generous and courageous acts of faith and obedience in her house of salvation, Joshua chapter 7, tells of Achan's acts of greed, disobedience, and a cover-up that would cost his life, the lives of his loved ones, and the loss of all that he had in verses 24-26. Great testing often came alongside great achievement or victory.

Israel celebrated incredible success. However, being prone to stray from God, and slow to learn from mistakes, she would stray (again) and suffer decades of bondage until she finally realized it was time to pray. Moreover, when she did call on the Lord, He answered her heartfelt *agreeing prayer* and sent Ehud, a brave deliverer whose anointed shofar would rally Israel's army to victory.

* * *

Why Shofars Wail in Scripture and Today—   By Mary A. Bruno, Ph.D.

121

Niagara Falls

The Brunos blew the shofar as they, proclaimed God's ownership of each country, province, state, point of interest, and all the people therein.

They declared God's blessings upon the people and the land, including the "Didgeridoo Couple" at Niagara Falls (mentioned in chapter 32).

Why Shofars Wail in Scripture and Today—   By Mary A. Bruno, Ph.D.

122

Chapter 15
Daring Deliverance

O bedience-challenged Israelites slipped back into their old ways, and grew sloppy about keeping God's Laws. They forgot why heathens were there, dumped God, married pagans, embraced false gods—and wondered why they were having problems.

> Now these *are* the nations which the LORD left, that He might test Israel by them, *that is,* all who had not known any of the wars in Canaan (*this was* only so that the generations of the children of Israel might be taught to know war, at least those who had not formerly known it).
>
> —Judg. 3:1–2

God knew that overcomers would need something to overcome. Therefore, He left a few heathen nations around for the Israelites to use as sparring partners to stay in shape for war. However, the Israelites relaxed their guard, decided to be lovers instead of fighters, and married pagans!

It was doubtful that any of them had asked God to bless marriage to an unbeliever. He would not bless what He had told them not to do. Since they enjoyed ungodly

Why Shofars Wail in Scripture and Today—   By Mary A. Bruno, Ph.D.

123

company, God turned them over ᵀᵒ Chushan-Rishathaim (*twice-wicked Chushan*) for eight years.

> Good understanding giveth favor, but the way of transgressors is hard.
>
> —Prov. 13:15 KJV

The way of evildoers was supposed to be hard, so they would quickly repent and return to where God's blessings flowed. Sadly, the slow learners failed their obedience tests and had to repeat the course.

After serving an *eight-year sentence* under Chushan-Rishathaim, the Israelites realized it was *time to pray* and *cried out* to the LORD. Merciful God answered their heartfelt prayer and raised up Othniel, Caleb's younger brother. The Holy Spirit came upon him in a great way in Judges 3:9–11, and Israel had 40 years of rest. However, the spiritually careless Israelites slipped back into sin (again) and suffered consequences that were a whole lot worse than before.

> So the children of Israel served Eglon king of Moab eighteen years.
>
> —Judg. 3:14

God handed down an 18-year sentence under "warden" Eglon, who had overcome Israel and taken Jericho.

They had won the Jericho prize by obedience but lost it by disobedience. Yet, when God's desperate, people *cried out* to Him (prayed) for help in Judges 3:15, He graciously raised up someone to lead them to victory. (God tends to be very nice about that sort of thing.) Bless Him!

> If my people, who are called by My name will humble themselves, and pray and seek My face, and **turn from**

Why Shofars Wail in Scripture and Today—   By Mary A. Bruno, Ph.D.

124

their wicked ways, then I will hear from heaven, and will forgive their sin and heal their land.

—2 Chron. 7:13–14, emphasis added

Ehud, a shofar-blowing Benjamite and God's man of the hour led a crew to deliver a tax payment to King Eglon.

> But when the sons of Israel cried to the LORD, the LORD raised up a deliverer for them, Ehud the son of Gera, the Benjamite, a left-handed man. And the sons of Israel sent tribute by him to Eglon the king of Moab. Ehud made himself a sword which had two edges, a cubit in length, and he bound it on his right thigh under his cloak. He presented the tribute to Eglon king of Moab. (Now Eglon *was* a very fat man.)
> —Judges 3:15–17 NASB

Everything was ready to load up in the morning. Ehud's evening may have unfolded as follows:

"What are you doing out there, Ehuddie? It is way past bedtime," Ehud's wife asked.

"Fret not, my Little Pomegranate. I'm finishing up a personal gift for the king."

Preparation

Ehud tightened his sash and kept on grinding. He worked with a great sense of destiny and finished the dagger/sword. It was exactly one cubit, the length from his elbow to his fingertip (about seventeen inches, including the handle). Perfect! He slipped the weapon into its sheath.

Early on tax day morning, Ehud fastened the sword under his clothing to hide it from any unreliable person who might accidentally disclose his mission.

Why Shofars Wail in Scripture and Today—   By Mary A. Bruno, Ph.D.

125

Heavy-laden camels sauntered along with the usual spitting, kicking, and licking. Ehud probably wondered if they sensed that this was a very special day for Israel.

The tax caravan arrived at King Eglon's office in rebuilt Jericho and the men lugged in the tribute. Ehud rode back with the rest of the team for part of the way and then sent them on. However, he returned to Jericho to settle the balance of their account with Eglon.

Presentation

Royal guards may have wondered why he was back so soon; nonetheless, they escorted him to the king's private room, as told in Judges 3:20–23. King Eglon may have rewarded himself with a celebratory snack after receiving the hefty payment. A refreshing breeze blew over cool marble floors as he dozed on his couch. Hearing footsteps in the corridor, he most likely brushed crumbs from his royal robe and let out a contented sigh that welcomed Ehud.

The king's dull brown eyes squinted beneath folds of fat that pressed his eyelids into narrow slits. He raised a bushy black eyebrow and cast a questioning gaze at the messenger. Ehud stood erect, spoke with authority, and stated that he was on a secret errand.

Was this why God had urged him to polish his sword making skills? What would his sweet *Little Pomegranate* think about all of this? Sensing God's help, Ehud's heart pounded as he inhaled, looked the doomed king straight in the slits and asserted, "I have a message from God for you."

As Eglon maneuvered his huge body back to his feet, Ehud seized the moment and thrust his sharp and sleek two-edged sword deep into Eglon's bulging belly that swallowed it beneath big brown folds of lumpy warm fat.

Why Shofars Wail in Scripture and Today—   By Mary A. Bruno, Ph.D.

126

Things got messy. Ehud gently closed the doors behind him, and then raced his camel out of Jericho.

> But Ehud had escaped while they delayed, and passed beyond the stone images and escaped to Seirah. And it happened, when he arrived, that he blew the trumpet in the mountains of Ephraim, and the children of Israel went down with him from the mountains; and he led them. Then he said to them, "Follow *me*, for the LORD has delivered your enemies the Moabites into your hand." So they went down after him, seized the fords of the Jordan leading to Moab, and did not allow anyone to cross over. And at that time they killed about ten thousand men of Moab, all stout men of valor; not a man escaped. So Moab was subdued that day under the hand of Israel. And the land had rest for eighty years.
>
> —Judg. 3:26–30

Shofar Calls

Ehud knew he had crushed the head of Israel's enemy, or in this case, *pierced* the belly. He hunched forward and raced his sweaty animal to Seirah near Ephraim's hills. He was not *running from* the enemy—he was *racing to* rally Israel's army to victory!

He raised his shofar and launched part three of his mission. Ehud's God-ordained shofar calls reverberated over Ephraim's hills, through Israel's warrior hearts, and awakened their sense of destiny. His soul-stirring shofar blasts compelled God's soldiers to rise up, line up, and follow up. They answered the call, rushed down slopes, and fell into order behind their new leader who cried, "Follow me for the Lord has delivered your enemies, the Moabites, into your hand" (Judg. 3:28 AMP).

Why Shofars Wail in Scripture and Today—   By Mary A. Bruno, Ph.D.

127

Board members got no vote. There were no committee meetings or elections. Warriors recognized a victory cry when they heard it. Ehud was God's answer to their prayer. It was time to move forward with God.

God's brave shofar blower led Israel's army to cut off the Moabites at Jordan's fords (The enemy's inroads or crossing places). News spread quickly that King Eglon was dead. His leaderless soldiers fell into confusion and went berserk while Israel's army came into divine order and went on the attack. The Bible does not mention how many Israelites were in that fight. When God was with them, even one was enough. However, it does say that about ten thousand Moabites died that day.

Ehud's victory brought peace that endured for *two generations*—because he had dared to move with God.

When God ushered in a new deliverer, He stayed with him until the end. Life was never dull when God came along to transform an unlikely person into a champion warrior. We shall see how that played out when Gideon, clothed with God's Holy Spirit, sounded his shofar. Shofar cries would pierce the darkness and scramble the enemy's plans.

* * *

Why Shofars Wail in Scripture and Today—   By Mary A. Bruno, Ph.D.

128

Chapter 16
Gideon's Preparation

J udges chapter six opens with Israel's plight, and when God empowered Gideon to sound a shofar. After forty years of peace, Israelites had lapsed into sin (again). Therefore, God had enrolled them for another class in the *School of Regrets and Remorse. Professors* Midian (strife) and Amalek (dweller in a valley) had "taught" a review course on *The Importance and Power of Prayer.*

All it took to sway God's people to hold a prayer meeting was seven years of poverty and misery under the two ruthless tyrants. When the sons of Israel (*the men*) prayed, the situation changed, and good things happened.

God heard and answered their prayers in Judges 6:7–10 and sent a prophet to remind them of how He had rescued them from their enemies. God could have scolded them; but instead of dwelling on their failures, He wanted them to dwell on His faithfulness and protection. Because He was their God, they would not need to fear the Amorites. Gideon was about to have company.

Why Shofars Wail in Scripture and Today—   By Mary A. Bruno, Ph.D.

129

> Now the Angel of the LORD came and sat under the terebinth tree which *was* in Ophrah, which *belonged* to Joash the Abiezrite, while his son Gideon threshed wheat in the winepress, in order to hide *it* from the Midianites. And the Angel of the LORD appeared to him, and said to him, "The LORD *is* with you, you mighty man of valor!"
> —Judg. 6:11–12

God's new *mighty man of valor* had a few questions. He wondered why they could be having so many problems if the God of Miracles was with them.

> Then Gideon said to him, "O my lord, if the LORD is with us, why then has all this happened to us? And where are all His miracles which our fathers told us about, saying, 'Did not the LORD bring us up from Egypt?' But now the LORD has abandoned us and given us into the hand of Midian." The LORD looked at him and said, "Go in this your strength and deliver Israel from the hand of Midian. Have I not sent you?"
> —Judg. 6:13–14 NASB

"*The LORD looked at him.*" (God gave him a *Fatherly look.*) Gideon had assumed the visitor was an angel. God had appeared *as* the Angel of the LORD.

> So he said to Him, "O my Lord, how can I save Israel? Indeed my clan *is* the weakest in Manasseh, and I *am* the least in my father's house."
> —Judg. 6:15

God gave Gideon strength, and Gideon gave God excuses. The LORD probably smiled and gave him a reason to believe. Gideon's faith, though limp as a rag, was still faith. God knew how to help build it up.

Why Shofars Wail in Scripture and Today—   By Mary A. Bruno, Ph.D.

130

But the LORD said to him, "Surely I will be with you, and you shall defeat Midian as one man." So Gideon said to Him, "If now I have found favor in Your sight, then show me a sign that it is You who speak with me. Please do not depart from here, until I come *back* to You, and bring out my offering and lay it before You." And He said, "I will remain until you return."

—Judg. 6:16–18 NASB

Potential

God may have hummed a marching tune as He suited Gideon up with Himself and prepped him to deliver Israel. Gideon's spark of potential had glistened as a nugget in a miner's pan while he was beating wheat in a winepress to hide it from the Midianites who had destroyed Israel's' crops (Judg. 6:3, 4) in an attempt to starve them out. God would fan Gideon's tiny spark into 300 victory flames.

Gideon's name means *hewer,* which means "one who could cut and gather, as to gather and cut wood, and to carve." God was ready to put him on the cutting edge and help him to gather and carve out an army for Israel.

The Angel of the LORD said God was with Gideon, and then called him a *valiant warrior.* Yet, Gideon focused on his problem and a lack of miracles instead of on God's Presence, promise, and potential. He may have forgotten that, with God, problems often lead to miracles.

God listened patiently to Gideon's concerns, gave him a *fatherly look,* and then, as stated previously, said, "Go in this your strength and deliver Israel from the hand[59] of Midian. Have I not sent you?"

---

[59] Cease Striving - In Touch, https://www.intouch.org/read/magazine/daily-devotions/cease-striving (accessed April 12, 2016).

Why Shofars Wail in Scripture and Today—   By Mary A. Bruno, Ph.D.

131

God spoke of *this—His strength*—which would empower Gideon. (Peter spoke of that kind of power in Acts 2:16–18, when he quoted Joel 2:28–29 regarding the Holy Spirit's outpouring.) Gideon would remember God's words when the Holy Spirit clothed him *with Himself.* That heavenly clothing became Gideon's uniform, equipment, empowerment, and authority.

Gideon explained why he was wrong for the job. Surely, God must have had a better man for the position. God promised to be with him and said Gideon *would* (not might) defeat Midian as one lone man. What the Angel of the LORD said sounded good; however, Gideon, new to hearing from God, craved confirmation and asked for a sign.

The new deliverer had failed to recognize one sure sign of being in God's Presence—a burning desire to give to God. He asked the Angel to wait for him to prepare an offering. The Angel (God) may have enjoyed Gideon's enthusiasm as he smiled and stayed a while to put His miracle blessing on Gideon's offering.

> So Gideon went in and prepared a young goat, and unleavened bread from an ephah of flour. The meat he put in a basket, and he put the broth in a pot; and he brought *them* out to Him under the terebinth tree and presented *them.* The Angel of God said to him, "Take the meat and the unleavened bread and lay *them* on this rock, and pour out the broth." And he did so. Then the Angel of the LORD put out the end of the staff that *was* in His hand, and touched the meat and the unleavened bread; and fire rose out of the rock and consumed the meat and the unleavened bread. And the Angel of the LORD departed out of his sight.
>
> —Judg. 6:19–21

Why Shofars Wail in Scripture and Today—   By Mary A. Bruno, Ph.D.

132

Offering

Gideon selected a young goat (about 50 pounds?) from the herd. It was not an old goat that nobody wanted, but one of the best that was tender and juicy. An ephah of flour (about 29-35 pounds or four to five dry gallons) was enough to fill a very large basket with flatbread cakes. He took the time to prepare his lavish gift and rushed back to the terebinth tree. The Angel of the LORD told him to lay his offerings on *this* rock, and then pour the broth over them.

At *that* rock, Gideon met God's Angel.

At *that* rock, he heard God's promises.

At that rock, he learned of his high calling.

At that rock, God changed him from the least of the least to a timely deliverer.

At that rock, he found strength, hope, and victory.

At that rock, he learned he could defeat the enemy.

At *that* rock, he poured out all of his offering and the flavorsome broth, which flowed over *that* rock.

Getting his saturated offering to burn was not a problem. The Angel of the LORD touched it with the tip of his staff (succulent sacrifice starter). Fire flashed up *from that rock* and consumed his offering. Holy fire blazed—when Gideon gave *all* of his offerings to God—*at that rock.*

God's fire that sprang from a wet rock and devoured a wet sacrifice settled Gideon's question about where were God's miracles. The Angel vanished.

> Now Gideon perceived that He *was* the Angel of the LORD. So Gideon said, "Alas, O Lord GOD! For I have seen the Angel of the LORD face to face." Then the LORD said to him, "Peace *be* with you; do not fear, you

Why Shofars Wail in Scripture and Today—   By Mary A. Bruno, Ph.D.

133

shall not die." So Gideon built an altar there to the LORD, and called it The-LORD-*Is*-Peace. To this day it *is* still in Ophrah of the Abiezrites.

—Judges 6:22–24

When the new deliverer realized he had seen the Angel of the LORD, he panicked and thought his life was over. God spoke peace and assured that he would be okay. Gideon's heart overflowed with praise and thanksgiving that compelled him to do more to honor God. He built an altar and named it "The LORD is Peace *(Jehovah Shalom)*." It was *at that rock*, where he met with God, where he heard from God, and where he gave all of his offering to God, that *Jehovah Shalom* (God of Peace) calmed Gideon's fears.

Could reports of Gideon's saturated sacrifice have triggered Elijah's confidence to soak another sacrifice with water and ask God to send fire when he faced off with 450 false prophets in 1 Kings chapter 18?

Before long, the enemy that Gideon once feared would run in holy terror—*to hide from him!*

Those events would have been enough blessings for any average mortal; however, God was not done. He stopped by at night and gave Gideon his first leadership order, which took courage, and involved a much larger sacrifice—a full-grown bull.

Since Gideon enjoyed giving to the LORD, God promoted him from giving his *fifty-pound* goat sacrifice, to giving an offering that weighed well over *a thousand pounds*. Suppose each pound represented about five dollars ($5). In that case, Gideon would have started out by blessing God with an offering worth over two-hundred-and-fifty

Why Shofars Wail in Scripture and Today—   By Mary A. Bruno, Ph.D.

134

dollars ($250) including the flour. That was terrific for a beginner. However, God knew He could rely on Gideon to follow through, and was setting him up to give a whole lot more than his first sacrificial gift. (These were not Gideon's tithes—they were sacrificial offerings.) Can God count on us to give joyfully and sacrificially as His Spirit leads?

The first offering was Gideon's idea. The next sacrifice was God's idea. Based on an estimate of five dollars per pound, his second offering could have been worth up to seven-thousand dollars ($5,000–$7,000). A mature bull could weigh far more than 1,000 pounds.

> Now it came to pass the same night that the LORD said to him, "Take your father's young bull, the second bull of seven years old, and tear down the altar of Baal that your father has, and cut down the wooden image that *is* beside it; and build an altar to the LORD your God on top of this rock in the proper arrangement, and take the second bull and offer a burnt sacrifice with the wood of the image which you shall cut down."
>
> —Judg. 6:25–26

Stronghold

Joash's unholy idol altar and costly wooden image of Baal signified generational strongholds of idolatry, spiritual confusion, and compromise. Strongholds have passed down through families that have worshiped statues and prayed to images, and saints (dead people). Joash and his idolatrous friends may have thought his handsome altar to Baal was a spiritual masterpiece. However, God despised the thing.

It was no surprise that Gideon was having a little trouble hearing from God and recognizing His voice. Joash's unholy spiritual mixture had brought spiritual confusion into his family. God knew how to change that.

Why Shofars Wail in Scripture and Today—   By Mary A. Bruno, Ph.D.

135

Oh, Gideon . . .

Gideon's next order from God and his second step to victory (after having laid down and poured out *all* of his first saturated sacrifice), was to destroy his father's *pagan idol* and his altar that *did not honor God*.

Gulp!

That was a huge order for someone who was new to hearing from God. Gideon would never forget his divine appointments. He dared to take another step of faith, flexed his sagging faith muscles, rounded up some help, and came up with an achievable plan.

> So Gideon took ten men from among his servants and did as the LORD had said to him. But because he feared his father's household and the men of the city too much to do *it* by day, he did *it* by night.
>
> —Judg. 6:27

His nighttime workout team obeyed God, even though they feared Joash and the town's Baal worshipers. Their victory by moonlight was sweet. However, Gideon wondered what would happen in the morning when everyone woke up and saw the blood, the destruction, and a handsome new altar to God that reeked of roasted bull.

The one who caused heaven to rejoice had aroused murderous thoughts in idolatrous hearts. Great testing has often come during moments of great obedience, great sacrifice, and great success.

> Then the men of the city said to Joash, "Bring out your son, that he may die, because he has torn down the altar

Why Shofars Wail in Scripture and Today—   By Mary A. Bruno, Ph.D.

136

of Baal, and because he has cut down the wooden image that *was* beside it."

—Judg. 6:30

How would Gideon's father handle the loss of his pricey idol and bull? The townsmen ordered Joash to hand Gideon over for slaughter.

Gideon wondered how this could have happened after he knew that he had heard and obeyed God.

Judges 6:31–32 tells of when Joash saved Gideon. His eyes must have beamed with fatherly pride (over his son who had dared to take such a bold stand for God). He bestowed Gideon's new name, *Jerubbaal, which meant,* Let Baal contend against him.

God was ready to ask Gideon to do some wilder and seemingly crazy, things with shofars that made no sense whatever to the natural mind.

* * *

Why Shofars Wail in Scripture and Today—   By Mary A. Bruno, Ph.D.

137

The Brunos declared God's ownership of, and blessings for, the White House in Washington, D.C., and over the nation.

Why Shofars Wail in Scripture and Today—   By Mary A. Bruno, Ph.D.

138

Chapter 17
Gideon's Shofars

When the sons of the east joined Midianites and Amalekites to fight Israel in Judges chapter 6, God had a plan, a provision, and a solution. It involved the Holy Spirit and Gideon's shofar.

> But the Spirit of the Lord clothed Gideon with Himself *and* took possession of him, and he blew a trumpet, and [the clan of] Abiezer was gathered to him.
> —Judg. 6:34 Amplified Bible Classic Edition (AMPC)

Being clothed with God's Holy Spirit gave Gideon dynamic empowerment. God's power supplemented Gideon's trumpet (shofar) blasts as they ricocheted throughout the countryside and stirred warriors' hearts. Everything changed for Gideon after God's Spirit embraced him. Warriors recognized his leadership and stood at attention when he spoke. The remarkable response to his Holy Spirit (Ruach Kodesh), anointed shofar blasts created a new problem for which God (as usual) had a solution. He gave Gideon a brief message (sermonette) for his troops.

Why Shofars Wail in Scripture and Today—   By Mary A. Bruno, Ph.D.

139

Now therefore, proclaim in the hearing of the people, saying, 'Whoever *is* fearful and afraid, let him turn and depart at once from Mount Gilead.'" And twenty-two thousand of the people returned, and ten thousand remained.

—Judg. 7:3

Wide-eyed Gideon had perked up and was all smiles when 32,000 ready men (Judg. 6:34–35, 7:3) answered his divinely enhanced shofar call to battle. God, preferred a smaller army. ("For **many are called**, but **few** *are* chosen" Mt. 22:14 emphasis added.) He would help Gideon to narrow it down to keep Israel humble about her victory.

The army assembled for Gideon's first public address, which was that, all who were afraid could go home. It must have brought a standing ovation with whistles, shouts, and cheers. Gideon stared as 22,000 soldiers (about two-thirds of his army!) spun their rides around and trotted off to their waiting wives and tasty falafels while 10,000 men stayed. God would help to thin them out as well.

Selection

In Judges 7:7–8, God showed Gideon how to recognize the chosen ones. He tested them one-by-one before His new General. Most bent down and slurped to drink, instead of lapping water from their hands so they could keep watch. God chose the three-hundred lappers, and Gideon excused the 9,700 slurppers. God did a few calculations and came up with something, even more, spectacular for Gideon's shofar.

While the men prepped their ram's horns (shofars) for the big attack, the LORD prepped Gideon to lead them.

God kept his fleece-seeking (Joshua 6:37–40), new

Why Shofars Wail in Scripture and Today—   By Mary A. Bruno, Ph.D.

140

deliverer steady and ready for battle. It was a lot for Gideon to absorb during a short time. However, God encouraged him that night and sent him out for some faith-building spying on a Midianite, who was telling his dream of what happened when Gideon rolled into camp.

Gideon's confidence soared when he heard his worried enemies discuss the dream. (The Hebrew word *sheber*, was translated here as *interpretation*,[60] and meant "destruction, crashing, breaking," as in "breaking the code.") God still helps His generals to crack enemy codes.

> And so it was, when Gideon heard the telling of the dream and its interpretation, that he worshiped. He returned to the camp of Israel, and said, "Arise, for the LORD has delivered the camp of Midian into your hand." Then he divided the three hundred men *into* three companies, and he put a trumpet into every man's hand, with empty pitchers, and torches inside the pitchers. And he said to them, "Look at me and do likewise; watch, and when I come to the edge of the camp you shall do as I do."
>
> —Judg. 7:15–17

During his big moment of breakthrough, Gideon's humble character was very evident. Instead of rushing to tell his men that God had given them victory, he humbly bowed and worshiped the LORD.

How precious that scene must have been to God. Gideon seemed to be no prize at the start, but his humble and thankful heart revealed why he was God's choice.

---

[60] "H7667 - sheber - Strong's Hebrew Lexicon (KJV)." Blue Letter Bible. Accessed 4 Jun, 2016.
https://www.blueletterbible.org//lang/Lexicon/Lexicon.cfm?Strongs=H7667&t=KJV

Why Shofars Wail in Scripture and Today—   By Mary A. Bruno, Ph.D.

141

Shofars

As it often does, God's move brought separation. Gideon divided the men into three companies of one hundred warriors[61] who awaited their weapons of warfare, which were not carnal, but spiritual and able to get the job done. God may have been thinking of this shofar-warfare strategy when He led Paul to write:

> For though we walk in the flesh, we do not war according to the flesh, for the weapons of our warfare are not of the flesh, but divinely powerful for the destruction of fortresses. *We are* destroying speculations and every lofty thing raised up against the knowledge of God, and *we are* taking every thought captive to the obedience of Christ.
>
> —2 Cor. 10:3–5 NASB

Gideon was a man of few words. He instructed his warriors on how and when to use their weapons, which boiled down to "Do as I do, when I do." The *trumpet* and *trumpets*[62] *i*n the next passage were both *shofars.*

> "When I blow the trumpet, I and all who *are* with me, then you also blow the trumpets on every side of the whole camp, and say, '*The sword of* the LORD and of Gideon!'"
>
> —Judg. 7:18

The event was reminiscent of victory at Jericho. However, this time, the men only had to blow their

---

[61] Judges 6-7 - Bible Study Daily, http://biblestudydaily.org/judges-6-7/ (accessed April 12, 2016).

[62] "H7782 - showphar - Strong's Hebrew Lexicon (KJV)." Blue Letter Bible. Accessed 4 Jun, 2016.
https://www.blueletterbible.org//lang/Lexicon/Lexicon.cfm?Strongs=H7782&t=KJV

Why Shofars Wail in Scripture and Today—   By Mary A. Bruno, Ph.D.

142

trumpets and say, *"The sword of* the LORD and of Gideon!"* God's enemies would flee, not because of shouts, but because warriors blew their shofars, spoke with the authority of His Word, kept their flesh under control, stayed in divine order, and dared to move with God.

Division

Gideon divided the remaining 300 warriors, which were less than one percent of the 32,000 first responders, into three companies. (Father Company? Son Company? Holy Spirit Company?) There were three divisions, but one army. They would fight against three groups (an unholy trio) that had banded against them: Midianites (strife), Amalekites (dweller in a valley), and sons of the East (of Arabia, "in the figurative sense of sterility"[63]).

> So Gideon and the hundred men who *were* with him came to the outpost of the camp at the beginning of the middle watch, just as they had posted the watch; and they blew the trumpets and broke the pitchers that *were* in their hands. Then the three companies blew the trumpets and broke the pitchers—they held the torches in their left hands and the trumpets in their right hands for blowing—and they cried, "The sword of the LORD and of Gideon!"
>
> —Judg. 7:19–20

That was the plan! They would hold an earthen vessel filled with God-ordained fire in one hand and a shofar that sent a wordless message in the other, and blow their shofars around the enemy's camp. This seemed counter-

---

[63] "H6152 - `Arab - Strong's Hebrew Lexicon (KJV)." Blue Letter Bible. Accessed 19 Jun, 2016. https://www.blueletterbible.org//lang/Lexicon/Lexicon.cfm?Strongs=H6152&t=KJV

Why Shofars Wail in Scripture and Today—   By Mary A. Bruno, Ph.D.

143

productive to military strategy. With both hands occupied, could anyone wield a sword? The Holy Spirit, perhaps?

> And take the helmet of salvation and the sword that the
> Spirit wields, which is the Word of God.
> —Eph. 6:17 AMPC

Gideon's men surrounded the camp with their readied shofars and fire-filled earthen vessels. At the right moment, and on his command, Gideon's three-part army shattered their pitchers, which sent breakthrough noises with flashing lights around the enemy's camp as their shofars wailed, and wailed, and wailed. Those blaring shofar blasts may have served as swords of the LORD, as the men *cried,* "A sword for the LORD and for Gideon."

Three-hundred shofars wailing t*a, ta, ta* by flashing torchlight fortified Israeli hearts, but rattled the enemy's camp with terror, confusion, and death by *friendly sword.*

Called Out

In Judges 7:20, the Hebrew word for *cried,*[64] is *qara,* which means, "to call out, to summon, invite, to call for, and to name." Gideon's army had *called out* their enemies. The fight was on! Opposition cries rang out. The Hebrew word used for their *crying (cried),*[65] in verse 21, is *ruwa,* which as we know means, "to shout a war cry or alarm for battle." God must have been waiting for those Teruah blasts. Because when they sounded, God was like a prowling lion

---

[64] "H7121 - qara' - Strong's Hebrew Lexicon (KJV)." Blue Letter Bible. Accessed 4 Jun, 2016.
https://www.blueletterbible.org//lang/Lexicon/Lexicon.cfm?Strongs=H7121&t=KJV
[65] "H7321 - ruwa` - Strong's Hebrew Lexicon (KJV)." Blue Letter Bible. Accessed 4 Jun, 2016.
https://www.blueletterbible.org//lang/Lexicon/Lexicon.cfm?Strongs=H7321&t=KJV

Why Shofars Wail in Scripture and Today—   By Mary A. Bruno, Ph.D.

144

stalking his prey until the moment was just right; then He sprang into action with His creative warfare attack.

> And every man stood in his place all around the camp; and the whole army ran and cried out and fled. When the three hundred blew the trumpets, the LORD set every man's sword against his companion throughout the whole camp; and the army fled to Beth Acacia, toward Zererah, as far as the border of Abel Meholah, by Tabbath.
>
> —Judg. 7:21–22

The enemies knew that troop leaders carried shofars. A numbers-minded person once concluded that by enemy calculations, if every shofar-blowing leader commanded up to 100 men, those 300 shofars could signify up to 30,000 warriors, which could equal disaster in the darkness. Frantic adversary minds may have thought each repeated shofar blast signified another 100 leaders, which equaled hundreds of thousands of warriors. When their *attack* (*ruwa*) cry went forth, it may have meant they were *under attack*. The attackers became "*attackees*" and fled.

God, the *Mighty Warrior*, had jumped into the fight and used those terrifying shofar sound waves as war weapons that scrambled enemy strategies. Imaginations ran wild as enemies turned their attack inward, slashed blindly at each other and ran bleeding into the night.

Oreb and Zeeb

> Then Gideon sent messengers throughout all the mountains of Ephraim, saying, "Come down against the Midianites, and seize from them the watering places as far as Beth Barah and the Jordan." Then all the men of Ephraim gathered together and seized the watering

Why Shofars Wail in Scripture and Today—   By Mary A. Bruno, Ph.D.

145

places as far as Beth Barah and the Jordan. And they captured two princes of the Midianites, Oreb and Zeeb. They killed Oreb at the rock of Oreb, and Zeeb they killed at the winepress of Zeeb. They pursued Midian and brought the heads of Oreb and Zeeb to Gideon on the other side of the Jordan.

—Judg. 7:24–25

During their victorious adventure with God, Gideon, and shofars, the men of Ephraim overthrew Midian's two leaders, Oreb (Raven) and Zeeb (Wolf). Oreb's head rolled at the rock of Oreb. Zeeb's head tumbled at the winepress of Zeeb. They should never have attacked God's people.

The mention of the *rock of Oreb* may have drawn Gideon's thoughts to another rock—*that rock*, where he had met with God when the holy fire came from *that rock* and consumed his saturated sacrifice.

The words *winepress of Zeeb* might have stirred Gideon's memories of when he had ground wheat in his father's winepress to rescue it from Zeeb's Amalekites. Gideon probably rested his hand on his shofar, as he gazed at the two villain s' dangling heads. He marveled at his encounters with God and the great victory that God had won for His beloved Israel—including the valuable watering holes, which were like liquid treasures in that arid land.

Gideon and his men had relied on God to bring victory from their nighttime shofar blasts that terrified the enemy's camp. His men with their broken—but fire-filled—vessels, had sounded their God-ordered shofars, proclaimed God's message, and had wisely trusted God to cover the rest.

Off in the distance, King Saul put a shofar to his lips.

* * *

Why Shofars Wail in Scripture and Today—   By Mary A. Bruno, Ph.D.

146

Chapter 18
King Saul Blew It!

Threthe shofar lineup continued with King Saul. The Israelites had hoped to be like other nations with a flesh and blood king. They wanted Saul to replace God as their king. Saul was a rather nice-looking fellow, much taller than the others were. All agreed that he *looked* right for the job; however, as the saying goes, "Handsome is as handsome does."

> Saul chose for himself three thousand *men* of Israel. Two thousand were with Saul in Michmash and in the mountains of Bethel, and a thousand were with Jonathan in Gibeah of Benjamin. The rest of the people he sent away, every man to his tent.
> And Jonathan attacked the garrison of the Philistines that *was* in Geba, and the Philistines heard *of it.* Then Saul blew the trumpet throughout all the land, saying, "Let the Hebrews hear!" Now all Israel heard it said *that* Saul had attacked a garrison of the Philistines, and *that* Israel had also become an abomination to the Philistines. And the people were called together to Saul at Gilgal.
> Then the Philistines gathered to fight with Israel, **thirty thousand chariots** and **six thousand horsemen**, and **people as the sand which *is* on the seashore in multitude.** And they came up and encamped in

Why Shofars Wail in Scripture and Today—   By Mary A. Bruno, Ph.D.

147

Michmash, to the east of Beth Aven. When the men of
Israel saw that they were in danger (for the people were
distressed), then the people hid in caves, in thickets, in
rocks, in holes, and in pits.

—1 Sam. 13:2–6, emphasis added

King Saul, clothed with his position and power, blew his shofar. His results were not as welcome as when Gideon, clothed with God's Holy Spirit and humility, blew his shofar that drew 32,000 ready warriors *to defend* Israel.

Results

Saul's fleshly shofar blasts drew enemies like flies to fresh meat. His result was enormous—*but the wrong army showed up!* Philistine warriors swarmed in with 30,000 chariots, 6,000 men on horses, and too many people to count. They were ready *to wage war against* Israel. However, Saul's divided and fainthearted army of 3,000 frightened men was shrinking with each passing moment.

Instead of instilling courage, Saul's shofar blasts brought fear and trembling. Instead of charging to attack their enemies, the Israelites ran and hid.

People soon realized that although Saul *looked* kingly, he was not a good leader. It took only 14 verses for him to mess up so badly that God sent the prophet Samuel to deliver a news flash (word from the LORD).

He gave Saul the plain facts version, which was that his disobedience had cost his kingdom. God, who always has a plan (and a solution), already had someone else (David) to take Saul's place. Events unfolded as follows:

Then he waited seven days, according to the time set by
Samuel. But Samuel did not come to Gilgal; and the

Why Shofars Wail in Scripture and Today—   By Mary A. Bruno, Ph.D.

148

people were scattered from him. So Saul said, "Bring a burnt offering and peace offerings here to me." And he offered the burnt offering.

—1 Sam. 13:8–9

Impatient

Restless Saul had grown tired of waiting for God's anointed and appointed prophet. He huffed, puffed, paced about, and then took it upon himself to perform Samuel's duty. However, no sooner did the sacrificial fat reach the fire than Samuel showed up fast and furious.

> As soon as he finished offering the burnt offering, behold, Samuel came; and Saul went out to meet him *and* to greet him. But Samuel said, "What have you done?" And Saul said, "Because I saw that the people were scattering from me, and that you did not come within the appointed days, and that the Philistines were assembling at Michmash, therefore I said, 'Now the Philistines will come down against me at Gilgal, and I have not asked the favor of the LORD.' So I forced myself and offered the burnt offering."
>
> —1 Sam. 13:10–12 NASB

Their meet-and-greet moment turned sour when Samuel ignored Saul's feeble excuse, which was *a lie in the skin of a reason*, and demanded a straight answer. His overstepping would not pass lightly. Saul was an earthly king, but Samuel answered to the *King of kings*.

Accountable

Saul tried to blame his actions on Samuel, but Samuel stared him down and demanded, "What have *you* done?"

Why Shofars Wail in Scripture and Today—   By Mary A. Bruno, Ph.D.

149

Saul made a feeble effort to save himself by blaming others and the enemy. One can almost hear him whine, "The Philistines made me do it."

> Samuel said to Saul, "You have acted foolishly; you have not kept the commandment of the LORD your God, which He commanded you, for now the LORD would have established your kingdom over Israel forever. But now your kingdom shall not endure. The LORD has sought out for Himself a man after His own heart, and the LORD has appointed him as ruler over His people, because you have not kept what the LORD commanded you."
> —1 Sam. 13:13–14 NASB

King Saul's smile and flimsy excuses held up about as well as trying to catch water in a sieve. Samuel's sharp and sure words pinned Saul down like a frog in a biology lab. He spewed one sharp *you* and *your* after another, that pierced Saul's soul like darts, seven of them in all.

As one may recall, seven is God's number of perfection or completion. Here, it indicated Saul was completely wrong and entirely accountable for what he had done. His arrogance had cost his kingdom. He seemed to be okay then, but if he thought[66] he could escape the outcome of Samuel's prophecy, he was wrong—dead wrong!

Counterfeit

Saul stayed in power after Samuel's visit, but God's Spirit withdrew from him. After God's voice had gone silent, Saul craved the thrill of supernatural guidance regarding warfare. So he consulted a medium (his version of a psychic

---

[66] Live from Brooklyn - blogspot.com, http://buriednova.blogspot.com/ (accessed April 12, 2016).

Why Shofars Wail in Scripture and Today—   By Mary A. Bruno, Ph.D.

150

hotline), which was a poor counterfeit of God's wise counsel. This was not his brightest idea. His spiritual experience was exciting, but the fun stopped when the medium predicted Saul would die the next day.

Saul left without apparent harm, but death followed him. It would not only destroy Saul but his army and his family members. Instead of pressing on in confidence, fear flooded the Israeli army. Saul's men fled and died on Mount Gilboa[67] (swollen heap). Saul, his three sons, his armorbearer, and all of his men[68] died in the desert at the southern plain of Jezreel. Their lifeless bodies must have become a *swollen heap*—on Mount Gilboa.

> Now the Philistines fought against Israel; and the men of Israel fled from before the Philistines, and fell slain on Mount Gilboa. Then the Philistines followed hard after Saul and his sons. And the Philistines killed Jonathan, Abinadab, and Malchishua, Saul's sons. The battle became fierce against Saul. The archers hit him, and he was severely wounded by the archers.
> Then Saul said to his armorbearer, "Draw your sword, and thrust me through with it, lest these uncircumcised men come and thrust me through and abuse me."
> But his armorbearer would not, for he was greatly afraid. Therefore Saul took a sword and fell on it. And when his armorbearer saw that Saul was dead, he also fell on his sword, and died with him. So Saul, his three sons, his armorbearer, and all his men died together that same day.
> And when the men of Israel who *were* on the other side of the valley, and *those* who *were* on the other side of the Jordan, saw that the men of Israel had fled

---

[67] "H1533 - Gilboa` - Strong's Hebrew Lexicon (KJV)." Blue Letter Bible. Accessed 4 Jun, 2016.
https://www.blueletterbible.org//lang/Lexicon/Lexicon.cfm?Strongs=H1533&t=KJV
[68] 1 Samuel 31:6 So Saul and his three sons and his armor .., http://biblehub.com/1_samuel/31-6.htm (accessed April 12, 2016).

Why Shofars Wail in Scripture and Today—   By Mary A. Bruno, Ph.D.

151

and that Saul and his sons were dead, they forsook the cities and fled; and the Philistines came and dwelt in them. So it happened the next day, when the Philistines came to strip the slain, that they found Saul and his three sons fallen on Mount Gilboa.

—1 Sam. 31:1–8

Saul foolishly sought a medium's advice and then killed himself the next day. On the other hand, David wisely inquired of the LORD and had terrific results. Three chapters later, he became king of Israel and Judah.

Then the men of Judah came and there anointed David king over the house of Judah.
—2 Sam. 2:4a NASB

Therefore all the elders of Israel came to the king at Hebron, and King David made a covenant with them at Hebron before the LORD. And they anointed David king over Israel.
—2 Sam. 5:3

Many knew that David honored the LORD and that God had called him to shepherd His Israelites and to rule over Israel. What better person could be their king? David did not need to submit his qualifications to the elders. They were aware of his walk with God and came to him.

We do not know if shofars sounded for either of David's coronations. However, he would play a major role in another big celebration that was coming up with many shofar blasts and a whole lot more.

* * *

Why Shofars Wail in Scripture and Today—   By Mary A. Bruno, Ph.D.

152

Chapter 19
David and the Ark

King David settled in and constructed some nice houses around Jerusalem, which had splendid views. Few would blame a king for erecting some villas here and there to enjoy Israel's great sights. David probably knew that Abigail, Bathsheba, Haggith, and especially Michal, would prefer to have their own homes.

> *David* built houses for himself in the City of David; and he prepared a place for the ark of God, and pitched a tent for it. Then David said, "No one may carry the ark of God but the Levites, for the LORD has chosen them to carry the ark of God and to minister before Him forever."
>
> —1 Chron. 15:1, 2

David chose a lovely location for the Ark of God and its tent and honored God's specifications. First Chronicles chapter 15 tells of when David rallied the Israelites to usher it to the tent. He gathered 862 men of the Levites and Kohathites and ordered leaders to consecrate themselves and their families to escort the Ark.

Why Shofars Wail in Scripture and Today—   By Mary A. Bruno, Ph.D.

153

> So the priests and the Levites sanctified themselves to bring up the ark of the LORD God of Israel. And the children of the Levites bore the ark of God on their shoulders, by its poles, as Moses had commanded according to the word of the LORD.
>
> —1 Chron. 15:14–15

David carefully followed God's instructions for the project. Only the Levites had Ark transport privilege.

Being an earnest worshiper and man after God's heart, David made sure there was plenty of triumphant worship to welcome the Ark of the Covenant to Jerusalem. He recruited the chief Levites, whose relatives were the best singers and musicians in town. They would provide abundant skillful and heart-stirring music.

David could hardly wait for the big occasion as he undoubtedly paced back and forth with a secretary taking rapid notes as he may have shouted out his ideas about who and what to include in the glorious and memorable event.

Harpists and Flutes!

Yes, your highness.

Loud sounding cymbals and Lyres!

Yes, sir.

Shofars and trumpets!

Yes, my lord.

Levites assembled a lively worship team with dozens of singers and musicians, and two guards for the Ark.

David, with Israel's elders and captains over thousands, escorted the Ark from Obed-edom's house. Glorious shouts rang out as everyone welcomed the sacred symbol of God's Holy Presence to Jerusalem. The people

Why Shofars Wail in Scripture and Today—   By Mary A. Bruno, Ph.D.

154

were not merely welcoming the Ark—they were welcoming God! The Lord must have been very pleased as He moved among their praises and scattered His blessings upon those who rejoiced in His Presence.

Contrary to a Hollywood movie's version of the event, David was *fully clothed* when he ushered in the Ark. God spelled out exactly what David wore during its return.

> Now **David was clothed with a robe of fine linen** with all the Levites who were carrying the ark, and the singers and Chenaniah the leader of the singing *with* the singers. **David also wore an ephod of linen.** Thus all Israel brought up the ark of the covenant of the LORD with shouting, and with sound of the horn, with trumpets, with loud-sounding cymbals, with harps and lyres.
> —1 Chron. 15:27–28 NASB, emphasis added

Shofars, Trumpets, and Shouts

In this verse, *showphar* translated as *horn*[69] and *chatsotsĕrah* as *trumpets*.[70] Shofars, trumpets, and the crowd's *teruwah* shouts sounded loudly before the Ark. Together they made a threefold sound of rejoicing.

Teruah Shout

The Hebrew word, *teruwah*, translated as "joyous shouting" in 1 Chronicles 15:28. The crowd's joyous roar pierced the heavens like billowing shofar blasts. Still, not all were happy about David's public worship and bold praise.

---

[69] "H7782 - showphar - Strong's Hebrew Lexicon (KJV)." Blue Letter Bible. Accessed 4 Jun, 2016.
https://www.blueletterbible.org//lang/Lexicon/Lexicon.cfm?Strongs=H7782&t=KJV
[70] "H2689 - chatsotsĕrah - Strong's Hebrew Lexicon (KJV)." Blue Letter Bible. Accessed 4 Jun, 2016.
https://www.blueletterbible.org//lang/Lexicon/Lexicon.cfm?Strongs=H2689&t=KJV

Why Shofars Wail in Scripture and Today—   By Mary A. Bruno, Ph.D.

155

It happened when the ark of the covenant of the LORD came to the city of David, that Michal the daughter of Saul looked out of the window and saw King David leaping and celebrating; and she despised him in her heart.

—1 Chron. 15:29 NASB

Contempt

During the festivity, David's heart overflowed with child-like love for God, while Michal's venomous heart spewed contempt for David. Longing for others to rejoice in the LORD with him, He lifted up his voice like a *teruwah*, blessed the LORD with his whole heart, and penned:

I will bless the LORD at all times;
His praise *shall* continually *be* in my mouth.
My soul shall make its boast in the LORD;
The humble shall hear *of it* and be glad.
Oh, magnify the LORD with me,
And let us exalt His name together.

—Ps. 34:1–3

Although Michal loathed her husband's bold gestures of love for God, the LORD cherished David's poetic love gifts.

King David's family problems worsened in the midst of his joyous celebration for the Ark's return. Absalom, one of his sons from Haggith, had defied him and tried to seize the throne. Shofars were involved.

* * *

Why Shofars Wail in Scripture and Today—   By Mary A. Bruno, Ph.D.

156

Chapter 20
Rebellious Spirits

Joab saw the tribes of Benjamin and Israel in combat. When Abner asked him to step in, Joab's shofar blasts in 2 Samuel 2:28 signaled a cease-slash. He told Abner that if he had kept silent (not asked for help), the bloodshed would have continued with heavy casualties.

Shofar Call for Peace

Shofars called for brethren to stop fighting among themselves. Sometimes, somebody with a voice of reason must lift his or her voice like a shofar, and call for peace. Joab's name came up later regarding a shofar when he and his brother Abishai led part of the army, and Ittai the rest.

> Now the king had commanded Joab, Abishai, and Ittai, saying, *"Deal* gently for my sake with the young man Absalom." And all the people heard when the king gave all the captains orders concerning Absalom.
>
> —2 Sam. 18:5

David ordered his three commanders, Joab, Abishai, and Ittai, to bring Absalom, his prideful and insubordinate son, back *alive.* We shall see how that turned out.

Why Shofars Wail in Scripture and Today—   By Mary A. Bruno, Ph.D.

157

Absalom

Deadly fighting conditions took 20,000 brave warriors' lives in the dense terrain mentioned in 2 Samuel 18:6–8. However, power-hungry Absalom spurred his swift mount through the dark forest. He could almost taste victory as he envisioned himself parading as king through Jerusalem in his rightful royal regalia.

Wisdom cried, "Wake up Absalom! Wake up!"

> Then Absalom met the servants of David. Absalom rode on a mule. The mule went under the thick boughs of a great terebinth tree, and his head caught in the terebinth; so he was left hanging between heaven and earth. And the mule which *was* under him went on.
>
> —2 Sam. 18:9

It was too late! Absalom was dangling high and helpless. One of David's men saw him and informed Joab.

> Then Joab said, "I cannot linger with you." And he took three spears in his hand and thrust them through Absalom's heart, while he was *still* alive in the midst of the terebinth tree. And ten young men who bore Joab's armor surrounded Absalom, and struck and killed him.
>
> —2 Sam. 18:14–15

Joab thought he knew best when he ignored David's order to spare his son. Joab murdered Absalom. When the time was right, David would settle that score.

> So Joab blew the trumpet, and the people returned from pursuing Israel. For Joab held back the people. And they took Absalom and cast him into a large pit in the woods,

Why Shofars Wail in Scripture and Today—   By Mary A. Bruno, Ph.D.

158

and laid a very large heap of stones over him. Then all Israel fled, everyone to his tent.

—2 Sam. 18:16–17

Joab's gory hands raised a shofar to his unruly lips and signaled to stop the fight. His bloodstained shofar would sound again four chapters later.

Sheba

Sheba, a power-hungry lowlife, and shofar-blowing rebel, had defied David and fled, as told in 2 Samuel 20:1–2. One might wonder if a spirit of rebellion had worked through Absalom until his dangling demise, and then moved on to Sheba, who also blew a shofar, defied David's authority, and seemed to follow in Absalom's wilful ways.

The upstart blew his own horn loud and often, which drew some foolish followers from David's forces and led to a disappointing outcome. His shofar blasting mutiny against David went well until Joab got involved. Joab observed Sheba but took care of a timewaster along the way.

And the king said to Amasa, "Assemble the men of Judah for me within three days, and be present here yourself." So Amasa went to assemble *the men of* Judah. But he delayed longer than the set time which David had appointed him.

—2 Sam. 20:4–5

Amasa

Amasa did not seem to grasp the meaning of *"Be here with the men in three days."* Royal servants had to follow all orders, show up on time and keep commitments.

Why Shofars Wail in Scripture and Today—   By Mary A. Bruno, Ph.D.

159

Meanwhile, David was dealing with several problems at the same time. He saw trouble brewing in Sheba's camp and closed off the escape routes.

> And David said to Abishai, "Now Sheba the son of Bichri will do us more harm than Absalom. Take your lord's servants and pursue him, lest he find for himself fortified cities, and escape us." So Joab's men, with the Cherethites, the Pelethites, and all the mighty men, went out after him. And they went out of Jerusalem to pursue Sheba the son of Bichri.
> —2 Sam. 20:6–7

Cherethites and Pelethites

Joab was bad enough, but oh, those guys who were with him! *Cherethites and Pelethites!* They were with a whole slew of *mighty men!* Those heavily armed muscle men were big, bad, and brutal. Amasa might have done better if he had arrived on time with the men. His indifference and sloppy lack of commitment drew disastrous results.

> Now Joab was dressed in battle armor; on it was a belt *with* a sword fastened in its sheath at his hips; and as he was going forward, it fell out. Then Joab said to Amasa, "*Are* you in health, my brother?" And Joab took Amasa by the beard with his right hand to kiss him.
> —2 Sam. 20:8b–9

Deception

Wisdom urged caution whenever a rival arrived with a friendly greeting and a kiss. However, Amasa, the careless and past-due procrastinator, was no friend of wisdom. He blundered blindly into Joab's sinister scheme.

Why Shofars Wail in Scripture and Today—   By Mary A. Bruno, Ph.D.

160

> But Amasa was not on guard against the sword which
> was in Joab's hand so he struck him in the belly with it
> and poured out his inward parts on the ground, and did
> not *strike* him again, and he died. Then Joab and Abishai
> his brother pursued Sheba the son of Bichri.
>
> —2 Sam. 20:10 NASB

With cunning in one hand and deadly deceit in the other, Joab seized the opportunity by the beard, and slit Amasa wide open. Savoring renewed job security, he wiped his bloody hands, bloody sword, and sticky sandals, and then chased Sheba through the northern country. The scene unfolded like an old western movie.

Right Woman

> Then they came and besieged him in Abel of Beth
> Maachah; and they cast up a siege mound against the
> city, and it stood by the rampart. And all the people who
> *were* with Joab battered the wall to throw it down.
> Then a wise woman cried out from the city, "Hear,
> hear! Please say to Joab, 'Come nearby, that I may
> speak with you.'"
>
> —2 Sam. 20:15–16

Citizens of Abel Beth Maacah cringed when Joab's men surrounded the town and battered their trusty wall of safety. A wise woman lifted up her voice like a shofar. Her words rang true as a bell through the battle's clamor. In 2 Samuel 20:17–20, she dared to speak up and confront Joab, the willful warrior, and coldblooded killer.

Right Spirit

Her appeal to Joab was reminiscent of Abigail's appeal to David in 1 Samuel chapters 25–31, when Nabal,

Why Shofars Wail in Scripture and Today—   By Mary A. Bruno, Ph.D.

161

her foolish, wine-sipping husband, had refused to let David's army pass through his land. Abigail's voice of wisdom saved lives when she brought God and provisions into the problem. Both women spoke with wisdom, humility, and reason, which kept David and Joab from violating their integrity. Even defiant and deadly Joab seemed to have displayed a dab of decency on that day.

> So the woman said to Joab, "Watch, his head will be thrown to you over the wall." Then the woman in her wisdom went to all the people. And they cut off the head of Sheba the son of Bichri, and threw *it* out to Joab. Then he blew a trumpet, and they withdrew from the city, every man to his tent. So Joab returned to the king at Jerusalem.
>
> —2 Sam. 20:21b–22

If the wise woman had not spoken up, there would have been major bloodshed. Wisdom and reason triumphed over tragedy. The city survived because she convinced its citizens to act. They severed Sheba's haughty head and hurled it (over or through a hole in the wall) to Joab.

Sheba's ruin began when he first entertained and came into agreement with an idea (spirit?) of rebellion. He exalted himself and cut ties with his righteous king, which was not wise. Sheba put a shofar to his rebellious lips and enjoyed an exhilarating rush of power. His defiant shofar blast drew the unwise into a revolt against King David.

Sheba soon understood that not all shofar cries conveyed God's blessing. His self-serving shofar blasts had the opposite effect and triggered his dreadful doom.

Why Shofars Wail in Scripture and Today—   By Mary A. Bruno, Ph.D.

162

Joab blasted out the victorious shofar proclamation that signaled Sheba's death. This was the last time that Joab's shofar sounded in Scripture.

Wrong Spirit

Again, one might wonder if it was a coincidence or the work of a defiant and rebellious spirit that oppressed or possessed obstinate Absalom and led to his tragic end. Had that same dark entity searched out another insubordinate vessel to oppress, inhabit, and destroy, such as Sheba, and then led him down a similar dark path to a violent end?

When one host perished, it seemed as though an oppressing spirit sought out, indwelt, and urged another power-hungry, God-defiant, self-centered rebel to ruin. Would it find a similar host to inhabit and destroy?

> Do you not know that to whom you present yourselves slaves to obey, you are that one's slaves whom you obey, whether of sin *leading* to death, or of obedience *leading* to righteousness?
>
> —Rom. 6:16 KJV

A shofar would announce good news when God's faithful Zadok the priest and reliable Nathan the prophet anointed a new king over Israel. However, a counterfeit coronation had convened across town.

More shofars were ready to wail.

* * *

Why Shofars Wail in Scripture and Today—   By Mary A. Bruno, Ph.D.

163

The Brunos blew their shofar from a favorite spot on the side of a mountain and prayed (again) at the edge of town for God's blessings upon the people of Caposele, an ancient town where Rocco grew up.

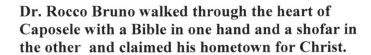

Dr. Rocco Bruno walked through the heart of Caposele with a Bible in one hand and a shofar in the other and claimed his hometown for Christ.

Why Shofars Wail in Scripture and Today—   By Mary A. Bruno, Ph.D.

164

Chapter 21
Solomon – Part 1

T he Book of Kings opens with a bedroom scene. David, aged warrior king, psalmist, and man after God's own heart shivered under death's relentless chill. Abishag, his strikingly beautiful health aid, could not warm him. Israel would soon need a new king. David had promised Bathsheba that Solomon would be the one to reign in his stead.

Adonijah

Across town, Adonijah, David's other son from Haggith had tried to seize the throne. One might wonder if Haggith had instilled belief in her sons that *they* would be king. She may have hoped to rule beside them. However, Absalom's rebellion had failed. He was dead and buried; yet, Adonijah's blatant takeover celebration was going strong.

> Then Adonijah the son of Haggith exalted himself, saying, "I will be king"; and he prepared for himself chariots and horsemen, and fifty men to run before him. (And his father had not rebuked him at any time by saying, "Why have you done so?" He *was* also very good-looking. *His mother* had borne him after

Why Shofars Wail in Scripture and Today—   By Mary A. Bruno, Ph.D.

165

Absalom.) Then he conferred with Joab the son of Zeruiah and with Abiathar the priest, and they followed and helped Adonijah. But Zadok the priest, Benaiah the son of Jehoiada, Nathan the prophet, Shimei, Rei, and the mighty men who *belonged* to David were not with Adonijah.

—1 Kings 1:5–8

Adonijah followed Absalom's defiant example as he combed his dark hair and flashed himself a toothy smile. His brother had looked dashing when he paraded through Jerusalem in his fancy chariot with regal horses, and fifty runners. Adonijah promised himself, "I will be king!"

Haggith may have coached him on how to dress for success. She donned her new gown, shoes, and accessories, and then made sure every hair was in place. It was all happening so fast! She had her public smile and hand gestures perfected. All eyes would be on her and Adonijah. She would be first to address him as, *Your Majesty*.

Joab and Abiathar, the priest, had backed the revolt.

And Adonijah sacrificed sheep and oxen and fattened cattle by the stone of Zoheleth, which *is* by En Rogel; he also invited all his brothers, the king's sons, and all the men of Judah, the king's servants. But he did not invite Nathan the prophet, Benaiah, the mighty men, or Solomon his brother.

—1 Kings 1:9–10

Zoheleth

Adonijah, the power-pursuing, potential potentate pranced off to Zoheleth, a boundary stone near Jerusalem that meant, *creeping one* or *serpent stone*. He chose that place to usurp authority. Had a spirit of rebellion led him

Why Shofars Wail in Scripture and Today—   By Mary A. Bruno, Ph.D.

166

there to receive the serpent's help? He looked quite religious when he sacrificed sheep, oxen, and fatlings; but may have forgotten that doing so had cost Saul his kingdom.

Adonijah invited the whole *A-List* to his coronation. Traitors would soon wish they had declined. If he succeeded, Solomon and Bathsheba's lives would be in grave danger—because new kings were inclined to kill off all contenders for their thrones.

God sent in Nathan with a new strategy. Nathan went straight to the real woman behind the throne—Bathsheba. If Adonijah became king, the usurper would probably have assassinated her and Solomon in a heartbeat. Nathan urged Bathsheba to remind David of his promise that Solomon would be king after him and to ask why Adonijah was king.

Bathsheba

Bathsheba may have splashed on perfume, pinched her cheeks for color, and then selected an ideal piece of jewelry, a gift perhaps from David. She would have slipped it on, glanced in the mirror, savored its memories, and then inhaled, and hurried to the King's chamber.

Her once youthful appearance had withered since her first time there. Painfully aware that she was no longer the prettiest woman in the room, Bathsheba tried to ignore Abishag, whose full lips, slender frame, and smooth olive skin radiated a youthful glow.

She turned her thoughts back to when her shriveled skin had been silky smooth. King David had caught a peek of her bathing on what she had thought was a secluded corner of her rooftop. His servants summoned her to the palace.

Their meeting may have progressed to his balcony

Why Shofars Wail in Scripture and Today—   By Mary A. Bruno, Ph.D.

167

that overlooked Jerusalem, as she sipped fine wine from his golden chalice. He most likely stood beside her as they savored the sunset's orange and lavender hues on Jerusalem's beautiful domes. Did she feel weak when he took her hand and gazed deeply into her eyes? City lights flickered as darkness settled in.

Fascinated by her beauty, David would have draped her with exquisite jewels from his royal treasury. In his eyes, they must have paled in comparison to her beauty.

Uriah, her husband, was away at war. Would she, or could she, refuse her king? Their heated moment of passion produced an unplanned pregnancy.

Worried that the fruit of their intimacy might be exposed, David tried to cover it up. He summoned Uriah from battle, and hoped his night at home would resolve the problem. Uriah's righteous response would cost his life.

He was more concerned for the Ark of God's Covenant that rested in a temporary shelter, and for his comrades in arms who slept in open fields, than for his personal desires. He flatly refused the comforts of a wife and home while the Ark and his army friends endured hardship. David did what he felt he had to do, and[71] issued an order to abandon Uriah where he would die openly and alone in the hottest part of the battle.

After ordering Uriah's murder, David wed the widow (Bathsheba) and assumed their problem was resolved. However, God thought otherwise and sent Nathan to deliver a clear message. He confronted their sin and said the sword would never depart from David's house. Their baby died.

---

[71] Codoh.com | Notebook, http://codoh.com/library/document/3709/ (accessed April 12, 2016).

Why Shofars Wail in Scripture and Today—   By Mary A. Bruno, Ph.D.

168

Solomon

God saw their remorse and repentance, forgave their sin, tempered judgment with mercy, and gave them another son whom Bathsheba called Solomon (peace). However, the LORD loved the boy too and sent Nathan to name him *Jedidiah* (beloved of the LORD). Like an unused gift of God, this was the only mention of the name *Jedidiah* in Scripture.

Bathsheba focused on the current life or death crisis and her fading husband and king. David, the giant-killer, had been brave and strong in his youth. Dark circles under his sunken eyes warned that his candle of life was failing.

> So Bathsheba went into the chamber to the king. (Now the king was very old, and Abishag the Shunammite was serving the king.) And Bathsheba bowed and did homage to the king. Then the king said, "What is your wish?"
>
> —1 Kings 1:15–16

Bathsheba had barely filled David in on the takeover and pleaded for their lives when Nathan's loud voice echoed in the corridor. Bathsheba politely excused herself.

As was his custom, Nathan prostrated himself before his king, and then gave him the short and sharp version of Adonijah's claim to the throne, as recorded in 1 Kings 1:24–27. David swiftly barked out his commands.

> Then King David answered and said, "Call Bathsheba to me." So she came into the king's presence and stood before the king. And the king took an oath and said, "*As* the LORD lives, who has redeemed my life from every distress, just as I swore to you by the LORD God of Israel, saying, 'Assuredly Solomon your son shall be

Why Shofars Wail in Scripture and Today—   By Mary A. Bruno, Ph.D.

169

king after me, and he shall sit on my throne in my place,' so I certainly will do this day."

—1 Kings 1:28–30

Intercession

Bathsheba's garment may have complimented her hair's silver highlights as she adorned herself in the king's gifts and answered his call to intercede in his presence. David was waiting for her. Bathsheba walked as tall as she could. She entered his room, paused for her loving eyes to flash him a warm smile, and then waited before her king.

David's eyes brightened, and his heart raced with excitement that surged through him whenever she came near. He delighted in his majestic Bathsheba, adorned with the beauty of his love-gifts and strength of his promises. His eyes though dim with age, filtered lines from her face as he drank in the nectar of her loveliness. His dear bride was still the remarkable creature that captured his heart so long ago.

His warrior soul seethed with rage upon hearing of Adonijah's scheme. David's eyes grew cold as he unsheathed the sword of his word. Solomon, their son, would sit on the throne that very day! David summoned Zadok the priest, Nathan the prophet, and Benaiah, *the Captain of the guard— and Assassin!* Things would change *quickly*.

In First Kings 1:34–37, David ordered his servants to put Solomon on the royal mule and escort him to Gihon (a stream that supplied Jerusalem's water). Gihon flowed from Eden, where God had promised the Redeemer would come through Eve's seed, which included Solomon. The Messiah (Jesus) would come from Solomon's bloodline.

Why Shofars Wail in Scripture and Today—   By Mary A. Bruno, Ph.D.

170

Sweet Anointing

The name *Gihon* means, *bursting forth.* Solomon's day of *bursting forth and anointing* was by a stream of refreshing. It was a day of *breakthrough* for God's anointed, and for *Israel and Judah.* Zadok the priest and Nathan the prophet anointed Solomon as king of Israel and Judah. Together the priest and the prophet may have symbolized a double anointing—of godly wisdom and godly authority.

> So Zadok the priest, Nathan the prophet, Benaiah the son of Jehoiada, the Cherethites, and the Pelethites went down and had Solomon ride on King David's mule, and took him to Gihon. Then Zadok the priest took a horn of oil from the tabernacle and anointed Solomon. And they blew the horn, and all the people said, *"Long* live King Solomon!" And all the people went up after him; and the people played the flutes and rejoiced with great joy, so that the earth *seemed to* split with their sound.
>
> —1 Kings 1:38–40

Benaiah knew that Adonijah was attempting a murderous coup. The mighty man of courage acted swiftly to protect Solomon. He ordered the Cherethites and Pelethites to the anointing ceremony and posted them to protect their new king. Few would dare to challenge them.

The people stood in reverence when Zadok anointed Solomon, king. The entire horn of sweet anointing flowed over him. It was a type of God's Holy Spirit coming upon Solomon to empower him to lead God's people. As scholars have noted, the sweet-smelling anointing flowed over his head and shoulders, through his garments, dripped from his hands and touched his feet. The abiding fragrance of his anointing was a reminder of his royal presence that clung to all who walked closely with him. It also pictured the Holy

Why Shofars Wail in Scripture and Today—   By Mary A. Bruno, Ph.D.

171

Spirit's outpouring upon believers who would walk closely with Jesus Christ and continue His ministry on Earth.

Solomon's anointing involved two horns; one poured the anointing oil. Another (a shofar) joyfully proclaimed that God's will triumphed and His anointed reigned. The two horns may have announced his God-given position and God-given power that enabled Solomon to reign with God-given wisdom and God-given mercy. Solomon went down in history as the wisest man who ever lived.

His coronation shofar brought a breakthrough. It seemed like all heaven broke loose with the blaring shofar, flutes, and rejoicing. God's anointing brought great joy; however, shakeups followed. Wailing shofars announced the new king as Nathan the prophet and Zadok, the priest proclaimed, "Long live King Solomon!"

However, Adonijah's coronation celebration was still in progress on the other side of town. Shofar wails would interrupt his royal party.

* * *

Why Shofars Wail in Scripture and Today—   By Mary A. Bruno, Ph.D.

172

Chapter 22
Solomon – Part 2

Solomon felt the surge of God's abiding and equipping power that released a rush of excitement. Wailing shofars and the rhythmic clatter of royal mule hooves on cobblestones proclaimed his coming. The crowds cheered, paraded behind him, and chanted, "Long live King Solomon!" The rightful king had claimed his throne.

Adonijah's guests were still nibbling dessert crumbs and hoping for positions of power in his kingdom when blaring shofar blasts halted the merriment.

> Now Adonijah and all the guests who *were* with him heard *it* as they finished eating. And when Joab heard the sound of the horn, he said, "Why *is* the city in such a noisy uproar?" While he was still speaking, there came Jonathan, the son of Abiathar the priest.
> —1 Kings 1:41–42a

Shofar cries that stimulated shouts of joy in the just incited shrieks of terror in the rebels. Jonathan announced that Solomon was king. Petrified guests paled, panicked, and

Why Shofars Wail in Scripture and Today—   By Mary A. Bruno, Ph.D.

173

pushed through exits to distance themselves from Adonijah, the new King's half-brother and rival for the throne.

Horrified Adonijah fled under a barrage of shofar blasts that pierced his flesh like arrows and shattered Haggith's dreams. Her son was in hiding. Her bragging rights were gone. It was too late to stop the news releases.

After his failed takeover (which could have meant death for Solomon and Bathsheba) Adonijah got religious in a hurry in 1 Kings 1:49–53. He ran in, grabbed the horns of the altar, and begged Solomon to spare his life.

The new king granted mercy to his conniving brother from a different mother and let him live. Solomon established his reign over Israel and Judah and placed a throne next to his for Bathsheba, whose bold intercession had saved his throne, and their lives.

Seven Steps to Success
From his deathbed, King David gave Solomon seven steps to success, plus a death list, and then ordered him to bless some faithful men who had stood by him when times were tough, and to deal with Shimei (the curser).

> Now the days of David drew near that he should die, and he charged Solomon his son, saying: "I go the way of all the earth; be strong, therefore, and prove yourself a man. And keep the charge of the LORD your God: to walk in His ways, to keep His statutes, His commandments, His judgments, and His testimonies, as it is written in the Law of Moses, that you may prosper in all that you do and wherever you turn;"
> —1 Kings 2:1–3

Why Shofars Wail in Scripture and Today—   By Mary A. Bruno, Ph.D.

174

King David's *Seven Steps to Success* were clear:

1. Be strong.

2. Be a man and keep the charge of the LORD your God.

3. Walk in God's ways.

4. Keep God's statutes.

5. Keep God's commandments.

6. Keep God's ordinances.

7. Keep God's testimonies.

God's Book of the Law became Solomon's royal university that made him unusually wise and very prosperous. His insightful writings in the book of Proverbs can bring wisdom to each new generation of kings and priests to God.

Death List

After the spiritual matters, David issued a *death list* and urged Solomon to deal wisely with some ungodly men whose grace period would expire with David.

> "Moreover you know also what Joab the son of Zeruiah did to me, *and* what he did to the two commanders of the armies of Israel, to Abner the son of Ner and Amasa the son of Jether, whom he killed. And he shed the blood of war in peacetime, and put the blood of war on his belt that *was* around his waist, and on his sandals that *were* on his feet. Therefore do according to your wisdom, and do not let his gray hair go down to the grave in peace.
>
> "But show kindness to the sons of Barzillai the Gileadite, and let them be among those who eat at your table, for so they came to me when I fled from Absalom your brother.

Why Shofars Wail in Scripture and Today—   By Mary A. Bruno, Ph.D.

175

"And see, *you have* with you Shimei the son of Gera, a Benjamite from Bahurim, who cursed me with a malicious curse in the day when I went to Mahanaim. But he came down to meet me at the Jordan, and I swore to him by the LORD, saying, 'I will not put you to death with the sword.' Now therefore, do not hold him guiltless, for you *are* a wise man and know what you ought to do to him; but bring his gray hair down to the grave with blood."

—1 Kings 2:5–9

If Joab, first on the death list (He killed Absalom), thought his dastardly deception, defiance, and devious deeds had dodged David's attention, he was wrong—*definitely wrong*. David clearly remembered when Joab had killed Abner and Amasa, his fellow commanders. Innocent blood had gushed over Joab's belt and splattered his feet. David ordered Solomon to act wisely and not let Joab die in peace. Joab would plead for mercy and find none.

Bittersweet memories stirred David's heart regarding Barzillai's sons and their unwavering loyalty. They had stood by him, and had honored him when Absalom, his own son, had defied him. Solomon must always give them VIP status to dine at the royal table.

Shimei was last on the list. He seemed blind to a huge problem that his cursing had created. His cruel words still stung as David neared death.

Jesus may have been thinking of Shimei in the following passage from Matthew 12:36, when He warned about idle words that come from of one's mouth.

Why Shofars Wail in Scripture and Today—   By Mary A. Bruno, Ph.D.

176

But I say to you that for every idle word men may speak, they will give account of it in the day of judgment.

—Matt. 12:36

The meanings of the following words (explained in footnotes) are from Matthew 12:36, and deserve some consideration: idle[72]; word[73]; speak[74]; account[75].

David's promise to let Shimei live would not endure beyond the grave. He used the word "I" twice, and emphasized "you" four times when he charged Solomon to bring Shimei down to the grave—with blood. The death sentences were David's last recorded words in the book of First Kings.

Adonijah's sneaky character surfaced again in 1 Kings 2:13–21. He asked Bathsheba to urge Solomon to let him wed the gorgeous Abishag (David's attendant). Was he kidding? Ten percent of the selfish words in his request were "I, mine, me, my, I, me, and me." Adonijah still felt entitled to whatever he wanted.

Bathsheba must have known how her son, the King, would respond to his sly half-brother's appeal. Therefore, she graciously conveyed Adonijah's wish, which she suspected would ignite Solomon's wrath.

---

[72] "G692 - argos - (G692, argos: idle and barren...); Strong's Greek Lexicon (KJV)." Blue Letter Bible. Accessed 9 Jun, 2016. https://www.blueletterbible.org//lang/Lexicon/Lexicon.cfm?Strongs=G692&t=KJV

[73] "G4487 - rhēma - (G4487, rhema: word, saying, thing, that which has been uttered...); Strong's Greek Lexicon (KJV)." Blue Letter Bible. Accessed 9 Jun, 2016. https://www.blueletterbible.org//lang/Lexicon/Lexicon.cfm?Strongs=G4487&t=KJV

[74] "G2980 - laleō - (G2980, laleo: speak, say, tell, talk, preach, utter...); Strong's Greek Lexicon (KJV)." Blue Letter Bible. Accessed 9 Jun, 2016. https://www.blueletterbible.org//lang/Lexicon/Lexicon.cfm?Strongs=G2980&t=KJV

[75] "G3056 - logos - (G3056, logos: word, saying, account, speech, Word(Christ), thing. Strong's Greek Lexicon (KJV)." Blue Letter Bible. Accessed 9 Jun, 2016. https://www.blueletterbible.org//lang/Lexicon/Lexicon.cfm?Strongs=G3056&t=KJV

Why Shofars Wail in Scripture and Today—   By Mary A. Bruno, Ph.D.

177

> And King Solomon answered and said to his mother, "Now why do you ask Abishag the Shunammite for Adonijah? Ask for him the kingdom also—for he is my older brother—for him, and for Abiathar the priest, and for Joab the son of Zeruiah." Then King Solomon swore by the LORD, saying, "May God do so to me, and more also, if Adonijah has not spoken this word against his own life!
>
> —1 Kings 2:22–23

King Solomon reigned from his throne, next to Bathsheba, on her throne. His jaw clenched, and veins pulsated when he heard that Adonijah wanted Abishag.

Oh, no he doesn't! Not 'Abbie'!

He knew what that throne-stealer would have done if he had become king. Bathsheba's motherly hand may have covered a knowing smile as she lowered her eyes when Solomon confidently pronounced sentence.

His verdict for Adonijah was fast, furious, and final. Instead of Abishag, *his dream girl,* Adonijah got Benaiah, *his worst nightmare!* Instead of an adorable *woman,* he got *an able assassin!* Instead of n*ewlywed,* he became *newly dead!*

King Solomon must have been in quite a mood after issuing Adonijah's death sentence in 1 Kings 2:26–27. He fired Abiathar, the traitor priest, but let him live.

Joab, the shedder of innocent blood, was next on the *hit list.* He paled at the news of Adonijah's execution and searched for a place to hide. Oh yes, the horns of the altar—surely, Solomon would respect the tent of meeting, and he would be safe there. Well, maybe not . . . . Joab clung to the horns of the altar in 1 Kings 2:28–31 and said he would die there. Solomon graciously granted Joab's dying wish and

Why Shofars Wail in Scripture and Today—   By Mary A. Bruno, Ph.D.

178

sent in loyal Benaiah to finish him off. Joab's own blood would be the last to stain his sandals.

Solomon's motive for killing Joab was to overthrow the power and penalty of his evil crimes (the shedding of innocent blood) from David's bloodline.

> "Their blood shall therefore return upon the head of Joab and upon the head of his descendants forever. But upon David and his descendants, upon his house and his throne, there shall be peace forever from the LORD."
> —1 Kings 2:33

Joab's demise created a job opening in 1 Kings 2:35. Solomon put faithful Benaiah over the army and gave Abiathar's job to loyal Zadok, who had anointed him, King.

Bathsheba's Restoration

Bathsheba, seated on her throne next to her son, the wise king, was a shining example of God's restoration of a repentant heart as seen in the following passage.

> But God, who is rich in mercy, because of His great love with which He loved us, even when we were dead in trespasses, made us alive together with Christ (by grace you have been saved), and raised *us* up together, and **made *us* sit together in the heavenly *places* in Christ Jesus**, that in the ages to come He might show the exceeding riches of His grace in *His* kindness toward us in Christ Jesus. For by grace you have been saved through faith, and that not of yourselves; *it is* the gift of God,
> —Eph. 2:4–8, emphasis added

Why Shofars Wail in Scripture and Today—   By Mary A. Bruno, Ph.D.

179

Shimei

Solomon's eyes scanned his list. Shimei, the bad-mouthed king-curser, was next. Solomon extended an *olive branch* of peace to him, which contained a slight *thorn.*

> Then the king sent and called for Shimei, and said to him, "Build yourself a house in Jerusalem and dwell there, and do not go out from there anywhere. For it shall be, on the day you go out and cross the Brook Kidron, know for certain you shall surely die; your blood shall be on your own head."
> —1 Kings 2:36–37

Sure, sure, where do I sign? Shimei gladly took Solomon's offer to let him build a house in Jerusalem, and never leave town. The terms were easy enough; however, this was Shimei, who dared to curse King David to his face. All was well until Shimei's servants defied *his* authority in 1 Kings 2:39–40. Blinded by rage, he forgot his contract.

Wisdom urged Shimei to paste memos all over his donkey's harness that read: *Stay within the city limits! Do not leave town! Avoid the Brook Kidron!*

Instead of reining himself in, Shimei galloped off to Gath, grabbed the fugitives, and grinned his way home. Somebody in town must have leaked the news. Solomon called Shimei in on the royal rug.

First Kings 2:41–43 shows that dealing with kings was not Shimei's greatest strength. Solomon quizzed him and repeated the life and death terms of their contract. He asked why he had not kept his oath before God. Runaways were no excuse. For once, Shimei had nothing to say.

Solomon recounted Shimei's violations, in 1 Kings 2:44–46, and pronounced sentence. God would return evil

Why Shofars Wail in Scripture and Today—   By Mary A. Bruno, Ph.D.

180

upon Shimei's head, but He would bless Solomon and David's throne forever.

Wide-eyed Shimei gasped in horror when Solomon gave Benaiah *the signal*. There would be no automatic appeal and no hope of an extended stay on Death Row. King Solomon's word was fast and final.

Benaiah knew the drill, and quickly ridded the court-room and the world of Shimei. Thus, Solomon finished David's *Death list*, and established his own kingdom.

Gazing down the corridors of time, shofar blasts would sound again to herald a new king who would make a clean sweep in Israel. Shofars were ready to proclaim God's perfect will.

* * *

Why Shofars Wail in Scripture and Today—   By Mary A. Bruno, Ph.D.

181

Declaring God's blessings over Ohio

"Shofie"

Dr. Mary A. Bruno's silver-embellished Yemenite shofar (Shown on the cover of this book.) cried boldly through the United States of America, Canada, and Italy, to proclaim God's blessings and ownership of the land and His people.

The website has full-color photos from the Brunos' shofar-blowing ministry trip (Addressed in chapters 31-34). Photos include sounding the shofar at the Liberty Bell in Philadelphia, PA, near the White House in Washington, D.C., in dozens of US states, Canada, and Italy. Visit www.ministrylit.com.

Why Shofars Wail in Scripture and Today—   By Mary A. Bruno, Ph.D.

182

Chapter 23
Elijah and Jehu

God visited Elijah the prophet after the holy fire had fallen and consumed some very wet sacrifices. Elijah had killed 450 of Jezebel's Baal prophets, which put a huge dent in her team of phony ministers. She was furious and wanted to kill him.

After his huge miracle in ministry, Elijah fled for his life and was alone and depressed in the desert. Circumstances seemed unbearable. He moaned under a juniper tree (broom tree) and asked God to end his life in 1 Kings 19:1–4. Interestingly, that broom tree (mentioned twice in three verses) hinted of a clean sweep that God was ready to launch through Jehu.

An angel prepared a cake and gave it to Elijah with a jar of water. Elijah ate and rested for his 80-mile hike to Mount Horeb (Sinai, Mount of God) for further instructions.

> Then the LORD said to him: "Go, return on your way to the Wilderness of Damascus; and when you arrive, anoint Hazael *as* king over Syria. Also you shall anoint Jehu the son of Nimshi *as* king over Israel. And Elisha the son of Shaphat of Abel Meholah you shall anoint *as* prophet in your place.
>
> —1 Kings 19:15–16

Why Shofars Wail in Scripture and Today—   By Mary A. Bruno, Ph.D.

183

When God said, "Go, return on your way," He may have been telling Elijah that he would grant his request to leave this world. It was time to anoint two new kings, and a new prophet (Elisha) to fill his position. God's plans for Elijah's retirement did not include leaving his bones for jackals in the desert. God speeded up the exciting transition.

When Elijah obeyed God and draped his prophet's cape over Elisha, who was plowing in a field, the persistent plower became a powerful prophet.

Instead of giving Elijah an earthly retirement gift, God sent His flaming ride with supernatural horsepower that carried the faithful prophet away (alive) to enjoy a new adventure with God in Paradise.

Second Kings 8:7–15 tells of when Elisha, the new prophet, met with Hazael. Sometimes God shows His prophets things that are hard to bear. Elisha wept when God revealed what Hazael would do to the Israelites. However, Hazael's anointing was God's idea. Elisha had to obey.

Jehu

Jehu's anointing went a little better; however, Elisha may not have looked forward to another royal anointing so soon after his disappointment regarding Hazael. He delegated a prophet's son to carry it out.

> And Elisha the prophet called one of the sons of the prophets, and said to him, "Get yourself ready, take this flask of oil in your hand, and go to Ramoth Gilead. Now when you arrive at that place, look there for Jehu the son of Jehoshaphat, the son of Nimshi, and go in and make him rise up from among his associates, and take him to an inner room. Then take the flask of oil, and pour *it* on his head, and say, 'Thus says the LORD: "I have

Why Shofars Wail in Scripture and Today—   By Mary A. Bruno, Ph.D.

184

anointed you king over Israel.'" Then open the door and flee, and do not delay."

—2 Kings 9:1–3

Elisha's delegate took the horn of oil, tracked down Captain Jehu, and spoke privately to him.

> Then he arose and went into the house. And he poured the oil on his head, and said to him, "Thus says the LORD God of Israel: 'I have anointed you king over the people of the LORD, over Israel.'"

—2 Kings 9:6

The anointer blurted out his prophecy and then raised the horn of oil and emptied all of it on Jehu's head. The fragrant anointing dripped from the astonished new sovereign, who wondered why God had made him king. God's answer came immediately.

Mission Statement

The prophet's son stated God's message in 2 Kings 9:7–10, which was a seven-point *Who Does What List for God, Jehu, and the Dogs.*

Jehu would strike the house of Ahab. This was the top priority for King Jehu. God was sending him to destroy Ahab's evil dominion.

1. God would avenge Naboth's blood, who died at Jezebel's command. God's vengeance would come thru Jehu.
2. Jezebel would pay with her blood for spilling Naboth's blood.
3. Ahab's whole house would perish. God would use Jehu to wipe out Ahab's lineage.

Why Shofars Wail in Scripture and Today—   By Mary A. Bruno, Ph.D.

185

4. God would cut off all of Ahab's male heirs in Israel. Jehu may have been swinging the sword, but this was God's battle.

5. God would make Ahab's house like the house of Jeroboam, son of Nebat, and like the house of Baasha, son of Ahijah. Thru Jehu, God, would annihilate all of Ahab's kin.

6. Dogs would eat Jezebel in the territory of Jezreel. Thru Jehu and the dogs, God would devour Jezebel because she had devoured His prophets and servants by the sword. Dogs would devour her.

7. None would bury her. Jezebel's body would pass through the dog's and become litter on the land. (Naboth's land?)

After the uneasy messenger had privately administered the royal anointing (which happened to be an act of treason), he delivered his prophecy, then threw open the door, and dashed out of town.

Jehu's mind raced as he experienced God's anointing and pondered God's seven-point marching orders. The powerful prophecy replayed in his spirit.

Dazed Jehu returned to the captains, oblivious of the fragrant anointing that was upon him. In 2 Kings 9:11–13, his men realized something was going on and asked what happened. Jehu, hardly a pillar of truth, began his reign with a lie. The anointing that had set him apart, and equipped him to be king, did not make him righteous.

Jehu's fellow officers recognized the fragrant oil that was still dripping and exchanged knowing glances. They refused his lie, and demanded the truth. Jehu sheepishly

Why Shofars Wail in Scripture and Today—   By Mary A. Bruno, Ph.D.

186

admitted God had made him king over Israel. They hurried to protect their new sovereign who stood on a slippery step that hinted of Jehu's upcoming sly strategies.

His captains spread their garments over the oily steps, blew the shofar and proclaimed, "Jehu is king!" Their shofars announced God's prophetic word. King Jehu (as a stiff broom in God's hand) would sweep away the evil house of Ahab and overthrow his stronghold.

The new king experienced the equipping power of God's prophetic word that would achieve what He sent it to do (Isa. 55:10–11). Shofar blasts that rippled through Jehu's soul awakened his talents and abilities to *clean house* for Israel. Jehu's anointing stimulated a new or renewed love for God's Word, and determination to do His will.

Operation Clean Sweep

Jehu honored God and launched what we can think of as *Operation Clean Sweep.* Suddenly his focus was all about what God wanted. The prophetic words still blazed like holy fire in his spirit. Pleasing God and exterminating Ahab's heirs was of utmost urgency.

> So the watchman reported, saying, "He went up to them and is not coming back; and the driving *is* like the driving of Jehu the son of Nimshi, for he drives furiously!"
>
> —2 Kings 9:20

Jehu polished his chariot, possibly an eye-catching cherry red, royal edition with gold-plated wheels and a zebra skin seat. He slapped reins to rumps; gave a wild victory shout, and left a trailing cloud of dust behind. Jezreel's guards knew Jehu drove as if he were in a chariot

Why Shofars Wail in Scripture and Today—   By Mary A. Bruno, Ph.D.

187

race. His whole-hearted approach to all he did may have been why God chose him to be king.

> Then Joram said, "Get ready." And they made his chariot ready. Joram king of Israel and Ahaziah king of Judah went out, each in his chariot, and they went out to meet Jehu and found him in the property of Naboth the Jezreelite. When Joram saw Jehu, he said, "Is it peace, Jehu?" And he answered, "What peace, so long as the harlotries of your mother Jezebel and her witchcrafts are so many?"
>
> —2 Kings 9:21–22 NASB

Payback

King Joram (one of Ahab's sons) had come to Jezreel to mend from a previous battle and teamed up with Ahaziah, king of Judah. They lined up their fancy chariots and rode to meet Jehu at Naboth's land, which was still very heavy on God's mind.

God was out for vengeance. Wailing shofars probably sounded in unison as the three kings rode to their showdown. King Jehu had ruined any hope for peace when he stated Joram's mother (Jezebel) was a woman of harlotry and witchcraft. Jehu reached for his weapon.

His biceps bulged, and veins pulsated in 2 Kings 9:23–24, as he loaded his bow, took careful aim, pulled the arrow back—all the way back—then paused, and let it fly. Horrified Joram stared at the sharp arrow jutting from his heart, and collapsed dead on the floor of his expensive ride.

God's words about repaying Ahab on Naboth's land kept replaying in Jehu's heart as he checked Joram off his list in 2 Kings 9:25–26, and then told Bidkar to throw the

Why Shofars Wail in Scripture and Today—   By Mary A. Bruno, Ph.D.

188

remains on Naboth's land. Jehu inhaled and began the next phase of *Operation Clean Sweep.*

Expecting Jehu, Jezebel piled her hair high, precisely applied her eye shadow, batted her eyes, exhaled, and admired her reflection. She need not have bothered because, as the saying goes, "All that goes up must come down." Eunuchs locked eyes with Jehu from an upper window as the scene played out in 2 Kings 9:30–37.

Jehu's one-liner, "Throw her down!" was reason enough. They tossed the conniving queen down like a sack of trash. Jehu slapped reins to rumps, ran her down, and then went to dinner. His was not the only ferocious appetite in town. Perhaps while sprinkling cilantro onto his food, he may have reconsidered the fallen queen. He sent someone to bury her. However, the dogs had left nothing but her skull that had plotted evil, the palms of her hands that had worked evil, and the soles of her feet that had run to mischief. The dogs had finished her off before Jehu was done with his main course.

Operation Clean Sweep continued. In 2 Kings 10:1–5, Jehu, while near Jezreel, sent a letter with hard choices for the town. Guardians of Ahab's seventy adult sons caved like sand castles and begged for peace at any price. They obeyed Jehu's gory order in 2 Kings 10:6–8, and deposited all seventy of the princes' heads in baskets at the city's gates.

In 2 Kings 10:9–11, King Jehu, declared the people innocent of the slaughter. He said God's words through Elijah would happen regarding Ahab's house. None of Ahab's family, friends, leaders, or priests survived in Jezreel. Jehu killed another forty-two of Ahaziah's kin in 2 Kings 10:12–14, and then finished off the rest of them in Samaria.

Why Shofars Wail in Scripture and Today—   By Mary A. Bruno, Ph.D.

189

Baal Ball

Jehu, God's "stiff broom" cunningly claimed he would be a greater Baal enthusiast than Ahab was. For emphasis, in 2 Kings 10:18–24, he said, "Sanctify a solemn assembly for Baal." Fans packed out the place for the fancy affair. Of course, there was a death penalty for not attending. They all wore official Baal attire (which targeted them for death).

One might wonder why God's servants were at that pagan event—in Baal outfits, no less! Making merry with heathens could have gotten them all killed.

Jehu's men rounded up all of God's servants who were at the celebration and made them leave. When his signal rang out; *Let the sacrifices begin!* Jehu's men swiftly put every Baal celebrant to the sword.

Second Kings 10:29–31 shows that Jehu had God's anointing, but he lacked training in God's ways and failed to forsake idols. God chose an imperfect leader with good intentions and helped him to take vengeance on an evil king. Jehu was untruthful but managed to kill off Ahab's family, plus all of the Baal followers in Israel. He achieved everything on his mission statement.

God commended Jehu for doing what was right and promised that his children of the fourth generation would sit on Israel's throne. The dogs' reward for eating Jezebel was a spicy treat and honorable mention in God's Book.

A shofar would wail again as hammers clanged, and dust flew during an upcoming building project. Nehemiah's ready shofar-blower awaited his command.

* * *

Why Shofars Wail in Scripture and Today—   By Mary A. Bruno, Ph.D.

190

Chapter 24
Crumbled Walls

N ehemiah was cupbearer to King Artaxerxes at the castle in Shushan, Persia (Iran). He chose fine wines, protected his king against poisoning and earned one of the highest salaries in the land.

The Jubilee shofar blasts had sounded back in Tishri, (Sept. / Oct.). All was well until Hanani, Nehemiah's relative and a few men from Judah visited him at the palace during Kislev (Nov. 5–Dec. 3). They said Jerusalem was in distress with her fallen walls and burned gates.

Hanani's report set off Nehemiah's spiritual alarm that wailed like a shofar's Shevarim. Hot tears spilled down his face and onto his expensive tunic. He wept for days with fasting and prayer. God had a plan in the works.

> A time to kill and a time to heal;
> A time to tear down and a time to build up.
> —Eccl. 3:3 NASB

Nehemiah's lone voice sobbed in the castle over Jerusalem's ruin. As he moved with God, a sense of urgency compelled him to help. God had prepared him "for such a

Why Shofars Wail in Scripture and Today—   By Mary A. Bruno, Ph.D.

191

time as[76] this," which explained his hearty appetite for God's Law, and the terrific cupbearer job.

Fasting and Prayer

Nehemiah fasted with travailing prayer. As a lawyer would argue a case, he cited God's Word that supported his request for Jerusalem. He quoted God's kindness and mercy clause for those who obeyed the Great Lawgiver and Ruler of the Universe. He quoted God's promises and then used them as precedents for his petitions.

Nisan (March 3–April 11) arrived with Passover. Nehemiah recalled his fasting and intense prayer during Kislev, (about five months earlier). Hope and expectation had been high. However, Jerusalem was still in ruins. For a while, it had looked as if God[77] would help. However, nothing seemed to have changed, except the seasons.

Wisdom cried, "Hey, Nehemiah, snap out of it! You quoted a passage back in Kislev, about God having a time for everything. This is a new season! You will see His answer. Your hope was not in vain. God has heard your prayer, even though you have seen no signs of change."

Jerusalem's walls needed building up; therefore, God weakened the Kings' inner walls of resistance. It took a while, but Artaxerxes' heart was as soft as a ripe plum when Nehemiah entered the King's presence. One could almost hear God say, "He's ripe and ready, Nehemiah, go for it!" An avalanche of blessings was ready to break loose.

---

[76] How to Defeat Your Goliath | Kim the Career Coach, http://kimthecareercoach.com/2013/09/25/how-to-defeat-your-goliath/ (accessed April 12, 2016).
[77] Voting Machines - Elections - Ballots - Politics - The New ..., http://www.nytimes.com/2008/01/06/magazine/06Vote-t.html (accessed April 12, 2016).

Why Shofars Wail in Scripture and Today—   By Mary A. Bruno, Ph.D.

192

Artaxerxes watched as Nehemiah filled his glass. The edgy king stared at his wine and then eyed glum Nehemiah, who was usually a bundle of cheer. The wine could wait. He had to find out what was going on with his cupbearer.

Familiar with plots, he asked why Nehemiah looked so serious. He had to be sure his bodyguard was not planning his demise. Nehemiah explained that he was heartsick, and said, "Let the king live forever." Artaxerxes sighed in relief, took a sip, and asked what he needed.

Nehemiah shot up a short prayer to God and hoped his king would not notice his pounding heart. Wisdom prevailed as he voiced his daring request.

> I said to the king, "If it please the king, and if your servant has found favor before you, send me to Judah, to the city of my fathers' tombs, that I may rebuild it." Then the king said to me, the queen sitting beside him, "How long will your journey be, and when will you return?" So it pleased the king to send me, and I gave him a definite time. And I said to the king, "If it please the king, let letters be given me for the governors *of the provinces* beyond the River, that they may allow me to pass through until I come to Judah, and a letter to Asaph the keeper of the king's forest, that he may give me timber to make beams for the gates of the fortress which is by the temple, for the wall of the city and for the house to which I will go." And the king granted *them* to me because the good hand of my God *was* on me.
> —Neh. 2:5–8 NASB

Specifics

Nehemiah asked for *specific* time off. Wisdom helped to state the need without mentioning, "Jerusalem," which might have annoyed the king, who was not fond of that city.

Why Shofars Wail in Scripture and Today—   By Mary A. Bruno, Ph.D.

193

He merely said the city was in Judah. The King probably knew about Nehemiah's background but agreed to his request without hesitation. Feeling confident, the cupbearer also asked for *specific* royal letters to *specific* leaders, in *specific* places, granting him passage to a *specific* location (Judah). Artaxerxes approved the whole thing.

Nehemiah braced himself and asked for the big one, a royal letter to a *particular* person (Asaph, head of the king's Forestry Department), granting a permit to cut *enough* of the king's lush trees for the city's gates and walls—and *enough* timber for his house.

Artaxerxes most likely gulped, took a sip, folded his hands over his belly, raised an eyebrow, and gazed with a half-smile at Nehemiah, who knew he had already rejected a Jerusalem project. Something was different this time; for some reason, the king felt[78] lavishly generous. He approved everything, including his lovely trees. The Persian king exhibited a God-touched heart and joyfully gave to bless God's work. He even threw in a military escort.

Nehemiah 5:14; puts Nehemiah's promotion to the governor in the same year as his fasting and prayer. God did more than Nehemiah could ask or think. Godly wisdom and knowledge (spiritual gifts) had enabled him to know when, how, and what to ask, and what not to say.

God may have drenched Artaxerxes in His love, which, of course, would have prompted him to give. The king practically fell all over himself to bless Nehemiah. He gave him a huge promotion and then loaded him up with abundant provision, and protection for the project.

---

[78] News From Camp Leroy, http://campleroy.blogspot.com/ (accessed April 12, 2016).

Why Shofars Wail in Scripture and Today—   By Mary A. Bruno, Ph.D.

194

Divine enablement had escalated Nehemiah's promotion and equipped him to restore Jerusalem's fallen walls. Nehemiah smiled and tucked the king's letters into his bag (perhaps by his shofar). Yes, this was God's time to help Jerusalem. Nehemiah would rebuild her walls with God-given authority, God-given permits, God-given building materials, a God-given crew, and a God-given shofar blower at his side. He blessed the Lord and rode confidently toward the rubble and the trouble.

Sanballat and Tobiah—*certified mockers and scoffers*—were as swarming vermin feeding on ill will, contempt, and negativity. Geshem, an Arab, joined in on their feeding frenzy, but they could not distract God's man from his mission. Nehemiah surveyed Jerusalem, shared his vision, assured the people of God's blessings, and then put together a diligent and dedicated work crew.

Meanwhile, Sanballat, Tobiah, and Geshem made an unholy alliance to stop the work. (Unholy alliances often come in *threes*.) They wrongly assumed the new governor would run back home before his men could say *lamb shank*. They would be surprised to learn, shofar blasts that could bring walls down could also help to rebuild them.

Shofar Blower

Masons and mortar carriers rallied, took up arms, and labored with a trowel in one hand and weapon in the other. The ready shofar blower stayed by Nehemiah's side as he focused on the restoration, despite interruptions.

Somebody could have done something to protect Jerusalem during more than a century of neglect, but it looked as if nobody did. Living around rubble was no longer acceptable. Jerusalem was vulnerable. Nehemiah knew that

Why Shofars Wail in Scripture and Today—   By Mary A. Bruno, Ph.D.

195

he had to close off the enemy's inroads.

The people worked at an astonishing speed. Priests who lived by the gates repaired walls and gates closest to their homes. Jerusalem's twelve gates included the:

1. *Valley Gate* (Neh. 2:10–11)
2. *Dung Gate* (2:13)
3. *Fountain Gate* (2:14)
4. *Sheep Gate* (3:1)
5. *Fish Gate* (3:3)
6. *Old Gate* (3:6)
7. *Water Gate* (*3:26*)
8. *Horse Gate* (*3:27*)
9. *East Gate* (3:29)
10. *Inspection Gate or Miphkad Gate* (3:31)
11. *Gate of Ephraim* (8:14–16)
12. *Prison Gate* (12:39) or *Gate of the Guard* [79] (2 Kings 11:5, 19)[80]

Mockers

Sanballat, enraged over the restored walls and closed gates in Nehemiah 4:1, spewed ridicule and taunts. He twisted Nehemiah's intentions in Nehemiah 2:19, accused him of a revolt against the king, and then attacked with distractions and intimidations.

Nehemiah prayed in Nehemiah 4:4, and then faced the project and the enemy with a sharp sword fixed to one side and his secret weapon (a skilled shofar blower) close by the other.

---

[79] APPENDIX 59. THE TWELVE GATES OF JERUSALEM (NEH. CHS. 3 ..,
http://www.therain.org/appendixes/app59.html (accessed April 12, 2016).
[80] For more information regarding Jerusalem's gates, see R. Jones' articles at
http://www.talkjesus.com/devotionals/17945-12-gates-jerusalem.html.

Why Shofars Wail in Scripture and Today—   By Mary A. Bruno, Ph.D.

196

In Nehemiah 4:7–11, the enemy plotted to injure, cause confusion, and stop the work; but his plan went public. Nehemiah stuck with what he did best. He prayed, and then posted guards day and night. As laborers watched, worked, and prayed, discussion groups formed.

Judah's leaders said the laborers were fading and unable to continue. The enemies claimed the laborers would not know or see what happened until they had killed them and stopped the work. (They might reconsider that later.)

Neighboring Jews came (ten times) with the same message in Nehemiah 4:12 "You must return and guard us."

As a general commands his troops, Nehemiah urged them to be brave and take courage from God! *Fight for your brethren! Fight for your sons! Fight for your daughters! Fight for your wives! Fight! Fight! Fight!*

If they did not fight for their own, who would? Nehemiah's encouragement calmed their fears and brought them back to their senses. In Nehemiah 4:16–18, they strengthened themselves in the LORD and saw God upset the enemy's plans as everyone worked on the wall.

Where the Shofar Sounds

> "Wherever you hear the sound of the trumpet, rally to us there. Our God will fight for us."
>
> —Neh. 4:20

This verse (formerly without punctuation) might read as, "Wherever you hear the sound of the trumpet (shofar), rally to us. *There* our God will fight for us."

Nehemiah gave orders to rally to the shofar's call in Nehemiah 4:18–23. Labors knew it was a call to gather to

Why Shofars Wail in Scripture and Today—   By Mary A. Bruno, Ph.D.

197

worship, to come into unity, to finish the mission, and to back God's chosen leader. *Wherever the shofar sounded*, the people hurried there to see God fight for them. Miracles happened where God fought for His people.

Where?

Where the shofar called—at the place of miracles.

1. Where God fought for them
2. Where miracles happened
3. Where shofars sounded for God's glory
4. Where shofar blasts were welcome

Laborers worked double shifts, slept in their clothes with weapons in hand; and then got up and did it all again

Sweaty warriors got down and dirty, and rebuilt Jerusalem's wall—*in fifty-two grueling days!*—(seven weeks and three days) *a*fter it had lain in ruins for more than a century.[81] With God's help, miraculous changes happened in those seven and a half intense weeks.

Zechariah wrote of another glorious wall that was already committed for Jerusalem.

> "'For I,' says the LORD, 'will be a wall of fire all around
> her, and I will be the glory in her midst.'"
> —Zech. 2:5

The next shofar blast would declare great blessings and joy.

* * *

---

[81] PRESSURES WITHIN AND WITHOUT SERIES: THE MESSAGE OF NEHEMIAH, https://www.pbc.org/system/message_files/7758/4615.pdf (accessed April 12, 2016).

Why Shofars Wail in Scripture and Today—   By Mary A. Bruno, Ph.D.

198

Chapter 25
Five Insights

The shofars mentioned in Job and Psalms may shed new light on familiar passages.

1. The Horse

A chat between God and Job included God's observations of the warhorse and its response to shofar calls. Job had been going through a rough time, so God gave him a three-part pop quiz that perked up his perception.

> Have you given the horse his might? Have you clothed his neck with quivering *and* a shaking mane?
> Was it you [Job] who made him to leap like a locust? The majesty of his [snorting] nostrils is terrible. He paws in the valley and exults in his strength; he goes out to meet the weapons [of armed men].
> —Job 39:19–21 AMP

As if standing back to appreciate the splendid mount, God focused on its powerful neck, with a flowing mane that made a handy grab handle for riding bareback. We can think of the horse as the LORD'S mustang. God may have smiled as

Why Shofars Wail in Scripture and Today—   By Mary A. Bruno, Ph.D.

199

the horse whinnied, swished his tail, and pranced about as though eager for a challenge.

> He mocks at fear and is not dismayed *or* terrified;
> neither does he turn back [in battle] from the sword.
> The quiver rattles upon him, as do the glittering spear
> and the lance [of his rider]. [He seems in running to]
> devour the ground with fierceness and rage; neither can
> he stand still at the sound of the [war] trumpet.
> —Job 39:22–24 AMP

God's spirited mustang was no coward. The rattle of weapons stirred and spurred him to victory. He loved doing what God had created him to do. He ran to the war trumpet's (shofar) call, with power and a victorious mind. God's lean, mean, running machine's ears perked up at the shofar's call. Battle sounded sweet as he snorted in the enemy's face and jumped over obstacles.

The LORD may have smiled while observing the horse's smooth lines, superb form, and surges of power. He could have viewed it as living art. How much more must He esteem those created in His image? We are His beloved children—His handiwork—filled with His Presence, power, and praise. We are living reflections of His image.

> For we are His workmanship, created in Christ Jesus for
> good works, which God prepared beforehand that we
> should walk in them.
> —Eph. 2:10

Why Shofars Wail in Scripture and Today—   By Mary A. Bruno, Ph.D.

200

2. Clapping, Shouts, and Shofar blasts

> O clap your hands, all peoples;
> Shout to God with the voice of joy.

—Ps. 47:1 NASB

God's Word urges believers to clap their hands and praise Him. Clapping meant more than slapping one's hands together. We shall peek under the word *clap* in Psalm 47:1, and examine its root.

Ah, ha! Clap,[82] *taqa,* meant "to blow, clap, strike, sound, thrust, give a blow, a blast, to thrust or drive a weapon, blast of a horn, and to strike or pledge oneself." It translated as "cast" in Exodus 19:19 when God sent a powerful west wind, which *cast* locusts into the Red Sea.

The same word *taqa* (clap) also translated as *blow,* as in to blow a trumpet or shofar to sound the alarm; and as "blown" when the great trumpet (shofar) blew in Isaiah 27:13. The shofar called the outcasts of Egypt to worship the LORD in the holy mount at Jerusalem.

Clap translated twice as "thrust," *as* when Ehud *thrust* his dagger into Eglon's belly in Judges 3:27, and when Joab *thrust* three spears into Absalom's heart in 2 Samuel 18:14. It meant "smote," as when fearless Jael of Judges 4:21 *hammered* the nail (tent stake) through Sisera's temples.

Hand clapping served as a two-edged sword. It could be an act of worship to God or an act of spiritual warfare, or an expression of commitment. Because the Hebrew word

---

[82] "H8628 - taqa` - Strong's Hebrew Lexicon (KJV)." Blue Letter Bible. Accessed 4 Jun, 2016.
https://www.blueletterbible.org//lang/Lexicon/Lexicon.cfm?Strongs=H8628&t=KJV

Why Shofars Wail in Scripture and Today—   By Mary A. Bruno, Ph.D.

201

taqa, most often translated as "blowing," and blowing the trumpet or shofar; clapping could have a similar impact to that of worshiping, blowing a shofar, or thrusting a weapon.

> God has gone up with a shout,
> The LORD with the sound of a trumpet.
>
> —Ps. 47:5

This verse uses two names for *God*. The first, *Elohiym,*[83] is plural and stirs thoughts of the Holy Trinity. The second, LORD,[84] is *Jehovah*, God's proper name. Things changed when God arose. When He went up with a *shout,*[85] one might wonder what kind of shout. It was a *teruwah* shout—the alarm, battle cry, a shout of joy, and Jubilee shout—a shofar blast. Because God was near, a battle cry signaled victory. When He was with His people—they won!

The trumpet's sound came immediately after shouting. This trumpet,[86] *shofar,* was an animal horn that came into being, not by man, but by God. Shouting and shofar blowing captured God's attention. Therefore, He issued an important command.

God said it four times in Psalm 47:6, to make sure everyone understood the message, and then added, "*Sing praises* to God our King." In the midst of shouting for joy,

---

[83] "H430 - 'elohiym - Strong's Hebrew Lexicon (KJV)." Blue Letter Bible. Accessed 4 Jun, 2016. https://www.blueletterbible.org//lang/Lexicon/Lexicon.cfm?Strongs=H430&t=KJV
[84] "H3068 - Yĕhovah - Strong's Hebrew Lexicon (KJV)." Blue Letter Bible. Accessed 4 Jun, 2016. https://www.blueletterbible.org//lang/Lexicon/Lexicon.cfm?Strongs=H3068&t=KJV
[85] "H8643 - tĕruw`ah - Strong's Hebrew Lexicon (KJV)." Blue Letter Bible. Accessed 4 Jun, 2016. https://www.blueletterbible.org//lang/Lexicon/Lexicon.cfm?Strongs=H8643&t=KJV
[86] "H7782 - showphar - Strong's Hebrew Lexicon (KJV)." Blue Letter Bible. Accessed 4 Jun, 2016. https://www.blueletterbible.org//lang/Lexicon/Lexicon.cfm?Strongs=H7782&t=KJV

Why Shofars Wail in Scripture and Today—   By Mary A. Bruno, Ph.D.

202

and sounding the alarm, God said to sing, and sing, and sing, and sing. Then He added to *sing praises*, which totaled five commands to *sing* in two verses. God was emphasizing a point. He wants singing, shouting, clapping, and shofar blasts in His house of worship.

In Psalm 81 (a song), God *commanded* His people to worship Him. He did not need His ego stroked, but knew their faith would soar when they focused on Him.

3. Songs and Shouts

God likes loud worship. To hear the scriptural version of *loud*, unplug all of the microphones, musical instruments, and amplifiers, and let everyone shout, clap, play, and sing at their loudest. (No hearing loss occurred during the playing of what God called *loud* worship.) See: 2 Chronicles 30:21, Psalm 33:3, 98:4, and 150:4.

> Sing for joy to God our strength;
> Shout joyfully to the God of Jacob
> Raise a song, strike the timbrel,
> The sweet sounding lyre with the harp.
> Blow the trumpet at the new moon,
> At the full moon, on our feast day
> For it is a statute for Israel,
> An ordinance of the God of Jacob.
>
> —Ps. 81:1–4 NASB

Sing[87] for joy, *ranan,* means, "To overcome, cry out, shout for joy, and give a ringing cry." God wants His people to lay aside inhibitions and belt out lively praises in His direction. To cry out and shout for joy was not elevator music. Let us examine that pithy little passage.

---

87 "H7442 - ranan - Strong's Hebrew Lexicon (KJV)." Blue Letter Bible. Accessed 4 Jun, 2016.
https://www.blueletterbible.org//lang/Lexicon/Lexicon.cfm?Strongs=H7442&t=KJV

Why Shofars Wail in Scripture and Today—   By Mary A. Bruno, Ph.D.

203

Shout[88] joyfully, *ruwa*, means "shout, noise, alarm, cry, triumph, and to shout, raise a sound, cry out, give a blast, shout a war cry, or alarm of battle, shout in triumph, and shout in applause." God loves exuberant worship. It was His idea. More noise was coming. The timbrel (tambourine) and other percussion instruments had joyful sounds. God's order was to not just to shake them but *strike* them.

In verse three, *trumpet*,[89] meant *shofar.* The word *blow* also meant "to clap." The command (twice) was to blow the shofar, at the new moon (new beginning), at the full moon, and on our feast day. It was a statute and ordinance—strong legal terminology.

4. Songs and Trumpets

Oh, sing to the LORD a new song!
For He has done marvelous things.

—Ps. 98:1a

This psalm urges us to come up with a new song, and then, sing it to the Lord. Yes, it is scriptural to sing to God. The Ancient of Days abounds with life and does great things, including signs, wonders, and miracles while bestowing His Spirit, love, and gifts upon His people. God is pleased and listens closely when someone writes an original song of gratitude and then sings His praises in the sanctuary.

---

[88] "H7321 - ruwa` - Strong's Hebrew Lexicon (KJV)." Blue Letter Bible. Accessed 4 Jun, 2016.
https://www.blueletterbible.org//lang/Lexicon/Lexicon.cfm?Strongs=H7321&t=KJV
[89] "H7782 - showphar - Strong's Hebrew Lexicon (KJV)." Blue Letter Bible. Accessed 4 Jun, 2016.
https://www.blueletterbible.org//lang/Lexicon/Lexicon.cfm?Strongs=H7782&t=KJV

Why Shofars Wail in Scripture and Today—   By Mary A. Bruno, Ph.D.

204

With trumpets and the sound of a horn;
Shout joyfully before the LORD, the King.

—Ps. 98:6

God wants His people to sing and *shout* before Him while shofars and trumpets wail during worship services. Now that we know what He wants, how many of us will comply with His wishes? Maybe if we all obeyed, we might get to see *why* God said to sound shofars in *His* sanctuary.

The *horn*,[90] in this passage, was a *shofar*. Some translations said, "cornet," which as stated earlier, was a shofar. That kind of joyous singing and shouting, along with silver trumpet and shofar blasts, still resounds in some joyful houses of worship (and Eagles' Wings conferences).

Mary's Shofar Struggle

It was confession time! Mary wrote the part about the shofar from Psalm 81 on a Saturday night. The razor-sharp Sword of God's Spirit had cut her deeply and left her squirming in a pool of guilt while oozing Holy Spirit conviction. Knowing that God longed to hear wailing shofars in His sanctuary, she wrestled with the thought of taking theirs to church the next morning but put them in the car.

The worship team was practicing a song to exalt the Lord. It had an ideal place to sound their shofars. The pastor said God had blessed when they had blown the shofars previously, and invited them to do so again.

They blended their shofar blasts with the praise and worship. Rocco even gave his shofar a stirring *ta, ta, ta—ta, ta, ta—ta, ta, ta*. People told them afterward that the

---

[90] "H7782 - showphar - Strong's Hebrew Lexicon (KJV)." Blue Letter Bible. Accessed 4 Jun, 2016.
https://www.blueletterbible.org//lang/Lexicon/Lexicon.cfm?Strongs=H7782&t=KJV

Why Shofars Wail in Scripture and Today—   By Mary A. Bruno, Ph.D.

205

shofar's calls had touched their hearts. One man said he wept as something broke within him when they sounded. Even the children were excited and delighted to hear them.

5. God's Wants

> Praise the LORD!
> Praise God in His sanctuary;
> Praise Him in His mighty expanse.
> Praise Him for His mighty deeds;
> Praise Him according to His excellent greatness.
> —Ps.150:1–2 NASB

In case we missed God's point in His first 149 psalms, He saved the best for last and said it again in His grand finale for the whole Book of Psalms (Jewish hymnal). Since the shofar comes first on the list, God may want and expect shofars to open *His* praise and worship services.

> Praise Him with trumpet sound;
> Praise Him with harp and lyre.
> Praise Him with timbrel and dancing;
> Praise Him with stringed instruments and pipe.
> Praise Him with loud cymbals;
> Praise Him with resounding cymbals.
> —Ps.150:3–5 NASB

These *commands* expressed various ways to praise God, including the trumpet (shofar), harp, lyre, timbrel, and dancing. Have you heard any harps lately? Dancing is next to timbrel, and they are in a group! God accepts the tambourine and dancing as expressions of worship. He put it right there in verse four, next to stringed instruments and the pipe. He may find wind or breath instruments particularly pleasing because one's life-breath flows through them in praise. When God said to "Praise Him with

Why Shofars Wail in Scripture and Today—   By Mary A. Bruno, Ph.D.

206

trumpet (shofar) sound," He did not add, "unless, someone objects." Nor did He say, "If you feel like doing so."

God called for resonating cymbals, the noisy kind that kept on ringing, and ringing, and ringing. Attracted to fresh and lively praise, He may have smiled and then danced, and twirled with the other dancers as their tambourines and blaring shofars echoed through the sanctuary and up into the heavens. How many pastors, priests, rabbis, ministers, board members, or elders, will allow those kinds of expressions in *their* houses of worship?

Just suppose for a moment that one of God's bold, brave, and obedient spiritual leaders were to read,[91] believe, and obey God's orders and statutes (not suggestions) about the shofar. What might happen if that rabbi, pastor, priest, evangelist, etc., were to commit to, and follow, God's written commands regarding the shofar—in His house of worship—for one entire year? (To conduct services God's way—in God's house—for twelve noisy months!) Just think of how the results might affect houses of worship, cities, states, provinces, islands, and nations for God. It might even help God's people to rise up in His dynamis power and demolish demonic dominions that need to come down. Their radical obedience could usher in waves of praise and rejoicing that might wash away man's *different ideas* of how to orchestrate a service.

News of God's overflowing blessings and miracles could spread like wildfire. Shofar sounding houses of

---

[91] Do u think the world wil end by 2012? | Yahoo Answers, https://answers.yahoo.com/question/index?qid=20100216085324AAJkDrn (accessed April 12, 2016).

Why Shofars Wail in Scripture and Today—   By Mary A. Bruno, Ph.D.

207

worship could fill up quickly. Throngs of people might weep and praise God at the altars and not want to leave.

Noisy new believers could overflow with joyous outbursts of praise to God and might disrupt sermons. Church leaders might need to figure out whether to rent or buy a larger facility to hold God's swelling congregation.

My friend, are you a pastor, servant of God, or guardian of His flock? If so, what has the Lord been stirring in your spirit regarding His commands to sound the shofar in *His house* of worship? Have you dared (or will you dare) to welcome and release shofars to sound during your regularly scheduled worship celebrations?

> His lord said to him, 'Well *done*, **good and faithful servant**; you have been **faithful** over a few things, I will make you ruler over many things. Enter into the joy of your lord.'
> —Matthew 25:23

> Now the Lord is the Spirit, and where the Spirit of the Lord is, *there* is liberty.
> —2 Cor. 3:17 NASB

Isaiah and Jeremiah also mentioned the shofar.

* * *

It was, and still is, God's idea to blow the shofar in the house of the Lord.

Why Shofars Wail in Scripture and Today—   By Mary A. Bruno, Ph.D.

208

Chapter 26
Isaiah and Jeremiah

Isaiah the prophet urged the Israelites to swiftly heed and obey God's signs and the shofar's call.

> "When the shofar is blown, listen!"
>
> —Isa. 18:3b CJB

When anointed shofars wail—expect to hear from the LORD. Isaiah pleaded for the people to pay attention and obey the shofar's wordless messages that called them to come up higher and closer to God.

> It will come about also in that day that a great trumpet will be blown, and those who were perishing in the land of Assyria and who were scattered in the land of Egypt will come and worship the LORD in the holy mountain at Jerusalem.
>
> —Isa. 27:13 NASB

Father God saw His people in distant lands, far from the house of worship, far from His love and peace, where few cried out to Him. He called for His own, who had lost

Why Shofars Wail in Scripture and Today—   By Mary A. Bruno, Ph.D.

209

their way back to Him or were enslaved. He still calls to all who are ready to perish and to the unwanted. Some may sleep in alleys, under bridges, in prison cells, hospitals, five-star hotels, yachts, or mansions. God's loving arms yearn to embrace and restore His own unto Himself.

They had been captive for so long, but it was not too late! God's Spirit and His Word called through the great shofar to show them the way home. Shofars brought hope to weary hearts, as they seemed to cry, "This is the way, walk in it" (Isaiah 31:21a). God knew that when His lost sheep heard the shofar's call, they would return to the comfort of His loving arms, and He would receive them unto Himself.

Shofar Impact

Forty-one chapters later God called to set captives free and to "Lift up *your* voice *like* a trumpet" (*shofar*).

> Cry aloud, spare not. Lift up your voice like a trumpet and declare to My people their transgression and to the house of Jacob their sins!
> —Isa. 58:1 AMP

God wants our voices to have *shofar impact*. He wants us to proclaim His message with *dynamis* power that breaks yokes of bondage. God wants His fiery anointing to flow through us and melt cold hearts. He wants us to lift up dynamic cries that will pull down strongholds and dividing walls. He wants to release His floods of Living Water on barren souls, to set captives free, and to restore wavering souls to their heavenly callings.

Why Shofars Wail in Scripture and Today—   By Mary A. Bruno, Ph.D.

210

> [Rather] is not this the fast that I have chosen: to loose the bonds of wickedness, to undo the bands of the yoke, to let the oppressed go free, and that you break every [enslaving] yoke?
>
> —Isa. 58: 6 AMP

"Who, me?" a startled person might ask.

God's chosen fast sets captives free. When a person fasts, God will help him or her to break many different forms of bondage. The verb loose,[92] *pathach,* meant, "To open, to free, and let loose." God expects believers *(us)* to use our God-given power and authority to release those who need God's power to break free from the power of evil.

The word *bonds,*[93] *chartsubbah,* meant a bond or fetter, or pangs of grief. The Bible speaks of captives who wore fetters (shackles) of brass and iron that held their feet.

Grief is another form of captivity. Jesus came to heal the brokenhearted and to set captives free—free to walk in His liberty, love, and joy with a new calling and fruitful life.

Break Yokes

God wants His servants to break every enslaving yoke. A yoke was a wooden device that went around an animal's neck to control it. The yoke was a type of sin's cruel bondage and control. God wants His people (His exact word

---

[92] "H6605 - pathach - Strong's Hebrew Lexicon (KJV)." Blue Letter Bible. Accessed 4 Jun, 2016.
https://www.blueletterbible.org//lang/Lexicon/Lexicon.cfm?Strongs=H6605&t=KJV
[93] "H2784 - chartsubbah - Strong's Hebrew Lexicon (KJV)." Blue Letter Bible. Accessed 4 Jun, 2016.
https://www.blueletterbible.org//lang/Lexicon/Lexicon.cfm?Strongs=H2784&t=KJV

Why Shofars Wail in Scripture and Today—   By Mary A. Bruno, Ph.D.

211

is *you*) to *break* every enslaving yoke. Break meant to shatter or undo it and render it ineffective and inoperable.

Isaiah chapter 58 and the following passages have more about fasting and its rewards: Esther 14:6; Joel 1:14–15; Zechariah 8:19; First Corinthians 7:5; Daniel 9:3; Matthew 17:21 and Mark 9:29.

Shofar Alarm

In a time of national disaster, Jeremiah said to sound the shofar. It was time to blow the alarm for war. They were under attack. The *Trumpet* in these verses is a *shofar.*

> Declare ye in Judah, and publish in Jerusalem; and say, Blow ye the trumpet in the land: cry, gather together, and say, Assemble yourselves, and let us go into the defenced cities.
>
> —Jer. 4:5 KJV

Because of His mercy, God warned in Jeremiah 4:19–21 that an invasion was imminent. It was time for national repentance. People knew more about sin than the things of God. Merciful God sent an urgent shofar warning to get out of town and take cover. Judgment was coming.

Fed up with Jerusalem's wantonness, if she wanted to indulge in evil, God would not stop her. But, He would use another nation to teach her that she would have been better off to stick with Him. She still had time to return with her whole heart. God seemed to be calling, "Come on home, Honey. We were so happy. We can work this out. I still love you and miss you so much. I AM still here for you."[94]

---

[94] Colin's Corner, http://colinstuart.blogspot.com/ (accessed April 12, 2016).

Why Shofars Wail in Scripture and Today—   By Mary A. Bruno, Ph.D.

212

Thus says the LORD:

"Stand in the ways and see,
And ask for the old paths, where the good way *is*,
And walk in it;
Then you will find rest for your souls.
But they said, 'We will not walk *in it*.'"

—Jer. 6:16

Jerusalem stuck to her stubborn, self-indulgent ways, and disregarded God's urgent warning. He refreshed her memory of His servants who had urged her to obey the *shofar calls* that could keep her safe.

Also, I set watchmen over you, *saying,*
'Listen to the sound of the trumpet!'
But they said, 'We will not listen.'

—Jer. 6:17

The city had rejected her chance to repent. Disaster was coming. If she insisted, she could have her wish to hear no more of God's Word, and no more shofar cries. Instead of hearing godly lips magnify God's name and release soul-stirring shofar calls, she would hear enemy lips curse her people whose lips cried for mercy and found none.

Shofar Calls to Nations

Jeremiah's last shofar mention was during God's repayment time for Babylon. The shofar urged nations to separate unto the LORD and against Babylon. She would pay for her evil against Zion and would go down hard!

Lift up a signal in the land,
Blow a trumpet among the nations!

—Jer. 51:27a NAS

Why Shofars Wail in Scripture and Today—   By Mary A. Bruno, Ph.D.

It was time to appoint a leader who understood strategies and weapons of warfare. It was time for the *shofar* to call nations to gather unto God. God still calls today as He did in Isaiah's time.

> Then I heard the voice of the Lord, saying, "Whom shall I send, and who will go for Us?" Then I said, "Here am I. Send me!"
>
> —Isa. 6:8 NASB

In the time in which we live, God's[95] multi-generational army has risen up to sound shofars in places of worship and across their lands. They will continue to fast, pray, blow the shofar, proclaim God's Word, set people free and reaffirm His ownership of His creation.

If you have a shofar—this would be a good time to blow it! We shall explore what God said would happen when someone knew to blow the shofar but failed to do so.

* * *

---

[95] Isaiah 6:8 Then I heard the voice of the Lord saying ... http://biblehub.com/isaiah/6-8.htm (accessed April 12, 2016).

Why Shofars Wail in Scripture and Today—   By Mary A. Bruno, Ph.D.

214

Chapter 27
Warning!

Knowledge brought accountability when God took Ezekiel aside for a God-to-prophet chat in Ezekiel 33:1–6. God made sure His prophet knew why he should blow the shofar and sound warnings.

Ezekiel understood God's message. When a guard saw the sword (trouble) coming and blew his shofar to warn the people—*they* were accountable for how *they* responded. The shofar blower would have met his responsibility, and would not have been accountable for what would happen to anyone who ignored its call.

God told him in Ezekiel 33:7, "I have made you a watchman for the house of Israel." When Ezekiel heard God's message, he had to tell the people.

However, if a guard heard God's message and did not warn the wicked, the evil person would die in his or her sin. Still, God would require his blood from the one (including Ezekiel) who did not sound a warning. God stated the message in various ways, to make sure he understood.

Shofar Blasts—Judgment
Another shofar mention came when God told Hosea

Why Shofars Wail in Scripture and Today—   By Mary A. Bruno, Ph.D.

215

to blow the ram's horn at Gibeah because He was sending judgment upon sin. The ram's *Horn*[96] was a *shofar;* however, *trumpet,*[97] *chatsoterah,* was a straight trumpet.

"Blow the **ram's horn** in Gibeah,
The trumpet in Ramah!
Cry aloud *at* Beth Aven,
'*Look* behind you, O Benjamin!'"
—Hos. 5:8, emphasis added

In the following passage, God told Hosea to sound the trumpet (shofar). Judgment was coming because Israel had broken covenant with God and had rebelled against His law. The shofar that cried for mercy also warned of judgment. Israel's sin against God had weakened her defenses and made her vulnerable to an enemy attack.

"*Set* the trumpet to your mouth!
He shall come like an eagle against the house of the LORD,
Because they have transgressed My covenant
And rebelled against My law."
—Hos. 8:1

The prophet Joel called to blow a trumpet (shofar) in Zion to announce the day of the LORD is near.

---

[96] "H7782 - showphar - Strong's Hebrew Lexicon (KJV)." Blue Letter Bible. Accessed 4 Jun, 2016.
https://www.blueletterbible.org//lang/Lexicon/Lexicon.cfm?Strongs=H7782&t=KJV

[97] "H2689 - chatsotsĕrah - Strong's Hebrew Lexicon (KJV)." Blue Letter Bible. Accessed 4 Jun, 2016.
https://www.blueletterbible.org//lang/Lexicon/Lexicon.cfm?Strongs=H2689&t=KJV

Why Shofars Wail in Scripture and Today—   By Mary A. Bruno, Ph.D.

216

Blow the trumpet in Zion,
And sound an alarm in My holy mountain!
Let all the inhabitants of the land tremble;
For the day of the LORD is coming,
For it is at hand.

—Joel 2:1

Consecration

It was time to blow the trumpet (shofar) to consecrate a fast, to weep, and to pray. The shofar called for repentance, consecration, and mercy. God wanted to hear and answer prayer. Yet, for Him to do so, somebody had to pray. Attendance was mandatory for all ages.

Blow a **trumpet** in Zion,
Consecrate a fast, proclaim a solemn assembly,
Gather the people, sanctify the congregation,
Assemble the elders,
Gather the children and the nursing infants.
Let the bridegroom come out of his room
And the bride out of her *bridal* chamber.

—Joel 2:15–16 NASB, emphasis added

Moab's sins were piling up. God told Amos (a shepherd in Tekoa) that He was ready to deal with Moab's ever-increasing iniquity. Deadly fire was coming.

But I will send a fire upon Moab,
And it shall devour the palaces of Kerioth;
Moab shall die with tumult,
With shouting *and* trumpet sound.

—Amos 2:2

Why Shofars Wail in Scripture and Today—   By Mary A. Bruno, Ph.D.

If Moab kept overstepping her sin boundaries, she would die in an unrestrained fiery battle, amid terrifying battle cries and shofar[98] blasts.

> If a trumpet is blown in a city will not the people tremble?
>
> —Amos 3:6a NASB

Shofar wails that awakened human hearts caused an inner trembling that shattered barriers, crumbled hidden strongholds and opened a way for the Word of God, and for a move of God. No wonder the enemy strives to silence God ordained shofar cries in houses of worship!

Idol Worshipers, Priests, and Astrologers

The shofar sounded again when God's Word came to Zephaniah. Judgment was coming on idol worshipers, idolatrous priests, astrologers, devotees of false gods, on those who turned back from following God, and those who had never sought Him. Fenced cities and high towers could not save or protect them from God's wrath.

> Near is the great day of the LORD,
> Near and coming very quickly;
> Listen, the day of the LORD!
> In it the warrior cries out bitterly.
> A day of wrath is that day,
> A day of trouble and distress,
> A day of destruction and desolation,
> A day of darkness and gloom,

---

[98] "H7782 - showphar - Strong's Hebrew Lexicon (KJV)." Blue Letter Bible. Accessed 4 Jun, 2016.
https://www.blueletterbible.org//lang/lexicon/lexicon.cfm?Strongs=H7782&t=KJV

Why Shofars Wail in Scripture and Today—   By Mary A. Bruno, Ph.D.

218

A day of clouds and thick darkness,
A day of **trumpet** and battle cry
Against the fortified cities
And the high corner towers.
                    —Zeph. 1:14–16 NASB, emphasis added

That prophetic word did not bring a *gloriously* good time. Nevertheless, it may have saved someone's soul if they had repented and turned to God while there was still time. The trumpet,[99] in verse 16 is a *shofar*.

Zechariah 9:9–13, is loaded with restoration and drips with sweet blessings on every hand. The Lord Himself will blow the trumpet and protect His people.

Then the LORD will appear over them,
And His arrow will go forth like lightning;
And the Lord GOD will blow the **trumpet**,
And will march in the storm winds of the south.
The LORD of hosts will defend them.
                    —Zech. 9:14–15a NASB, emphasis added

God will enlighten us later about whether this is only a metaphor or if He will actually blow the shofar when He arises as Zion's Great Defender. Earth-shaking New Testament shofar blasts were already scheduled.

* * *

---

[99] "H7782 - showphar - Strong's Hebrew Lexicon (KJV)." Blue Letter Bible. Accessed 4 Jun, 2016.
https://www.blueletterbible.org//lang/Lexicon/Lexicon.cfm?Strongs=H7782&t=KJV

Why Shofars Wail in Scripture and Today—   By Mary A. Bruno, Ph.D.

**Rocco preached God's Word
with a new zeal in Caposele, Italy.**

Why Shofars Wail in Scripture and Today—   By Mary A. Bruno, Ph.D.

220

Chapter 28
Shofar Blasts Predicted – Part 1

Pastor Shawn Brix, in his article "The Final Sacrifice," cited shofars sounding as the Passover lambs were sacrificed when Jesus died on the cross.[100] He wrote:

The Bible tells us that Jesus drew his final breath at three o'clock in the afternoon (Luke 23:4446). That was an important time in Jerusalem, for it was the time of the afternoon sacrifice, and because it was Passover week, the Passover lambs were being sacrificed at the Temple.

It was customary also for the priest to blow a horn at the time of the sacrifice—a ram's horn, called a shofar. So at the same time when Jesus breathed his last, the shofar could be heard. At the sound of the horn, people would stop what they were doing and fall silent for a few moments. And In that time of silence Jesus died.
As the Passover lambs were being sacrificed in the Temple, the Lamb of God was being sacrificed on the

---

[100] Shawn Brix, "The Final Sacrifice," *Today* 61, no. 2, March/April 2011 (Palos Heights, Illinois: ReFrame Media, a division of Back to God Ministries International), http://today.reframemedia.com/archives/the-final-sacrifice-2011-04-22. Used by permission.

Why Shofars Wail in Scripture and Today—   By Mary A. Bruno, Ph.D.

221

cross. In God's plan, never again would an afternoon sacrifice be needed . . .

Salpigx / Shofar

In the New Testament, the Greek word *salpigx,* is a *shofar*, "Trumpet"[101] in Matthew 24:31. It also translated as *trumpet* (nine times), and twice as, *trump*, in eleven verses of the KJV. It appeared, at least, fourteen times in the CJB. Notice who or what will sound the shofar. (If anyone plans to blow a shofar, now would be the time.)

First New Testament (N.T.) Shofar Mention

This horn, *The Great Trumpet*—is a shofar.

> He will send out his angels **with a great *shofar*;** and they will gather together his chosen people from the four winds, from one end of heaven to the other.
>   —Matt. 24:31 CJB

Second N.T. Shofar Mention

The next mention happened when Paul used the shofar as an example while discussing prophecy, tongues, and interpretation of tongues.

> Indeed, if a shofar gives an unclear trumpet call, who will prepare himself for krav (battle)?
>   —1 Cor. 14:8 OJB

Paul included a shofar with other spiritual or prophetic expressions that drew believers closer to God.

---

[101] "G4536 - salpigx - Strong's Greek Lexicon (KJV)." Blue Letter Bible. Accessed 4 Jun, 2016.
https://www.blueletterbible.org//lang/Lexicon/Lexicon.cfm?Strongs=G4536&t=KJV

Why Shofars Wail in Scripture and Today—   By Mary A. Bruno, Ph.D.

222

Third N.T. Shofar Mention

This shofar has a blast that will raise the dead. The passage does not specify who will blow that shofar.

> It will take but a moment, the blink of an eye, at the final *shofar*. For the *shofar* will sound, and the dead will be raised to live forever, and we too will be changed.
> —1 Cor. 15:52 CJB

Fourth N.T. Shofar Mention

A fourth mention involved God's shofar. *Yes, God has a shofar! Since* He has one, He probably intends to blow it.

> For the Lord himself will come down from heaven with a rousing cry, with a call from one of the ruling angels, and with God's *shofar*; those who died united with the Messiah will be the first to rise; then we who are left still alive will be caught up with them in the clouds to meet the Lord in the air; and thus we will always be with the Lord.
> —1 Thess. 4:16–17 CJB

God's *rousing cry*[102] in verse 16 merits study. This word appeared once in the New Testament. God must have reserved it for that special verse.

The *rousing cry* of 1 Thessalonians 4:16 was from, keleusma, which can mean *an order, a command, and a stimulating cry.* It can also indicate a signal given to men or to soldiers by a commander, or as a loud summons, or trumpet call. The word meaning of the Lord's *shout (rousing*

---

[102] "G2752 - keleusma - Strong's Greek Lexicon (KJV)." Blue Letter Bible. Accessed 4 Jun, 2016.
https://www.blueletterbible.org//lang/Lexicon/Lexicon.cfm?Strongs=G2752&t=KJV

Why Shofars Wail in Scripture and Today—   By Mary A. Bruno, Ph.D.

223

cry) includes a trumpet call that will sound when the Lord calls believers to Himself.

Fifth N.T. Shofar Mention

This mention happened in Hebrews 12:14–17 after the writer had taught about walking in peace and turning from sin. He wrote of the terror that people felt when the shofar first sounded when God's Covenant came from Mount Sinai. He associated it with Jesus, the Messiah and Mediator of a new covenant of peace with God, made possible by *His* shed blood.

> For you have not come to a tangible mountain, to an ignited fire, to darkness, to murk, to a whirlwind, to the sound of a *shofar*, and to a voice whose words made the hearers beg that no further message be given to them.
> —Heb. 12:18–19 CJB

Mary's Warning

When Mary first began to realize that, it was time to take God seriously, something a Bible teacher had said offended her. The next morning, while washing dishes, listening to a Christian radio broadcast, and resenting the teacher, God got involved. Near-blinding rays of what she had thought were sun rays, streamed through the window as a minister's voice warned over the radio:

> See to it that you do not refuse Him who is speaking. For if those did not escape when they refused him who warned *them* on earth, much less *will* we *escape* who turn away from Him who *warns* from heaven.
> —Heb. 12:25 NASB

Why Shofars Wail in Scripture and Today—   By Mary A. Bruno, Ph.D.

224

Mary heard the Lord say, "Those were My words that she spoke to you."

Shaken by the awfulness of her mistake, she fell to her knees, soapsuds and all, and apologized to God.

That heavenly warning gave the grace to make the significant changes that were necessary for Jesus to become Lord of her life. She admits to having stumbled many times since then but says God's cleansing Word has wailed like an inner shofar that helped her to get back up and keep on trying—as she learned how to recover and walk in victory.

Voice like a Trumpet

Sixth N.T. Shofar Mention

John heard a sound like the voice of a shofar while he was on the Isle of Patmos. This verse does not say John heard a trumpet (shofar). It says he heard a *voice* like the sound of a trumpet (shofar). Jesus' words were as soul-searching *shofar cries* to John.

> I heard behind me a kol gadol (a loud voice), like the blast of a shofar.
>
> —Rev. 1:10b OJB

John heard the Lord Jesus Christ (Yeshua)—the Messiah—as heaven's scene unfolded with what the Alpha and Omega's shofar-sound-alike voice said to him.

> Then I turned to see the voice that was speaking with me. And having turned I saw seven golden lampstands; and in the middle of the lampstands *I saw* one like a son of man, clothed in a robe reaching to the feet, and girded across His chest with a golden sash. His head and His hair were white like white wool, like snow; and His eyes

Why Shofars Wail in Scripture and Today—   By Mary A. Bruno, Ph.D.

225

were like a flame of fire. His feet *were* like burnished bronze, when it has been made to glow in a furnace, and His voice *was* like the sound of many waters. In His right hand He held seven stars, and out of His mouth came a sharp two-edged sword; and His face was like the sun shining in its strength.

—Rev. 1:12–16 NASB

God showed these things to John and told him to write them in a book. His specially revealed truths were for His church—His called out ones.

God's voice may come as a stirring shofar cry that will ripple through one's spirit, humble the heart, and reveal rich insights. He still urges those who hear His voice to write books that will honor Him and strengthen believers.

When I saw Him, I fell at His feet like a dead man. And He placed His right hand on me, saying, "Do not be afraid; I am the first and the last, and the living One; and I was dead, and behold, I am alive forevermore, and I have the keys of death and of Hades. Therefore write the things which you have seen, and the things which are, and the things which will take place after these things.

—Rev. 1:17–19 NASB

Seventh N.T. Shofar Mention

This shofar brought a message from God with an opened door in heaven. John heard what sounded like a shofar speaking to him. The OJB has, "voice like a shofar." whereas the NASB used the word "trumpet."

After these things I looked, and behold, a door *standing* open in heaven, and the first voice which I had heard, like *the sound* of a trumpet speaking with me, said, "Come up here, and I will show you what must take

Why Shofars Wail in Scripture and Today—   By Mary A. Bruno, Ph.D.

226

place after these things." Immediately I was in the Spirit; and behold, a throne was standing in heaven, and One sitting on the throne. And He who was sitting *was* like a jasper stone and a sardius in appearance; and *there was* a rainbow around the throne, like an emerald in appearance.

—Rev. 4:1–3 NASB

The precious stones in the above passage are jasper, a dark opaque green (the color of living things). Jasper is comparable to an emerald; sardius is a fiery red stone; and an emerald is a clear green stone.

Come Up Higher

The heavenly shofar-sounding voice invited John to come up higher to see what would happen. Suddenly John was in the Spirit beholding God's throne.

A shofar's call may urge us to come up higher through heaven's open door, to see the splendor and majesty of our Heavenly Bridegroom. It may call a believer to the place where the heart overflows and all one can utter is: "Holy! Holy! Holy!—Holy is the LORD God Almighty!"

When the Lamb broke the seventh seal, there was silence in heaven for what seemed like half an hour. Then I saw the seven angels who stand before God, and they were given seven *shofars*.

—Rev. 8:1–2 CJB

A holy hush fell over heaven when the Lamb of God broke the seventh seal. The silence lasted for about thirty wide-eyed, heart-pounding minutes. Each of the seven angels before God's throne held a trumpet (shofar) and stood at attention. They were waiting for the perfect

Why Shofars Wail in Scripture and Today—   By Mary A. Bruno, Ph.D.

227

moment to launch their blasts—when the saints' prayers and incense would flame on God's[103] holy altar.

> Another angel came and stood at the altar, holding a golden censer; and much incense was given to him, so that he might add it to the prayers of all the saints on the golden altar which was before the throne. And the smoke of the incense, with the prayers of the saints, went up before God out of the angel's hand. Then the angel took the censer and filled it with the fire of the altar, and threw it to the earth; and there followed peals of thunder and sounds and flashes of lightning and an earthquake.
>
> —Rev. 8:3–5 NASB

Burning Prayers

Unlike when an angel took a coal from the altar and touched Isaiah's lips in Isaiah 6:5–8, When this angel takes fire from God's altar and throws it to earth, thunder, lightning, and an earthquake will follow. Angels watched as the Lamb of God came near. The tension was building. The stage was set for seven more shofar blasts—by angels.

A voice (with shofar impact) that sounded like a shofar would speak.

* * *

---

[103] U.S. Men's And Women's Soccer Teams Are Fighting, And .., http://www.thepostgame.com/daily-take/201604/americas-mens-and-womens-soccer-tea (accessed April 12, 2016).

Why Shofars Wail in Scripture and Today—   By Mary A. Bruno, Ph.D.

228

Chapter 29
Shofar Blasts Predicted – Part 2

T he sounds of seven inhaling angels ready to launch shofar blasts hinted that something big was coming. What follows will be like a science fiction thriller, except it will be real, with no pauses and no escape. The Bible tells of what the blasts will release on earth.

Eighth N.T. Shofar Mention—First Angel's Shofar

At the eighth New Testament shofar mention, the first of the seven angels will blow his shofar, which will release a burning with hail, fire, and blood, that will affect weather and vegetation. Failed crops may trigger famines. Food prices will soar. Lush forests will become charred clumps of stumps. National parks will scorch and burn. Green lawns will turn to gray.

> The first one sounded his *shofar*; and there came hail and fire mingled with blood, and it was thrown down upon the earth. A third of the earth was burned up, a third of the trees were burned up, and all green grass was burned up.
>
> —Rev. 8:7 CJB

Why Shofars Wail in Scripture and Today—   By Mary A. Bruno, Ph.D.

229

Ninth N.T. Shofar Mention—Second Angel's Shofar

A second angel's shofar blast will destroy a third of the sea creatures and ships. Seafood and shipping prices will soar. International trade will suffer.

> The second angel sounded his *shofar*, and what looked like an enormous blazing mountain was hurled into the sea. A third of the sea turned to blood, a third of the living creatures in the sea died, and a third of the ships were destroyed.
> —Rev. 8:8–9 CJB

Naval strength will weaken. Coastal countries may be at risk. Winds will fan the repulsive stench of rotting sea creatures that will have washed up on beaches.

Tenth N.T. Shofar Mention—Third Angel's Shofar

When a third angel's shofar sounds, a third of the water supplies will become deadly.

> The third angel sounded his *shofar*; and a great star, blazing like a torch, fell from the sky onto a third of the rivers and onto the springs of water. The name of the star was "Bitterness," and a third of the water became bitter, and many people died from the water that had been turned bitter.
> —Rev. 8:10–11 CJB

Water purification plants may not be able to keep up with the demand. Friends and loved ones will die. Crops will suffer. Scientists might call the blazing torch an asteroid. Another shofar blast was ready to wail.

Why Shofars Wail in Scripture and Today—   By Mary A. Bruno, Ph.D.

230

Eleventh N.T. Shofar Mention—Fourth Angel's Shofar

A fourth angel's shofar blast will dim earth's light. (Has anyone noticed that this sounds very similar to the plagues in the book of Exodus?)

> The fourth angel sounded his *shofar*; and a third of the sun was struck, also a third of the moon and a third of the stars; so that a third of them were darkened, the day had a third less light, and the night likewise.
> —Rev. 8:12 CJB

Global cooling will skyrocket utility bills. Crops will struggle from fewer hours of light. Food prices will rise even higher. Beachfront businesses will stagnate. Crime will increase from muggings, burglaries, robberies, and violence.

Overloaded power grids may fail and plunge cities into darkness. Mental health facilities will overrun with people in depression from living in reduced light and fear. Crops will fail. Meat and poultry prices will be unaffordable to many. More shofar blasts and woes coming.

> Then I looked, and I heard a lone eagle give a loud cry, as it flew in mid-heaven, "Woe! Woe! Woe to the people living on earth, because of the remaining blasts from the three angels who have yet to sound their *shofars*!"
> —Rev. 8:13 CJB

Twelfth N.T. Shofar Mention—Fifth Angel's Shofar

A fifth angel's shofar blast will release five months of smoke, pain, and misery on those without God's seal. (All who have received Christ have God's seal of protection.)

> In Him you also *trusted,* after you heard the word of truth, the gospel of your salvation; in whom also, having

Why Shofars Wail in Scripture and Today—   By Mary A. Bruno, Ph.D.

231

believed, you were sealed with the Holy Spirit of promise,

—Eph. 1:13

And do not grieve the Holy Spirit of God, by whom you were sealed for the day of redemption.

Eph.—4:30

Those without God's seal will endure great misery.

The fifth angel sounded his *shofar*; and I saw a star that had fallen out of heaven onto the earth, and he was given the key to the shaft leading down to the Abyss. He opened the shaft of the Abyss, and there went up smoke from the shaft like the smoke of a huge furnace; the sun was darkened, and the sky too, by the smoke from the shaft. Then out of the smoke onto the earth came locusts, and they were given power like the power scorpions have on earth. They were instructed not to harm the grass on the earth, any green plant or any tree, but only the people who did not have the seal of God on their foreheads. The locusts were not allowed to kill them, only to inflict pain on them for five months; and the pain they caused was like the pain of a scorpion sting. In those days people will seek death but will not find it; they will long to die, but death will elude them.

—Rev. 9:1–6 CJB

The fifth angel's shofar blast will free a star that will plunge to earth. When the angel opens the abyss, billowing smoke will darken the sky. Hospitals will overflow with those seeking medical attention for painful locust wounds, eye problems, and breathing issues. Crops will struggle.

There will be no death. Human misery will escalate from burns, accidents, disease, failed abortions, failed euthanasia, failed murders, failed suicides and executions.

Why Shofars Wail in Scripture and Today—   By Mary A. Bruno, Ph.D.

232

Thirteenth N.T. Shofar Mention—Sixth Angel's Shofar

The sixth angel's shofar blast will release a vast army of killers—a multimillion-man death squad.

> The sixth angel sounded his *shofar*, and I heard a voice from the four horns of the gold altar before God, saying to the sixth angel, the one with the *shofar*, "Release the four angels that are bound at the great river Euphrates!" And they were released. These four angels had been kept ready for this moment, for this day and month and year, to kill a third of mankind; and the number of cavalry soldiers was two hundred million! — I heard the number.
>
> —Rev. 9:13–16 CJB

Death will return when an army of *two hundred million* soldiers exterminates a third of earth's population. Their uniform colors will be—*red, purplish blue, and greenish yellow*. Do you know of an army with those colors?

> And thus I saw the horses in the vision: those who sat on them had breastplates of fiery red, hyacinth blue, and sulfur yellow; and the heads of the horses *were* like the heads of lions; and out of their mouths came fire, smoke, and brimstone. By these three *plagues,* a third of mankind was killed—by the fire and the smoke and the brimstone which came out of their mouths. For their power is in their mouth and in their tails; for their tails *are* like serpents, having heads; and with them they do harm.
>
> —Rev. 9:17–19

Some people never seem to learn. The next few verses are like a replay of hardheaded idolaters down through the ages who trusted in lifeless idols, played with demons, and stubbornly refused to repent before God.

Why Shofars Wail in Scripture and Today—　　　　By Mary A. Bruno, Ph.D.

233

But the rest of mankind, who were not killed by these plagues, did not repent of the works of their hands, that they should not worship demons, and idols of gold, silver, brass, stone, and wood, which can neither see nor hear nor walk. And they did not repent of their murders or their sorceries or their sexual immorality or their thefts.

—Rev. 9:20–21

Fourteenth N.T. Shofar Mention—Seventh Angel's Shofar

At the fourteenth New Testament shofar blast, a seventh angel's shofar blast will bring joy to believers, and anguish to those who have not received Jesus Christ—God's Messiah—and do not have God's seal.

The seventh angel sounded his *shofar*; and there were loud voices in heaven, saying,

"The kingdom of the world
has become the Kingdom
of our Lord and his Messiah,
and he will rule forever and ever!"
Then the Temple of God in heaven was opened, and the Ark of the Covenant was seen in his Temple; and there were flashes of lightning, voices, peals of thunder, an earthquake and violent hail.

—Rev. 11:15, 19 CJB

For those who have been wondering about the Ark of the Covenant's location, wonder no more. God has it!

Recap

Shofar blasts have called through the ages, urging God's servants to humble themselves, abandon idols, and obey His Word. Shofars cried in desert places to show the way of the Lord and to help believers to move with God. They sounded by the Ark of the Covenant, pointing the way

Why Shofars Wail in Scripture and Today—   By Mary A. Bruno, Ph.D.

234

to God's Presence, power, and provision. On the Day of Jubilee, they announced release and restoration.

Warriors answered shofar calls and followed godly leaders. Ehud's shofar echoed over Ephraim's hills and drew an army that defeated the enemy and cut off his inroads. Gideon's men's shofars encouraged his 300 chosen soldiers, yet those same shofar cries drove their enemies crazy enough to attack and kill each other in the darkness. Shofar wails at Jericho brought breakthrough and victory.

Nehemiah's loyal shofar blower called to rally where God fought for them, which bolstered workers to rebuild Jerusalem's walls—in 52 grueling days.

King Saul's shofar blasts sent so much fear through his army that they ran and hid. Other rebels blew their shofars to launch revolts (which triggered their demise).

David ordered shofars to welcome the Ark of the Covenant to Jerusalem. Shofars proclaimed that Solomon the anointed king had claimed his throne. Shofar blasts also broke up Absalom's counterfeit coronation and sent him and his guests running for cover.

The horse rejoiced to hear a shofar's call. Eager to run his race, he soared over obstacles and helped to win victory on the battlefront.

God delights in the sound of shofar wails in His sanctuary, with tambourines, loud-sounding cymbals, singing, shouting, clapping, and dancing.

Shofars sound warnings, call to set captives free, and to restore the outcasts to peace with God. They urge us to humble ourselves before God, to remember His blessings, to rejoice in His presence, and to sing praises to His name.

Why Shofars Wail in Scripture and Today—   By Mary A. Bruno, Ph.D.

Shofars proclaim new beginnings and call us to come up higher through heaven's open door and into God's glorious Presence. One day, a long-awaited shofar blast will split the sky with joy when Jesus comes for those who look for His return. Resurrected believers and those who are alive on earth will rise to meet Him in the air at the great catching away *"Rapture"* of the Church.

Now is the time to ask God to soften our loved one's hearts and help them to believe[104] and receive Jesus Christ—the Messiah—as Lord and Savior, and to receive God's seal. God expects us to lift up our voices (with shofar impact) and proclaim the acceptable day of the[105] Lord.

One may wonder what to say to someone who needs to receive peace with God. The following chapter will explain how to speak and pray with someone who wants to receive Jesus Christ, to become born again, and to receive God's seal.

May the Lord anoint you to lift up your voice like a great shofar to show the way of salvation—and make you a highly effective soul winner in His Kingdom.

"He who is wise wins souls"
(Pr. 11:30b NASB).

* * *

---

[104] Examining Ourselves Before the Passover - ucg.org, http://www.ucg.org/sermons/examining-ourselves-before-the-passover (accessed April 12, 2016).

[105] Evangelicals in the Episcopal Church | Refreshing .., https://barnabasproject.wordpress.com/ (accessed April 12, 2016).

Why Shofars Wail in Scripture and Today—   By Mary A. Bruno, Ph.D.

236

Chapter 30

How to Lift up Your Voice as a Shofar
(How to Lead a Soul to Peace with God)

One way to start discussions about peace with God is to ask people if they were to die today, where would they spend eternity.[106] Ask why they believe that to be true. Explain that sin has been in all of us since Adam and Eve. Sin cannot enter heaven; however, God figured out a way to get rid of the sin, so that we can be part of His family, with a future home in heaven. His Word says,

> For all have sinned and fall short of the glory of God.
> —Rom. 3:23

However, some very Good News was coming!

"But the cowardly, unbelieving, abominable, murderers, sexually immoral, sorcerers, idolaters, and **all liars** shall

---

[106] YOU WOULD NOT BELIEVE! - Rejoice Marriage Ministries, Inc, https://www.rejoiceministries.org/charlyne-cares-daily-devotional/2010/11/09/you (accessed April 12, 2016).

Why Shofars Wail in Scripture and Today—   By Mary A. Bruno, Ph.D.

237

have their part in the lake which burns with fire and brimstone, which is the second death."
—Rev. 21:8, emphasis added

Do not be deceived; neither fornicators, nor idolaters, nor adulterers, nor effeminate, nor homosexuals, nor thieves, nor *the* covetous, nor drunkards, nor revilers, nor swindlers, will inherit the kingdom of God. **Such were some of you; but you were washed, but you were sanctified, but you were justified** in the name of the Lord Jesus Christ and in the Spirit of our God.
—I Cor. 6:9b–11 NASB, emphasis added

God made a way to clean up those sinners, and us. "Washed, sanctified, and justified," sounds good for those who qualify for that list. How many lies does it take to make a liar? (One.)[107] How many sins does it take to make a sinner? Actually, we were all born with sin at work in us. That sounded like bad news—but there is some good news.

For the wages of sin *is* death, but the **gift** of God *is* eternal life in Christ Jesus our Lord.
—Rom. 6:23, emphasis added

It is true! You will be born again and experience eternal life the moment you believe and *receive* Jesus Christ. This will happen, not because of any good work that you have done, but because of what Jesus did for you (that you were unable to do for yourself).

---

[107] In Florida how many lies does it take to make a Conspiracy?, http://hubpages.com/politics/In-Florida-how-many-lies-does-it-take-to-make-a-Con (accessed April 12, 2016).

Why Shofars Wail in Scripture and Today—   By Mary A. Bruno, Ph.D.

238

"Unless one is born again, he cannot see the kingdom of God."

—John 3:3b

But as many as received Him, to them He gave the right to become children of God, to those who believe in His name.

—John 1:12

Many believe—but fail to receive. Even demons believe in God (James 2:19). We must *accept* (receive) Jesus Christ—the Messiah. Is it enough to believe and receive? God says it is, because Jesus paid a high price for that gift *(your gift)*. Soldiers *nailed* Him to a cross, pushed a (mock) crown of thorns on His head, and stabbed Jesus while He was paying the debt for every sin that we ever have, or ever will, commit. However, Jesus overthrew death's power and lives again.

His blood that seeped into the ground that day, as a great shofar, it still proclaims God's mercy and forgiveness for all believers. Each of us, including you, will choose to either receive or reject God's love gift of salvation. Our choices will determine where we spend eternity.

For God so loved the world that He gave His only be-gotten Son, that whoever believes in Him should not perish but have everlasting life. For God did not send His Son into the world to condemn the world, but that the world through Him might be saved.

—John 3:16–17

If you confess with your mouth the Lord Jesus and believe in your heart that God has raised Him from the dead, you will be saved.

—Rom. 10:9

Why Shofars Wail in Scripture and Today—   By Mary A. Bruno, Ph.D.

239

For by grace you have been saved through faith, and that not of yourselves; *it is* the gift of God, not of works, lest anyone should boast.

—Eph. 2:8–9

No Second Chance

Some wrongly think that if they miss God now, they will have another chance after death. It will be too late then.

And as it is appointed for men to die once, but after this the judgment.

—Heb. 9:27

Behold, now *is* the accepted time; behold, now *is* the day of salvation.

—2 Cor. 6:2b

Jesus is the only way. He is waiting for each of us to receive Him. When we do, He will live within us with lasting peace, joy, and love. He will also keep us from falling.

Nor is there salvation in any other, for there is no other name under heaven given among men by which we must be saved.

—Acts 4:12

Peace I leave with you, My peace I give to you; not as the world gives do I give to you. Let not your heart be troubled, neither let it be afraid.

—John 14:27

Why Shofars Wail in Scripture and Today—   By Mary A. Bruno, Ph.D.

240

Confess

If you sin again,[108] God will forgive you and bestow His grace to overcome that temptation. As an inner fountain, Jesus' blood will keep cleansing us as we walk with Him. (The key word here is to *walk with Him*—and not *wallow* in sin.)

> Let the wicked forsake his way, and the unrighteous man his thoughts: and let him return unto the LORD, and he will have mercy upon him; and to our God, for he will abundantly pardon.
>
> —Isa. 55:7 KJV

> But if we walk in the light as He is in the light, we have fellowship with one another, and the blood of Jesus Christ His Son cleanses us from all sin.
>
> —1 John 1:7

It is important to own up when you do something that offends God and quickly ask for His forgiveness. Something very powerful happens when you speak the name of your sin(s) aloud to God. For example: "Dear Lord; I lied; I stole; I was mean to someone; I took Your name in vain; I gossiped; I watched porn; I cheated, I committed a sexual sin; I prayed to an idol; I committed gluttony, I used . . . . Please forgive me and help me to never do that again."

God will forgive, cleanse, and restore, as though you had never sinned. He will also fill you with His power to live a holy life. If there were no temptations, there would be no overcomers. It is not a sin to be tempted. Sin happens when

---

[108] LET NOT YOUR HEART BE TROUBLED; NEITHER LET IT BE AFRAID .., http://chrisreimersblog.com/2010/04/29/let-not-your-heart-be-troubled-neither-le (accessed April 12, 2016).

Why Shofars Wail in Scripture and Today—   By Mary A. Bruno, Ph.D.

241

you resist[109] God, and yield to temptation instead of resisting temptation, and yielding to God.

If we confess our sins, He is faithful and just to forgive us our sins and to cleanse us from all unrighteousness.
—1 John 1:9, emphasis added

If you slip up and sin, God's Word tells you to admit (tell Him) what you did, and He will forgive and cleanse you.

After receiving the Lord, it is important to attend a church that teaches salvation through faith in Christ, and then request baptism in water. You will enjoy telling others about what Jesus has done in your life.

"Therefore whoever confesses Me before men, him I will also confess before My Father who is in heaven. But whoever denies Me before men, him I will also deny before My Father who is in heaven."
—Matt. 10:32–33

Phillip, the evangelist, helped an Ethiopian eunuch to understand a passage that he was reading from the book of Isaiah, which spoke of Jesus Christ. The man believed, received the Lord, and wanted to be baptized right away. The baptizer and baptizee both got wet when they both stepped down into the water.

And he ordered the chariot to stop; and they both went down into the water, Philip as well as the eunuch, and he baptized him.
—Acts 8:38 NASB

---

[109] WHAT TO DO ABOUT TEMPTATION - e-Catholic 2000, http://www.ecatholic2000.com/cts/untitled-704.shtml (accessed April 12, 2016).

Why Shofars Wail in Scripture and Today—   By Mary A. Bruno, Ph.D.

242

Helper

Jesus sent His Holy Spirit to help us. (He gives us the same Holy[110] Spirit Who helped Him to do His Father's will.) The Holy Spirit will help us to understand God's Word, and will give us holy courage, and spiritual gifts. John the Baptist, when speaking of Jesus, said,

> "He will baptize you with the Holy Spirit and fire."
> —Matt. 3:11b NASB

Forty days after Jesus[111] rose from the dead, and just before He ascended in a cloud to His Father in heaven, 500 people heard His command—not a suggestion.

> And gathering them together, He **commanded** them not to leave Jerusalem, but to wait for what the Father had promised, "which," *He said*, "You heard from Me; for John baptized with water, but you shall be baptized with the Holy Spirit not many days from now. . . . But you shall receive power when the Holy Spirit is come upon you; and you shall be My witnesses both in Jerusalem, and in all Judea, and in Samaria, and even to the remotest part of the earth."
> —Acts 1:4, 5, 8 NASB, emphasis added

Several verses later in Acts 2:1-4, about 120 of the 500 persons (around 20 percent) obeyed, waited in an upper room, and received the promised Holy Spirit. God's gift of His Holy Spirit is for all who believe. "All who are afar

---

[110] 13. The Ethiopian Eunuch (Acts 8:26-40) | Bible.org, https://bible.org/seriespage/13-ethiopian-eunuch-acts-826-40 (accessed April 12, 2016).

[111] FullArticle - Seeking God's Love, http://www.seekinggodslove.com/Articles/FullArticle/1 (accessed April 12, 2016).

Why Shofars Wail in Scripture and Today—   By Mary A. Bruno, Ph.D.

243

off" in the following passage includes believers everywhere, including those who are alive today.

> And Peter *said* to them, "Repent, and each of you be baptized in the name of Jesus Christ for the forgiveness of your sins; and you will receive the gift of the Holy Spirit. For the promise is for you and your children and for all who are far off, as many as the Lord our God will call to Himself."
>
> —Acts 2:38–39 NASB

You can know that if you were to die today, your sins would be forgiven and gone, and that your spirit would go to be with God in heaven. The main part is to believe *and* receive. There is no special prayer to say. As you make room in your heart (life) for God, He will be right there to hear and answer your prayer—even while you are still speaking, He will answer. (See Isaiah 65:24)

> [Jesus said,] "All that the Father gives Me will come to Me, and the one who comes to Me I will by no means cast out"
>
> —John 6:37

Jesus—the Messiah—was talking with some Jewish people in the temple one day, and telling them about being sent by the Father in Heaven. He told them very plainly; as a matter of fact, He said it *twice in one sentence that they would die in their sins* if they did not believe that He is the One sent by God.

> And He said to them, "You are from beneath; I am from above. You are of this world; I am not of this

Why Shofars Wail in Scripture and Today—   By Mary A. Bruno, Ph.D.

244

world. Therefore I said to you that you will die in your sins; for if you do not believe that I am *He,* you will die in your sins."

─John 8:23, 24

Right after sharing God's promises with someone would be a good time to ask, "Are you ready to[112] pray to receive the Lord Jesus Christ (Yeshua) as your Savior and Lord?" Then add, "To help you get started, just repeat this start-up prayer after me, and mean it with your whole heart." Then lead the person in the following sample prayer (or pray it for yourself). Wait for him or her to repeat each line as it is spoken.

This involves more than just saying and repeating a set of words to meet God's requirements for escaping Hell. It is a matter of trusting God's Holy Spirit to unveil His truth and love. He will be working with you to help a person to believe and receive Jesus Christ—the Messiah—and His amazing peace and joy that will exceed all that words can express or the heart can contain.

Prayer to Make Peace with God

Dear Lord Jesus,

I believe You *are* God's Son, the Messiah.

Thank You for bearing *my* sin on the cross.

I believe You died, rose again, and *live* today.

I receive You right now as *my* Savior and Lord.

Please forgive me, and make me clean.

---

[112] Jesus - ccmonte.com, http://www.ccmonte.com/believe/jesus/ (accessed April 12, 2016).

Why Shofars Wail in Scripture and Today—   By Mary A. Bruno, Ph.D.

245

Thank You, for *receiving me* into God's family.

Holy Spirt, I *receive* You now.

Please help *me* to live a life that pleases God.

(Invite the person to add what else he or she wants to say to God, and then conclude as follows.)

In *Jesus' name*, I pray. Amen.

Encourage the person to write in his or her Bible the date and time that he or she prayed to receive Christ. The individual will cherish that life-changing date forever.

It is important to tell others (family, friends, etc.) about the joys of one's new life in Christ, and help them to receive the Lord. Jesus loves them too and wants to welcome them into God's family.

> Go therefore and make disciples of all the nations, baptizing them in the name of the Father and of the Son and of the Holy Spirit, teaching them to observe all things that I have commanded you; and lo, I am with you always, *even* to the end of the age." Amen.
> —Matt. 28:19-20

> So Jesus said to them again, "Peace to you! As the Father has sent Me, I also send you." And when He had said this, He breathed on *them,* and said to them, "Receive the Holy Spirit.
> —John 20:21-22

The Christian Hope Network will be happy to pray with you, or a new believer/receiver, and will send information to help in one's new walk with God.

Why Shofars Wail in Scripture and Today—   By Mary A. Bruno, Ph.D.

246

Call the Hope Connection Prayer Line:
(718) 238–4600 (EST).
Visit the website at www.chn.cc,

Or write to the

Christian Hope Network
P.O. Box 280196
Brooklyn, New York 11228

The soul-winning tips in this chapter are available in a tract entitled, "Is My Heart Right with God?"(How to Have Peace With God), by Dr. Mary A. Bruno through her website at www.ministrylit.com.

If you have received the Lord Jesus as your Savior or have recommitted your life to Him, or if God has ministered to you in some other way, while reading this book, please write and tell Dr. Bruno. She will rejoice to know that you have become part of God's family, and that He is pouring out His blessing in your life.

Contact her by visiting the website:
www.ministrylit.com.
Email: drmaryabruno@ministrylit.com

Or write to:

Dr. Mary A. Bruno, Vice President
Interdenominational Ministries International
P.O. Box 2107
Vista, CA 92085-2107 USA

Why Shofars Wail in Scripture and Today—   By Mary A. Bruno, Ph.D.

247

She has asked the Lord to pour out His special blessings and to release His spiritual gifts and callings, with a fresh anointing of His Holy Spirit upon each person who reads this book, which includes you. Her desire is for you to enjoy a greater awareness of God's sweet presence, power, and joy in your life.

The next four chapters are about an adventure that the Brunos thought would be a routine road trip from California to New York—with a shofar in the trunk of their car. Then God came along and got involved, which meant that it was time to take Shofie (shofar) out of the trunk and let her proclaim God's blessings and victory throughout the land.

Rocco declared God's blessings for New Mexico.

Why Shofars Wail in Scripture and Today—   By Mary A. Bruno, Ph.D.

248

Chapter 31
Shofar Trip – Part 1: Northern Route

I n May 2012 Rocco was planning another ministry trip to Caposele, his hometown in Southern Italy. Struggling with writer's block, Mary was secretly hoping for some time alone to work on her shofar book.

"Do you have any sermons ready?" Rocco asked almost daily. "Will you be joining me on this trip?"

"No, Dear, God has given me nothing for Italy," was her usual reply.

However, John Welsh, retired Baptist minister, and a member of San Diego Christian Writers' Guild, mentioned in a critique group, "Us fellas kind of like to have our wives around when we preach."

God used his timely words to prod Mary into a life-changing, shofar-blowing adventure with, her hubby.

"Rocco, although God has given me nothing for Caposele, I will come along to back *you* in prayer."

His face brightened with a happy smile.

They made plans to drive to New York, visit Dr. Barbara A. Yovino, store the car, fly to Italy, and blow the

Why Shofars Wail in Scripture and Today—   By Mary A. Bruno, Ph.D.

249

shofar by the Liberty Bell on the way home.

First Shofar Blast

Day One, May 29—With the luggage and Shofie, their thirty-two-inch silver trimmed Yemenite shofar, tucked safely in the trunk of the car; they drove up the Interstate (I–15) toward Utah. At Mesquite, Nevada, near the Arizona and Utah borders, Mary sensed a sudden urge to blow the shofar. Rocco stopped and pulled Shofie out.

The desert air felt hot as a branding iron, as burning heat waves rose up from the near-melting asphalt. They seemed to be pushing the shofar blasts back into the horn as Mary's lungs struggled to force the sounds through. She proclaimed that land belonged to God, and then targeted a few more blasts toward a casino that was across the street.

Shofie stayed within easy reach as they drove through the rugged Virgin River Gorge. Mary blew the shofar again by the Arizona state line and asserted the land was God's turf. Shofie wailed again in Utah. They feasted on buffalo burgers and spent the night in Cedar City. Mary pondered Rocco's very considerate driving.

Divine Appointment—Colorado

Day Two—Like stubborn squatters, surges of blistering heat waves resisted them at Devil's Gorge, Utah. Shofie's blasts invaded their turf and echoed in the vast red canyon. Mary shouted, "Devil, one day, a great shofar blast is coming that will signal the Lord's return—and your doom!" Strangers stared, but so what! It felt good to invade the enemy's turf and smear God's Word in his face.

Rocco snapped pictures by Colorado's rustic brown sign as Mary blew the shofar in all directions. God was up to

Why Shofars Wail in Scripture and Today—   By Mary A. Bruno, Ph.D.

250

something. A van full of people pulled up. A woman rolled down a window, pointed to the blaring shofar, and asked,

"What is that thing you're blowing?"

"It is a shofar. The Bible speaks of them," Mary said.

"It does?"

"Yes, Jewish Traditionalists believe God blew one on Mount Sinai when He gave the Ten Commandments. The shofar sounded to announce the Day of Jubilee, to sound the alarm for war, and to anoint a new king. It still rings out on the Day of Atonement as a call to repentance, and on many other occasions. It seemed to work as a spiritual *'Now hear this!'* when God was ready to speak."

"How can you tell which is a shofar in the Bible?"

"Well, that is easy enough if you have a *Strong's Exhaustive Concordance of the Bible.*"

"Oh, OK." She seemed familiar with it.

"Just look up the words, *trumpet, trump, horn, and cornet* in the Strong's. A number for the Hebrew, Aramaic, or Greek word will be by each reference."

"Uh huh, go on."

"Go to the back of the book, and[113] look up the definition for that word number to find which horn was used."

The woman seemed to be taking notes. Her excitement reminded Mary of her first shofar purchase.

---

[113] Making Peach Upside Down Cake for Dinner Guests, http://reluctantentertainer.com/making-peach-upside-down-cake-for-dinner-guests/ (accessed April 12, 2016).

Why Shofars Wail in Scripture and Today—   By Mary A. Bruno, Ph.D.

251

Supernatural Changes at Iowa

Days Three–Six—Emerald landscapes replaced desert scenes by Vail, Colorado. Deer glided through a green meadow. Shofie confirmed God's ownership there, and again at Nebraska's welcoming border.

Something was unusually sweet about the peaceful way Rocco and Mary were interacting. He took I–80 East toward Des Moines, Iowa, while she navigated. A CD with the book of Joshua was their spiritual feast of the day, along with an Italian language course that Mary hoped to master. Rocco was a fantastic help with pronunciation.

At Iowa, with no place to stop, Mary pushed Shofie halfway out of the window and launched several blasts that brought startled looks from drivers in the next lane. Things changed at Council Bluffs, Rocco grabbed Shofie and took her for a whirl in a green grassy field where he released a hearty string of shofar blasts (for the first time on this trip).

Together, God's daring servants boldly declared His blessing over Council Bluffs, took pictures, and affirmed His ownership of that land, as they had done in other cities, states, and points of interest, and then continued their journey. They would find out later that those random photos in that beautiful green field had captured a life-changing and ministry-changing moment.

They soon realized that God must have done something very special when Rocco stepped up and blew the shofar at Council Bluffs. A new sense of supernatural unity filled them. Whatever God had done through Rocco's shofar blasts had brought sweet peace.

Shofie announced God's blessings by Illinois' rain splattered welcome sign and again in Indiana and Michigan.

Why Shofars Wail in Scripture and Today—   By Mary A. Bruno, Ph.D.

252

Day Seven—They had planned to go through Buffalo, New York, to Niagara Falls, but a banking stop in Michigan made it easier to go by way of Canada. They smiled when Shofie's blasts drew a guard's curious glance at the international border. A few hours later, US flags led them back into the USA and toward a lovely hotel by the Falls.

Strawberry- and plum-colored spotlights lit the massive falls and reflected into towering columns of rising mist that looked like glowing puffs of cotton candy against the night sky. God must have been grinning in the background because He was definitely planning something.

Divine Appointment—Niagara Falls

Day Eight—A young couple clad in jeans and warm jackets strolled through the park in the crisp morning air. The man carried an odd-looking twisted bamboo horn.

"It's a portable didgeridoo from Israel," he explained. "I brought it along to blow at the falls."

"Could you show us how it sounds?" Mary asked.

"Sure!" He smiled and gave a stunning recital of its different sounds that were reminiscent of when somebody blew one in a Crocodile Dundee film.

"So, what's that thing you've got in your hand?" he asked Rocco and pointed to Shofie. She did not seem to mind his curious[114] stare, or that he called her a *thing*. She was ready to release her own *loftier* sounds.

---

[114] A Plate of Cookies Chapter 1: Silence is Golden, an ...,
https://www.fanfiction.net/s/5681123/1/A-Plate-of-Cookies (accessed April 12, 2016).

Why Shofars Wail in Scripture and Today—   By Mary A. Bruno, Ph.D.

253

"It's a shofar. They sounded in Bible times and still do today. My wife can tell you more," Rocco said as he passed the horn over to Mary.

"Do you know how to blow it?" the man asked.

"Yes, we both do. The Bible mentions shofars. Jewish tradition claimed God blew one when He gave the Ten Commandments," Mary explained.

"The Israelites were at Mount Sinai's base, which was like a giant amphitheater. Imagine what it must have been like[115] to wake before dawn to lightning flashes, rolling thunder, and wailing shofar blasts reverberating through their trembling tents."

"I want to know more; please go on!"

Sunlight flashed on Shofie's silver trimmings as Mary tilted the horn toward heaven. Shofie's finest Tekiah, Shevarim, Teruah, and a hearty Tekiah-Gedolah turned the discussion to shofars on the Day of Atonement, at Jericho, with Gideon, and then to Jesus Christ and God's salvation.

"We've never heard anyone talk about these things or say them in the way that you did!"

"This was a divine appointment for you. God wanted to touch your lives in a special way today and show that He loves you. Remember, 'whosoever will' includes you too."

"You were actually preaching to them!" Rocco said, knowing that Jesus was with them on that garden path. (God seems to like garden paths.) His Holy Spirit had brought those points to life for that particular couple who

---

[115] Personality Quiz: Which Beatle Are You? | Anglophenia .., http://www.bbcamerica.com/anglophenia/2014/01/personality-quiz-beatle/ (accessed April 12, 2016).

Why Shofars Wail in Scripture and Today—   By Mary A. Bruno, Ph.D.

254

were certainly hungry for more of God. Rocco and Mary savored God's Presence, knowing He had used their change of plans to lead them to that particular place at that given time for a God-ordained appointment with that particular couple. He was probably busy lining up other yielded servants for the next phases of His plan for their lives. (God has a very special plan for your life as well.)

More Blasts

Days Nine–Ten—Shofie wailed God's blessings in Maine, New Hampshire, and Connecticut. The Brunos sipped iced tea at the Boston Harbor, site of the famous Boston Tea Party, which was a tax revolt. Having fun and feeling playful, Rocco took pictures as Mary poured a glass of tea into the harbor, tilted Shofie high, released a few blasts, and boldly proclaimed, "May we all live tax-free!"

Dr. Barbara Yovino welcomed them to her lovely (three-story) Brooklyn home across from the Atlantic Ocean and treated them like royalty. They enjoyed visiting face-to-face without having to bother with e-mails. However, Mary had tweaked her back, which made walking or climbing stairs a bit of a challenge.

Their flight to Italy was a day or so away.

* * *

Why Shofars Wail in Scripture and Today—   By Mary A. Bruno, Ph.D.

255

Rocco took Shofie for a whirl in a meadow when he first blew the shofar during their trip.

As pictured above, they were unaware of God's amazing changes in their marriage and ministry that began that moment in Council Bluffs, Iowa.

"Oh, **magnify the LORD with me**,
And let us exalt His name together" (Psalm 34:3).

Why Shofars Wail in Scripture and Today—   By Mary A. Bruno, Ph.D.

256

Chapter 32
Shofar Trip – Part 2: Italy

S aturday, June 9, 2012. Pasquale Ceres, Rocco's gracious nephew, whisked Rocco and Mary from the airport to his home in Rome. Loving relatives greeted them with kisses on both cheeks and a tasty Italian feast. He chauffeured them the next day on a four-hour drive down to Caposele, population 3,500 (during tourist season). It was about 70 miles past Naples.

A flight of green marble stairs led to their cozy abode in the historic part of town. Stairs were difficult for Mary's aching back, but she clung to the railing and toughed it out.

Their house adjoined Concetta's (Rocco's sister). The balconies overlooked busy cobblestone streets and downtown events. The village clock's bell (half a block on the left) and church bell (half a block to the right) announced the time, church services, deaths, etcetera.

Michela
Tuesday, June 12—Pastor Geremia Albano, Senior Pastor of Chiesa Evangelica di Caposele (which his father Pasquale Albano had founded around 1945) took Rocco and Mary to pray for Michela, his beloved wife. She was still

Why Shofars Wail in Scripture and Today—   By Mary A. Bruno, Ph.D.

257

hospitalized from a recent surgery. Others were there to pray and encourage her. God blessed, and everyone enjoyed sweet fellowship.

Mary shared uplifting words as fast as God put them in her heart. She said God was going to raise Michela up and that she would have a significant new dynamic of the Holy Spirit that would surprise people and cause them to wonder what had happened to her. Mary had no hint of the testing that would follow those words in the weeks ahead.

Although Michela was very frail, she smiled bravely and gave Mary's hand a faint squeeze. She promised to cook dinner for the Brunos when she got well. Mary could tell that Michela was one of God's extra special people and hoped they would enjoy a lasting friendship.

While climbing the stairs to home that evening, Mary walked in the middle of the broad steps instead of clinging to the railing. "Look, Rocco! I can climb the stairs without holding the rail, and my back does not hurt!"

"It happened to you, as it did with Job," Rocco said. "God healed him when he prayed for his friends. Sometimes, God works in mysterious ways. When we ask Him to heal someone else, He heals us. And that is a mystery of God."

Drifting off to sleep that night, Mary pondered Rocco's new wave of sweet eloquence and charm.

Thursday, June 14—They strolled by the cozy white house where Rocco was born, and then hiked up the side of a nearby mountain that was practically in their back yard. After blowing the shofar over Caposele, and reading from the Scriptures, they pulled down strongholds and prayed for revival. Shofie sounded again near a path where water surged from the side of a granite mountain.

Why Shofars Wail in Scripture and Today—   By Mary A. Bruno, Ph.D.

258

Concetta had a huge feast waiting after their three-hour walk, prayer, and shofar outing.

Rocco preached mightily on prayer that night. Mary assumed his new dynamic was because he spoke in Italian.

At the close of his message, Concetta applauded, and shouted, *"Bravo! Bravo, Mio Fratello!* (My brother)"

They were shocked to see such zeal pouring from his conservative sister. She had heard Rocco preach before, but had never reacted like that. Rocco was definitely different.

Good Preaching

Sunday, June 17—Rocco ministered again at the Chiesa Evangelica di Caposele. His sermon was about how Father God had lovingly unveiled Eve's exquisite beauty to Adam when He presented her as his bride and made them one. That message was drenched in God's love!

People told Rocco his sermon was among the best they had heard. Something new and wonderful had happened to, and through, him. His eyes were bright and full of zeal as he paced about and powerfully proclaimed God's Word with holy fervor. God must have smiled as Rocco boldly preached in the church he had mocked in his youth. Rocco stayed right on point—when loud church bells rang nonstop for seven intense minutes during his sermon. Mary wondered how he managed to stay so focused.

She Understood the Words

June 18–20—People came to the house to visit, and some, including family members, received the Lord in the Brunos' kitchen. As was the case with Rocco's cousin, Antonietta Merola (married to Carmine Merola), God led Mary to share a brief salvation message, which Rocco

Why Shofars Wail in Scripture and Today—   By Mary A. Bruno, Ph.D.

259

interpreted phrase-by-phrase. When they got to the part when it was time for Antonietta to *receive* Christ as her Savior, she began to tremble and staggered to a chair. She had sensed that God was in that kitchen with them, and was stunned because she suddenly understood what Mary was saying in English—before Rocco interpreted it to Italian.

"It is the most wonderful thing that has ever happened to me!" she told everyone later.

Holy Spirit Outpouring — in the Kitchen
A young man came to visit late one Saturday night and said he wanted God to baptize him with the Holy Spirit. Jesus granted his heart's desire, and he left rejoicing.

Shofar Blasts in Church
Thursday, June 21—Pastor Geremia invited Mary to address his congregation (with an interpreter). She spoke about some of the shofar occurrences in Scripture and then launched a few shofar blasts during appropriate places.

Rocco spoke next and delivered another powerful sermon that hit home with the people. God had come through with Holy Spirit unction. A greatly blessed woman jumped up and proclaimed she wanted to be a preacher. She went on and on about how God's Word had touched and stirred her heart as Rocco spoke.

Ministering in the same service with Rocco in Italy was wonderful for Mary. However, she could not figure out what had caused her very reserved husband to come alive with that remarkable new dynamic.

Sunday, June 23—Concetta said someone else from the church had gone throughout Caposele telling others about Rocco's soul-stirring preaching. Yes, something was

Why Shofars Wail in Scripture and Today—   By Mary A. Bruno, Ph.D.

260

very different on this trip to Italy. However, what could have contributed to his magnificent change?

God had shown them through His Word that shofar blasts called for separation and sanctification. They also stirred up the spirit of idolatry, so that leaders could identify and purge it from the camp. A message on tithing and idolatry erupted in Mary's heart like a fire-spouting volcano. Rocco offered to translate.

They held hands during daily strolls through town. Rocco had a new smile and twinkle in his eye as ongoing compliments dripped from his lips like honey. Mary eyed him cautiously, unsure of what was going on with the mellow fellow who had been her husband for decades. He was so different. It was as though God had grabbed him by the collar, unzipped his chest, yanked out the old Rocco, tossed him aside, dropped in a whole new person, and then zipped him back up again. Not that she was complaining; the *New Guy* would do fine.

They hiked up to a favorite scenic point that overlooked Caposele. While taking turns blowing the shofar, they asserted God's authority over spirits of idolatry and fear of man, and prayed again for a mighty wave of revival.

Prayer for Michela

Sunday, June 24—Rocco preached another heart-warming message. Mary encouraged him on a job well done. After church, they stopped at Pastor Geremia's home and prayed for Michela. She had come home from the hospital on Friday but had to return that afternoon because her condition had worsened. Twelve days had passed since they had met at the hospital when Mary had shared encouraging words that she believed were from God. The Brunos' still

Why Shofars Wail in Scripture and Today—   By Mary A. Bruno, Ph.D.

261

did not know the cause of Michela's health issue. Mary had assumed that it was too personal to mention.

Missing Walls

June 26–July—Rocco was sweeter than ever. Invisible divisive walls that had bristled between them during decades of marriage had vanished. They enjoyed a delightful sense of unity as they worked on a bilingual message for Sunday. It was time to pull down the strongholds of idolatry and fear of man from Caposele so that God's work could flourish. God led Mary to fast until Sunday. (Dear Concetta was new to fasting and kept offering little portions of food.)

God's holy fire from on high graced Rocco's preaching on Thursday evening. Mary stared and wondered where this dynamic evangelist had been hiding.

God's peace and guidance prevailed as they slashed Sunday's bilingual message to thirty-five minutes. Rocco did an excellent job of interpreting. People received the message well as shofar blasts reverberated off walls and through their yielded hearts.

After the service, a woman in leadership said God had led her to do a study on tithing and idolatry. She asked for and received their complete set of the bilingual notes.

God revealed more insights regarding shofar blasts, and how they crumbled walls and strongholds. The Brunos must have been slow learners. They had no hint that stepping up together to blow the shofar so often to honor God and reaffirm His turf in three countries could have had anything to do with Rocco's new touch from God, or with the crumbling walls between them. Mary wondered if

Why Shofars Wail in Scripture and Today—   By Mary A. Bruno, Ph.D.

262

blowing the shofar might also help to shatter the barriers to writing about Jericho's walls for her book.

Something fresh and new had permeated their relationship since they first embarked on their shofar-blowing mission. They were relaxed and at peace with one another and walked in unexpected unity and joy. Rocco went around with blissful eyes and a warm smile. One afternoon he took Mary's hand, and then danced and twirled them both around in their kitchen. He swung her in a backward dip, raised one arm high and proclaimed, "I have fallen in love with *my wife!*" Whoa!

Good-Bye to Italy

July 4–9—Dino Ceres, Rocco's other nephew from Rome (a lay minister for the Catholic Church) drove them back to Rome in time for a night of rest before their return flight to New York.

* * *

Why Shofars Wail in Scripture and Today—   By Mary A. Bruno, Ph.D.

263

Pastor Geremia Albano, and his lovely wife, Michela.

**With a boyish grin and twinkle in his eyes,
Pastor Geremia shared his testimony and secret.**

Why Shofars Wail in Scripture and Today—   By Mary A. Bruno, Ph.D.

264

Chapter 33
Shofar Trip – Part 3: Southern Route

The Brunos had hoped to attend the Eagles' Wings' 2012 East Coast Conference, with Dr. Yovino before driving back to California. However, the timing was off, so they headed for the Liberty Bell instead.

July 10, 2012—The GPS guided them to Philadelphia, Pennsylvania and a nice parking place near the Liberty Bell.

Liberty Bell

She hung there in gorgeous metallic splendor, suspended from a sturdy yoke of rugged American elm. Her deep-grained wood was very rough and dark, almost black. Light from a glass wall behind her gave an almost halo effect to that national treasure. Her smooth dome-like top gently curved out, and then nipped in for a hint of a waistline, then flared out to her sturdy, albeit cracked, rim that boasted twelve feet in circumference. She weighed over 2,000 pounds but wore them well. Her inscription boldly quoted Leviticus 25:10 from the Holy Bible. The raised letters, just below the rim of her crown declared, "Proclaim Liberty throughout all the Land unto all the inhabitants thereof. . . ."

Why Shofars Wail in Scripture and Today—   By Mary A. Bruno, Ph.D.

265

Shofar Wails at the Liberty Bell

Rocco asked permission to blow the shofar by the bell and take pictures. The guard wanted to know what tie the shofar had with the Liberty Bell. They explained that the shofar had captured people's attention when God was ready to issue a proclamation, such as the Ten Commandments. It also sounded on the Day of Jubilee, when He initiated freedom for captives, and restoration of houses, lands, and family. The guard seemed pleased that God's Word came with shofar blasts on the Day of Jubilee.

Mary stood in front of the huge bell, gazed at its cracked rim, and raised Shofie high. The Liberty Bell's size did not intimidate Shofie. She was up for the challenge and ready to make her own history. Her silver trim flashed as the visitor-filled room resonated with several of her glorious wails, along with a hefty Tekiah Gedolah that sent a hearty wordless *Amen* to God's engraved proclamation.

"*Hallelujah*!" boomed a man's deep southern voice in the midst of spontaneous applause, whistles, and cheers that erupted with the shofar blasts. Once again, something very special had happened when anointed shofar blasts had gladdened hearing hearts.

As they left, Rocco heard the guard telling another group of tourists, "The shofar sounded on the Day of Jubilee when God gave this proclamation from the Bible. As you can read on this inscription, it says right here on our Liberty Bell, 'Proclaim Liberty throughout all the Land . . .'"

Tripped

While walking toward their car, Mary's foot caught on what felt like a banana-sized root. *Kerplop*! She did a dusty belly flop and landed face down at the base of a tree,

Why Shofars Wail in Scripture and Today—   By Mary A. Bruno, Ph.D.

266

with both hands keeping her upper body out of the dirt. Suddenly, an invisible force pressed her head and torso downward and then ground her face into the dirt. Rocco quickly helped her back on her feet.

Embarrassed by the public display, she brushed the dirt from her dark-blue clothes.

"That scrape on your nose is bleeding quite a bit. You might want to go to the restroom and clean it up," a man said, offering several moist baby wipes. The three-quarter-inch scrape on the bridge of her nose—would not ordinarily have made contact with a flat surface.

They had started to leave but walked back to snap a picture of the root to document that part of the journey. A brick walkway framed the four-foot square area of earth at the base of the tree. There was *no root*—nothing but smooth, flat, neatly raked dirt.

What unseen force could have tripped her, shoved her forward, and then ground her face into the dirt? Had they hit a spiritual nerve while citing God's Word, blowing the shofar by the Liberty Bell, and influencing the guard to explain God's Jubilee blessings? Might that trip, fall, and dirt grinding have been a form of spiritual retaliation?

Danger on the Freeway
Back on the road again, they had barely settled into an open lane, when out of nowhere, a speeding black car cut them off and barely missed hitting the left front fender. Their hearts were still pounding when another car, which seemed to be going over 100 miles per hour nearly sideswiped them on the right side. They cried out for God to protect them and to surround their car with angels. Mary sent a quick prayer request (via cell phone) for Barbara and

Why Shofars Wail in Scripture and Today—   By Mary A. Bruno, Ph.D.

267

CHN's intercessors to pray for their immediate protection. They had expected nothing like that when they came to blow the shofar and reaffirm God's turf at the Liberty Bell.

Rocco boldly declared, "We stepped on what the Devil thought was his territory. He was not happy about that and tried to harm us, but God saved us. Greater is He that is in us than he that is in the world! God is our Defender and has surely rescued us on this day!"

Divine Appointment—Alabama

July 12–13—Shofar blasts rang again in front of the White House in Washington, D.C., where they prayed and asserted God's ownership of the United States of America. Shofie wailed in Maryland as they headed toward Tennessee. The fertile countryside was a feast for their eyes. Shofie's blasts sounded during an unexpected route change that added an extra 60 miles to their day's journey but rewarded them with a clean hotel at Livingston, Alabama.

They enjoyed chatting with a young man who was working at a nearby Mexican restaurant. He was from Escondido, California, about 10 miles from the Brunos' home. Soon after moving there to be with his brother, the brother's job had transferred him to Hawaii. He wondered why he was stuck there, alone and far from home.

A suggestion that God might have had a different reason for bringing him there captured his attention. He said he was ready to ask God to reveal His purpose for the move, and to grant wise decisions regarding his situation.

"I had never thought of doing anything like[116] that!" he exclaimed, with hope and joy in his eyes.

---

[116] Herbed Compound Butter - Hilah Cooking, http://hilahcooking.com/herbed-compound-butter/ (accessed April 12, 2016).

Why Shofars Wail in Scripture and Today—   By Mary A. Bruno, Ph.D.

268

His bright smile assured that he would be fine. The encounter felt like another divine appointment, which took them 60 miles further than they had planned.

Saturday, July 14— Shofie wailed in Mississippi, near clusters of magnolia trees with huge white blossoms. A light mist christened her blasts in New Orleans, Louisiana. White horse-drawn Cinderella carriages clattered happy tourists thru crowded streets amid jugglers, stilt walkers, and percussion bands that drew curious crowds to their lively Cajun beats. New Orleans was exciting; however, thoughts of home tugged at their hearts.

* * *

They had cut their sermon to almost bare verses, but God helped them.

Why Shofars Wail in Scripture and Today—   By Mary A. Bruno, Ph.D.

269

Mary had a blast by the Liberty Bell.

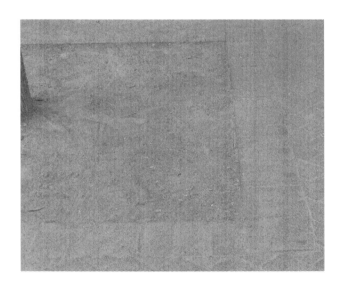

There was no banana size root, nothing but smooth, flat, neatly raked dirt!

Why Shofars Wail in Scripture and Today—   By Mary A. Bruno, Ph.D.

270

Chapter 34
Shofar Trip – Part 4:
Home, Italy, and Miracles

July 16–19, 2012. The Brunos drove through Oklahoma, and the Choctaw Nation then took the I–40 West; sounding shofar blasts along the way through Texas and New Mexico. Traveling with Rocco was like riding with a charming stranger. His uplifting talk and considerate driving set Mary's heart at ease. What could have made this refreshing change in them? They wanted more. One thing that they had not done on previous trips was to blow the shofar and pray at cities, state lines, and points of interest. This time, they had *both* sounded it for God's glory and proclaimed His ownership and blessings.

Fountains of Blessings

They wondered if when they had put Shofie to their lips, if her blasts had become as fountains of blessings for the land, and for *them.* Shofie wailed again in Arizona and California as they neared San Diego County and home.

Their personal refreshing was not merely due to taking a trip, or to being in beautiful places. They had done that many times. During a recent two-day road trip, shortly

Why Shofars Wail in Scripture and Today—   By Mary A. Bruno, Ph.D.

before their shofar-blowing adventure, they had returned so stressed that they barely spoke; and Mary had growled through clenched teeth, *"N-e-v-e-r again!"* (This explained her hesitation to sign up for another trip.)

Yet, this seven-week journey was very different. God had used it to shatter destructive patterns and replaced them with His loving words of kindness and peace. Changes began when they blew the shofar *together* and prayed as *a team* at state lines, etc. Their breath through the shofar had marked those places for God. However, while doing so, God had also marked *them* for His peace, unity, and blessings. He had crumbled their walls of contention and replaced them with His protective walls of peace and joy. The changes continued in Caposele as they blew the shofar on a mountain, during strolls, in church, and from their balcony.

Well, Mary may have gone a little wild one day while blowing Shofie's brains out from their balcony. It took place during a high-noon face off with Caposele's clanging town clock—but that only happened once.

God was tearing down and building up within them. They were thankful for changes that were more than they could have ever asked or thought. Jesus, the Prince of Peace, had come along (He was invited) and used a shofar-blowing ministry journey to change them! That was so like Him!

A passage about God being able to do abundantly above all that we could ask or think kept replaying in Mary's spirit. It became her daily prayer for others, along with a request for God to manifest His Glorious Presence.

> Now to Him who is able to do far more abundantly beyond all that we ask or think, according to the **power** that works within us, to Him *be* the glory in the church

Why Shofars Wail in Scripture and Today—   By Mary A. Bruno, Ph.D.

272

and in Christ Jesus to all generations forever and ever. Amen

—Eph. 3:20–21 NASB, emphasis added

A study of that passage revealed the word for the "power[117] that works within us" is *God's dynamis power.*

Vision of Michela

On or about August 12, 2012, God had more. While walking through their family room in Vista, Michela's face suddenly appeared in full color before Mary.

Michela's eyes were pleading, and her lips did not move, but Mary heard her spirit say, *"Help me."*

She speaks Italian, but Mary heard her in English.

Michela was desperate! Mary knew it was time to fast and pray for her—*immediately*! Being human, and prone to pamper the flesh, Mary's first thought was to go on an easy forty-day Daniel fast. However, God squelched that idea as quickly as it came and plainly said,

"No! You do not have time."

"Oh."

She immediately began a three-day fast from all food and asked God to help Michela. Her prayer started with, "Lord, Your servant Michela needs Your help. . ."

Concetta called from Italy and said the doctors had given Michela **"two days to live,"** and then transferred her to a different hospital.

---

[117] "G1411 - dynamis - Strong's Greek Lexicon (KJV)." Blue Letter Bible. Accessed 4 Jun, 2016.
https://www.blueletterbible.org//lang/Lexicon/Lexicon.cfm?Strongs=G1411&t=KJV

Why Shofars Wail in Scripture and Today—   By Mary A. Bruno, Ph.D.

273

"Two days to live?" How could this have happened after all of the[118] beautiful things God had urged Mary to tell Michela when they had all prayed in her hospital room?

Two days to live? Michela was not supposed to die! She was supposed to recover and rise up in new strength to share her amazing testimony of God's greatness—and to be a living example of His handiwork!

Two days to live? Mary was sure that God had given her those words to say to Michela when they were at that hospital. She had blurted them out as fast as they came. She and Michela had such a lovely kindred spirit! Mary longed to stand by Michela in their church as she blessed the Lord.

Two days to live? Mary wondered if she could have been that far off base regarding what she believed God had said. Could she ever bring herself to tell anyone else what she thought He was urging her to say?

Rocco's Ministry

Knowing this could seriously affect Rocco's ministry was crushing. People might say he had married a false prophet. He could suffer ridicule and a closed door of ministry in Caposele—his hometown! Mary kept fasting and asking God to heal His servant, as did Rocco, Michela's loved ones, churches in their region, and CHN's intercessors.

Concetta called three weeks after the vision and fast. She said Michela was back home, and gaining weight! She returned to work soon after.

---

[118] Avoiding the Mistake of Materialism sermon page 2 ..,
http://www.sermoncentral.com/sermons/avoiding-the-mistake-of-materialism-david-o (accessed April 12, 2016).

Why Shofars Wail in Scripture and Today—   By Mary A. Bruno, Ph.D.

274

Tests and Tears

May–June 2013—Eight months later, Rocco and Mary returned to minister in Caposele. Michela told them that her doctor had retested her **deteriorated pancreas** regularly since she had been near death and had tested her again right before they arrived. She said that while she was still under the examining machine, she saw tears in her doctor's eyes as he reviewed her test results. Michela braced herself for what he was going to tell her.

He said this was his first time to witness anything like what happened to her. Her doctor informed her that she had **a new pancreas!**

As promised on the day they had met at the hospital, Michela prepared a delicious meal for Rocco and Mary. That woman can cook! She said that every day at the hospital where she works, people come over and ask her to tell them about her miracle healing from God.

New Miracle

During dinner, it was a joy to hear of Michela's miracle healing from the previous year. However, Mary told Pastor Geremia, that she wanted to hear about a new miracle—*just one new miracle*—from the current trip. She looked him in the eye and said,[119] "I can run for a long time on one new miracle—*just one miracle!*" He just smiled, and nodded, but kept his secret to himself.

In church the next morning, every minute counted because Rocco and Mary had slashed another bilingual message down to almost bare verses. The service moved

---

[119] Proverbs 7:13-22, Holy Bible: Easy-to-Read Version (ERV .., https://www.bible.com/bible/406/pro.7.13-22.erv#! (accessed April 12, 2016).

Why Shofars Wail in Scripture and Today—   By Mary A. Bruno, Ph.D.

275

along nicely, with just enough time for what was left of the whittled down sermon. Then, Pastor Geremia stepped up to the mike and announced he was going to share his testimony. Mary assumed he was going to tell of his salvation from fifty years ago. God was in charge, and they would have to talk faster or leave more out.

Pastor Geremia's Secret

With a big boyish grin and twinkle in his eye, Pastor Geremia spilled his big secret. He said he had needed gallbladder surgery over a year earlier when Michela became ill. He had to postpone it because she was so sick. However, his doctor said the stones had gotten bigger and had to come out. (Pastor Geremia had asked Rocco and Mary to pray for him a week or so earlier.) Once again, they had prayed as God led but sensed no great manifestation of His Presence or power. (Thankfully, God's power does not flow in proportion to anyone's feelings or sensations.)

A few days later, the doctor called Pastor Geremia in for one last test before scheduling surgery. His doctor examined the test results and was very confused because— they showed *no gallstones!* Pastor Geremia grinned and told him confidently, *"The same God who healed my wife's pancreas also **healed me of gallstones!**"*

His was the new miracle Mary had hoped to see. Sermon length was not a problem. During a packed response to an invitation to pray at the close of that Sunday service, Michela helped Pastor Geremia, Rocco, and Mary to pray for the people. As Michela stretched forth her hands in ministry, God granted Mary's desire to stand with her as she ministered to their congregation. Michela told them later that this was her first time to do anything like that. It will

Why Shofars Wail in Scripture and Today—   By Mary A. Bruno, Ph.D.

276

probably not be her last. Rocco's open door of ministry in Caposele should not be a problem.

On this, their first shofar blowing trip, the Brunos had only intended to sound their shofar by the Liberty Bell. However, God, being Himself, and full of surprises, came along, made Himself comfortable, and then mapped out His own plans after a few hours into their journey.

Next time they will take two shofars. They look forward to seeing what kind of miracles and divine appointments God has scheduled for their 2016 shofar-sounding mission, which will include another Eagles' Wings[120] Conference in New York.

During that new adventure with God, they plan to sound the shofar and affirm His ownership of the land and people in another few dozen states within the USA, plus Canadian provinces, Italy, and wherever else God leads.

THE END

Also I heard the voice of the Lord, saying: "**Whom** shall I send, And **who will go for Us**?" Then I said, "Here *am* I! Send me" (Isaiah 6:8).

---

[120] www.eagleswings.to

Why Shofars Wail in Scripture and Today—   By Mary A. Bruno, Ph.D.

277

Dare to Write a Review!

May God bless you for reading *Why Shofars Wail in Scripture and Today—The Exciting Stories and Miracles!* by Mary A. Bruno, Ph.D. If you have enjoyed this book, she would like to see your review on www.Amazon.com. She reads every one.

As Barbara Anne Waite,[121] author of *Elsie's Mountain,* once mentioned, "Many people are unaware of the enormous boost that even a few words from a reader can mean for an author. Every review helps, no matter how brief."

Your notes will not only bless Dr. Bruno and others, but may help to boost sales. Your review could even help someone to find peace with God, and to lift up his or her voice as a shofar.

How To Write A Review—It's Easy!

1. Type, www.amazon.com on your browser.
2. Type, *Mary A. Bruno,* Ph.D., on Amazon's search bar, and then click on the magnifying glass.
3. Click on the book's title: *Why Shofars Wail in Scripture and Today—The Exciting Stories and Miracles!*
4. Click on the *customer reviews,* (blue writing), by the yellow rating stars (next to a picture of the book).
5. Read a few of the reviews to get an idea of what goes into one.
6. Click on the (gray) *Write A Customer Review* box, and then complete the *Sign In* box that pops up.
7. Dare to wax eloquent and compose your review with your unique observations and style.

For a writer, knowing that a reader has taken the time to compose a brief comment is equal to having received an extremely generous tip. Thank you!

---

[121] www.barbaraannewaite.com

Why Shofars Wail in Scripture and Today—   By Mary A. Bruno, Ph.D.

278

Appendix

Shofar References in Scripture

For the reader's sake, Old Testament and New Testament references to the shofar, trumpet, etc., with the word number and definition from *Strong's Exhaustive Concordance of the Bible* (Strong's) were grouped together in this section.

Trumpet:[122]   Strong's   H7782   -   Showphar (shō-far')
Seventy-two (72) mentions of the shofar in the following sixty-three (63) verses are from the *Blue Letter Bible.*
In the following references from the King James Version of the Bible (KJV), where H7782 Showphar was used, the translated word for "Showphar" will be emboldened and the word Showphar will be in brackets, i.e. *trumpet* [Showphar]. (Italics added by author.) In some instances, the singular word (*Showphar*) may include the plural if indicated by a preceding word.

---

[122] "H7782 - showphar - Strong's Hebrew Lexicon (KJV)." Blue Letter Bible. Accessed 4 Jun, 2016. https://www.blueletterbible.org//lang/lexicon/lexicon.cfm?Strongs=H7782&t=KJV

Cornet translated from *Showphar* in three passages. See: Hos. 5:8, 1 Chron. 15:28, and 1 Chron. 15:14.

Dictionary and word search for *showphar* (Strong's 7782). *Blue Letter Bible.* http://www.blueletterbible.org/lang/lexicon/lexicon.cfm?Strongs=H7782&t=KJV.

1. Ex. 19:16, 19 KJV — "And it came to pass on the third day in the morning, that there were thunders and lightnings, and a thick cloud upon the mount, and the voice of the **trumpet [showphar]** exceeding loud; so that all the people that [was] in the camp trembled."

2. Ex. 19:19 KJV — "And when the voice of the **trumpet [showphar]** sounded long, and waxed louder and louder, Moses spake, and God answered him by a voice."

3. Ex. 20:18 KJV — "And all the people saw the thunderings, and the lightnings, and the noise of the **trumpet,** [**showphar]** and the mountain smoking: and when the people saw [it], they removed, and stood afar off."

4. Lev. 25:9 KJV — "Then shalt thou cause the **trumpet [showphar]** of the jubile to sound on the tenth [day] of the seventh month, in the day of atonement shall ye make the **trumpet [showphar]** sound throughout all your land."

5. Josh. 6:4 KJV — "And seven priests shall bear before the ark seven **trumpets [showphar]** of rams' **horns [yowbel]**: and the seventh day ye shall compass the city seven times, and the priests [H3548] shall blow with the **trumpets [showphar]**."

Why Shofars Wail in Scripture and Today—   By Mary A. Bruno, Ph.D.

6. **Josh. 6:5 KJV** — "And it shall come to pass, that when they make a long [blast] with the **ram's horn [qeren]**, [and] when ye hear the sound of the **trumpet [showphar]**, all the people shall shout with a great shout; and the wall of the city shall fall down flat, and the people shall ascend up every man straight before him."

7. **Josh. 6:6 KJV** — "And Joshua the son of Nun called the priests, and said unto them, Take up the ark of the covenant, and let seven priests bear seven **trumpets [showphar] of rams' horns [yowbel]** before the ark of the LORD."

8. **Josh. 6:8 KJV** — "And it came to pass, when Joshua had spoken unto the people, that the seven priests bearing the seven **trumpets [showphar]** of **rams' horns [yowbel]** passed on before the LORD, and blew with the **trumpets [showphar]**: and the ark of the covenant of the LORD followed them."

9. **Josh. 6:9 KJV** — "And the armed men went before the priests that blew with the **trumpets [showphar]**, and the rereward came after the ark, [the priests] going on, and blowing with the **trumpets [showphar]**."

10. **Josh. 6:13 KJV** — "And seven priests bearing seven **trumpets [showphar]** of **rams' horns [yowbel]** before the ark of the LORD went on continually, and blew with the **trumpets [showphar]**; and the armed men went before them; but the rereward came after the ark of the LORD, [the priests] going on, and blowing with the **trumpets [showphar]**."

11. **Josh. 6:16 KJV** — "And it came to pass at the seventh time, when the priests blew with the **trumpets [showphar]**, Joshua said unto the people, Shout; for the LORD hath given you the city."

12. **Josh. 6:20 KJV** — "So the people shouted when [the priests] blew with the **trumpets: [showphar]** and it came to pass, when the people heard the sound of the **trumpet, [showphar]** and the people shouted with a great shout, that the wall fell down flat, so that the people went up into the city, every man straight before him, and they took the city."

13. **Judg. 3:27 KJV** — "And it came to pass, when he was come, that he blew a **trumpet [showphar]** in the mountain of Ephraim, and the children of Israel went down with him from the mount, and he before them."

14. **Judg. 6:34 KJV** — "But the Spirit of the LORD came upon Gideon, and he blew a **trumpet [showphar]**; and Abiezer was gathered after him."

15. **Judg. 7:8 KJV**— "So the people took victuals in their hand, and their **trumpets [showphar]**: and he sent all [the rest of] Israel every man unto his tent, and retained those three hundred men: [H376] and the host of Midian [H4080] was beneath him in the valley."

16. **Judg. 7:16 KJV** — "And he divided the three hundred men [into] three companies, and he put a **trumpet [showphar]** in every man's hand, with empty pitchers, and lamps within the pitchers."

17. **Judg. 7:18 KJV** — "When I blow with a **trumpet [showphar]**, I and all that [are] with me, then blow ye the **trumpets [showphar]** also on every side of all the camp, and say,

Why Shofars Wail in Scripture and Today—   By Mary A. Bruno, Ph.D.

280

[The sword] of the LORD, and of Gideon."

18. **Judg. 7:19 KJV** — "So Gideon, and the hundred men that [were] with him, came unto the outside of the camp in the beginning of the middle watch; and they had but newly set the watch: and they blew the **trumpets [showphar]**, and brake the pitchers that [were] in their hands."

19. **Judg. 7:20 KJV** — "And the three companies blew the **trumpets [showphar]**, and brake the pitchers, and held the lamps in their left hands, and the **trumpets [showphar]** in their right hands to blow [withal]: and they cried, The sword of the LORD, and of Gideon."

20. **Judg. 7:22 KJV** — "And the three hundred blew the **trumpets, [showphar]** and the LORD set every man's sword against his fellow, even throughout all the host: and the host fled to Bethshittah in Zererath, [and] to the border of Abelmeholah, unto Tabbath."

21. **1 Sam. 13:3 KJV** — "And Jonathan smote the garrison of the Philistines that [was] in Geba, and the Philistines heard [of it]. And Saul blew the **trumpet [showphar]** throughout all the land, saying, Let the Hebrews hear."

22. **2 Sam. 2:28 KJV** — "So Joab blew a **trumpet [showphar]**, and all the people stood still, and pursued after Israel no more, neither fought they any more."

23. **2 Sam. 6:15 KJV** — "So David and all the house of Israel brought up the ark of the LORD with shouting, and with the sound of the **trumpet [showphar]**."

24. **2 Sam. 15:10 KJV** — "But Absalom sent spies throughout all the tribes of Israel, saying, As soon as ye hear the sound of the **trumpet [showphar]**, then ye shall say, Absalom reigneth in Hebron."

25. **2 Sam. 18:16 KJV** — "And Joab blew **the trumpet [showphar]**, and the people returned from pursuing after Israel: for Joab held back the people."

26. **2 Sam. 20:1 KJV** — "And there happened to be there a man of Belial, whose name [was] Sheba, the son of Bichri, a Benjamite: and he blew a **trumpet [showphar]**, and said, We have no part in David, neither have we inheritance in the son of Jesse: every man to his tents, O Israel."

27. **2 Sam. 20:22 KJV** — "Then the woman went unto all the people in her wisdom. And they cut off the head of Sheba the son of Bichri, and cast [it] out to Joab. And he blew a **trumpet [showphar]**, and they retired from the city, every man to his tent. And Joab returned to Jerusalem unto the king."

28. **1 Kings 1:34 KJV** — "And let Zadok the priest and Nathan the prophet anoint him there king over Israel: and blow ye with the **trumpet [showphar]**, and say, God save king Solomon."

29. **I Kings 1:39 KJV** — "And Zadok the priest took an horn of oil out of the tabernacle, and anointed Solomon. And they blew the **trumpet [showphar]**; and all the people said, God save king Solomon."

30. **I Kings 1:41 KJV** — "And Adonijah and all the guests that [were] with him heard [it] as they had made an end of eating. And when Joab heard the sound of the **trumpet**

Why Shofars Wail in Scripture and Today—   By Mary A. Bruno, Ph.D.

[showphar, he said, Wherefore [is this] noise of the city being in an uproar?"

31. **2 Kings 9:13 KJV** — "Then they hasted, and took every man his garment, and put [it] under him on the top of the stairs,
and blew with **trumpets [showphar]**, saying, Jehu is king."

32. **1 Chron. 15:28 KJV** — "Thus all Israel brought up the ark of the covenant of the LORD with shouting, and with sound of the **cornet [showphar]**, and with trumpets, and with cymbals, making a noise with psalteries and harps."

33. **2 Chron. 15:14 KJV** — "And they sware unto the LORD with a loud voice, and with shouting, and with trumpets, and with **cornets [showphar]**."

34. **Neh. 4:18 KJV** — "For the builders, every one had his sword girded by his side, and [so] builded. And he that sounded the **trumpet [showphar]** [was] by me."

35. **Neh. 4:20 KJV** — "In what place [therefore] ye hear the sound of the **trumpet [showphar]**, resort ye thither unto us: our God shall fight for us."

36. **Job 39:24 KJV** — "He swalloweth the ground with fierceness and rage: neither believeth he that [it is] the sound of the **trumpet [showphar]**,"

37. **Job 39:25 KJV** — "He saith among the **trumpets [showphar,** Ha, ha; and he smelleth the battle afar off, the thunder of the captains, and the shouting."

38. **Ps. 47:5 KJV**— "God is gone up with a shout, the LORD with the sound of a **trumpet [showphar]**."

39. **Ps. 81:3 KJV** — "Blow up the **trumpet [showphar]** in the new moon, in the time appointed, on our solemn feast day."

40. **Ps. 98:6 KJV** — "With trumpets and sound of **cornet [showphar]** make a joyful noise before the LORD, the King."

41. **Ps. 150:3 KJV** — "Praise him with the sound of the **trumpet [showphar]**: praise him with the psaltery and harp."

42. **Isa. 18:3 KJV** — "All ye inhabitants of the world, and dwellers on the earth, see ye, when he lifteth up an ensign on the mountains; and when he bloweth a **trumpet [showphar]**, hear ye."

43. **Isa. 27:13 KJV** — "And it shall come to pass in that day, [that] the great **trumpet [showphar]** shall be blown, and they shall come which were ready to perish in the land of Assyria, and the outcasts in the land of Egypt, and shall worship the LORD in the holy mount at Jerusalem."

44. **Isa. 58:1 KJV** — "Cry aloud, spare not, lift up thy voice like a **trumpet [showphar]**, and shew my people their transgression, and the house of Jacob their sins."

45. **Jer. 4:5 KJV** — "Declare ye in Judah, and publish in Jerusalem; and say, Blow ye the **trumpet [showphar]**, in the land: cry, gather together, and say, Assemble yourselves, and let us go into the defenced cities."

46. **Jer. 4:19 KJV** — "My bowels, my bowels! I am pained at my very heart; my heart maketh a noise in me; I cannot hold my peace, because thou hast heard, O my soul, the sound of the **trumpet [showphar]**, the alarm of war."

Why Shofars Wail in Scripture and Today—   By Mary A. Bruno, Ph.D.

282

47. **Jer. 4:21 KJV** — "How long shall I see the standard, [and] hear the sound of the **trumpet [showphar]**?"

48. **Jer. 6:1 KJV** — "O ye children of Benjamin, gather yourselves to flee out of the midst of Jerusalem, and blow the **trumpet [showphar]** in Tekoa, and set up a sign of fire in Bethhaccerem: for evil appeareth out of the north, and great destruction."

49. **Jer. 6:17 KJV** — "Also I set watchmen over you, [saying], Hearken to the sound of the **trumpet [showphar]**. But they said, We will not hearken."

50. **Jer. 42:14 KJV** — "Saying, No; but we will go into the land of Egypt, where we shall see no war, nor hear the sound of the **trumpet [showphar]**, nor have hunger of bread; and there will we dwell:"

51. **Jer. 51:27 KJV** — "Set ye up a standard in the land, blow the **trumpet [showphar]** among the nations, prepare the nations against her, call together against her the kingdoms of Ararat, Minni, and Ashchenaz; appoint a captain against her; cause the horses to come up as the rough caterpillers."

52. **Ezek. 33:3 KJV** — "If when he seeth the sword come upon the land, he blow the **trumpet [showphar]**, and warn the people;"

53. **Ezek. 33:4 KJV** — "Then whosoever heareth the sound of the **trumpet [showphar]**, and taketh not warning; if the sword come, and take him away, his blood shall be upon his own head. "

54. **Ezek. 33:5 KJV** — "He heard the sound of the **trumpet [showphar]**, and took not warning; his blood shall be upon him. But he that taketh warning shall deliver his soul."

55. **Ezek. 33:6 KJV** — "But if the watchman see the sword come, and blow not the **trumpet [showphar]**, and the people be not warned; if the sword come, and take [any] person from among them, he is taken away in his iniquity; but his blood will I require at the watchman's hand."

56. **Hos. 5:8 KJV** — "Blow ye the **cornet [showphar]** in Gibeah, [and] the trumpet in Ramah: cry aloud [at] Bethaven, after thee, O Benjamin."

57. **Hos. 8:1 KJV** — "[Set] the **trumpet [showphar]** to thy mouth. [He shall come] as an eagle against the house of the LORD, because they have transgressed my covenant, and trespassed against my law."

58. **Joel 2:1 KJV** — "Blow ye the **trumpet [showphar]** in Zion, and sound an alarm in my holy mountain: let all the inhabitants of the land tremble: for the day of the LORD cometh, for [it is] nigh at hand;"

59. **Joel 2:15 KJV** — "Blow the **trumpet [showphar]** in Zion, sanctify a fast call a solemn assembly:"

60. **Amos 2:2 KJV** — "But I will send a fire upon Moab and it shall devour the palaces of Kerioth: and Moab shall die with tumult, with shouting, [and] with the sound of the **trumpet [showphar]**:"

61. **Amos 3:6 KJV** — "Shall a **trumpet [showphar]** be blown in the city, and the people not be afraid? Shall there be evil in a city, and the LORD hath not done [it]?"

62. **Zeph. 1:16 KJV** — "A day of the **trumpet [shophar]** and alarm

Why Shofars Wail in Scripture and Today—   By Mary A. Bruno, Ph.D.

against the fenced cities, and against the high towers."

63. Zech. 9:14 KJV — "And the LORD shall be seen over them, and his arrow shall go forth as the lightning: and the Lord GOD shall blow the **trumpet [showphar]**, and shall go with whirlwinds of the south."

Trumpet:[123] Strong's H3104 - Yowbel (yō-vāl)

Strong's Hebrew word H3104 - Yowbel, occurs twenty-seven (27) times in twenty-five (25) verses in the KJV. (Italics added by author.) It translated as **Jubilee** twenty-one times, as **ram's horn** five times, and as **trumpet** one time.

Where H3104 - *yowbel* was used, the translated word for *yowbel* has been emboldened by the word *yowbel* in brackets, i.e. *jubilee* (H3104 – *yowbel*). In some instances, the singular word (yowbel) may also include the plural if indicated by a preceding word. Passages are in the order in which they occur in the Old Testament. Dictionary and word search for *yowbel* (Strong's H3104). *Blue Letter Bible.* http://www.blueletterbible.org/lan g/lexicon/lexicon.cfm?Strongs=H31 04&t=KJV.

1. Ex. 19:13 KJV — "There shall not an hand touch it, but he shall surely be stoned, or shot through; whether [it be] beast or man, it shall not live: when the **trumpet [yowbel]** soundeth long, they shall come up to the mount."

---

[123] "H3104 - yowbel - Strong's Hebrew Lexicon (KJV)." Blue Letter Bible. Accessed 4 Jun, 2016. https://www.blueletterbible.org//lang/le xicon/lexicon.cfm?Strongs=H3104&t= KJV

2. Lev. 25:10 KJV — "And ye shall hallow the fiftieth year, and proclaim liberty throughout [all] the land unto all the inhabitants thereof: it shall be a **jubilee [yowbel]** unto you; and ye shall return every man unto his possession, and ye shall return every man unto his family."

3. Lev. 25:11 KJV — "A **jubilee [yowbel]** shall that fiftieth year be unto you: ye shall not sow, neither reap that which groweth of itself in it, nor gather [the grapes] in it of thy vine undressed."

4. Lev. 25:12 KJV — "For it [is] the **jubilee [yowbel]**; it shall be holy unto you: ye shall eat the increase thereof out of the field."

5. Lev. 25:13 KJV — In the year of this **jubilee [yowbel]** ye shall return every man unto his possession."

6. Lev. 25:15 KJV — "According to the number of years after the **jubilee [yowbel]** thou shalt buy of thy neighbour, [and] according unto the number of years of the fruits he shall sell unto thee:"

7. Lev. 25:28 KJV — "But if he be not able to restore [it] to him, then that which is sold shall remain in the hand of him that hath bought it until the year of **jubilee [yowbel]**: and in the **jubilee [yowbel]** it shall go out, and he shall return unto his possession."

8. Lev. 25: 30 KJV — "And if it be not redeemed within the space of a full year, then the house that [is] in the walled city shall be established for ever to him that bought it throughout his generations: it shall not go out in the **jubilee [yowbel]**."

9. Lev. 25:31 KJV — "But the houses of the villages which have no wall

Why Shofars Wail in Scripture and Today—   By Mary A. Bruno, Ph.D.

284

round about them shall be counted as the fields of the country: they may be redeemed, and they shall go out in the **jubilee [yowbel]**."

10. **Lev. 25: 33 KJV** — "And if a man purchase of the Levites, then the house that was sold, and the city of his possession, shall go out in [the year of] **jubilee [yowbel]**: for the houses of the cities of the Levites [are] their possession among the children of Israel."

11. **Lev. 25:40 KJV** — " [But] as an hired servant, [and] as a sojourner, he shall be with thee, [and] shall serve thee unto the year of **jubilee [yowbel]**:"

12. **Lev. 25:50 KJV** — "And he shall reckon with him that bought him from the year that he was sold to him unto the year of **jubilee [yowbel]**: and the price of his sale shall be according unto the number of years, according to the time of an hired servant shall it be with him."

13. **Lev. 25:52 KJV** — "And if there remain but few years unto the year of **jubilee [yowbel]**, then he shall count with him, [and] according unto his years shall he give him again the price of his redemption."

14. **Lev. 25:54 KJV** — "And if he be not redeemed in these [years], then he shall go out in the year of **jubilee [yowbel]**, [both] he, and his children with him."

15. **Lev. 27:17 KJV** — "If he sanctify his field from the year of **jubilee [yowbel]**, according to thy estimation it shall stand."

16. **Lev. 27:18 KJV** — "But if he sanctify his field after the **jubilee [yowbel]**, then the priest shall reckon unto him the money according to the years that remain, even unto the

year of the **jubilee [yowbel]**, and it shall be abated from thy estimation."

17. **Lev. 27:21 KJV** — "But the field, when it goeth out in the **jubilee [yowbel]**, shall be holy unto the LORD, as a field devoted; the possession thereof shall be the priest's."

18. **Lev. 27:23 KJV** — "Then the priest shall reckon unto him the worth of thy estimation, [even] unto the year of the **jubilee [yowbel]**: and he shall give thine estimation in that day, [as] a holy thing unto the LORD."

19. **Lev. 27:24 KJV** — "In the year of the **jubilee [yowbel]** the field shall return unto him of whom it was bought, [even] to him to whom the possession of the land [did belong]."

20. **Num. 36:4 KJV** — "And when the **jubilee [yowbel]** of the children of Israel shall be, then shall their inheritance be put unto the inheritance of the tribe whereunto they are received: so shall their inheritance be taken away from the inheritance of the tribe of our fathers."

21. **Josh. 6:4 KJV** — "And seven priests shall bear before the ark seven trumpets of rams' **horns [yowbel]**: and the seventh day ye shall compass the city seven times, and the priests shall blow with the trumpets."

22. **Josh. 6:5 KJV** — "And it shall come to pass, that when they make a long [blast] with the **ram's [yowbel] horn**, [and] when ye hear the sound of the trumpet, all the people shall shout with a great shout; and the wall of the city shall fall down flat, and the people shall ascend up every man straight before him."

Why Shofars Wail in Scripture and Today— By Mary A. Bruno, Ph.D.

23. Josh. 6:6 KJV — "And Joshua the son of Nun called the priests, and said unto them, Take up the ark of the covenant, and let seven priests bear seven trumpets of **rams' horns [yowbel]** before the ark of the LORD."

24. Josh. 6:8 KJV — "And it came to pass, when Joshua had spoken unto the people, that the seven priests bearing the seven trumpets of **rams' horns [yowbel]** passed on before the LORD, and blew with the trumpets: and the ark of the covenant of the LORD followed them."

25. Josh. 6:13 KJV — "And seven priests bearing seven trumpets of **rams' horns [yowbel]** before the ark of the LORD went on continually, and blew with the trumpets: and the armed men went before them; but the rereward came after the ark of the LORD, [the priests] going on, and blowing with the trumpets."

Trumpet:[124] **Strong's G4536 - Salpigx (sä'l-pĕnks)**
Dictionary and word search for *salpigx* (Strong's G4536). *Blue Letter Bible.*
http://www.blueletterbible.org/lan g/lexicon/lexicon.cfm?Strongs=G45 36&t=KJV.
Strong's Greek Word G4536 - *Salpigx* (pronounced sä'l-pĕnks) was used for "trumpet" or "trump" in the following passages. Bold added for emphasis. Salpigx occurs eleven (11) times in eleven (11) New Testament verses of the KJV.

---

[124] "G4536 - salpigx - Strong's Greek Lexicon (KJV)." Blue Letter Bible. Accessed 4 Jun, 2016. https://www.blueletterbible.org//lan g/lexicon/lexicon.cfm?Strongs=G45 36&t=KJV

Vine's Expository Dictionary of New Testament Words indicates the following definition for Strong's G4536, salpigx (salpinx) a noun: See: http://www.blueletterbible.org/lan g/lexicon/lexicon.cfm?Strongs=G45 36&t=KJV.

Trump, Trumpet:
It is used:
(1) of the **natural instrument,** 1 Cr. 14:8;
(2) of the supernatural accompaniment of divine interpositions,
  (*a*) at Sinai, Heb. 12:19;
  (*b*) of the acts of angels at the second advent of Christ, Mat. 24:31;
  (*c*) of their acts in the period of divine judgments preceding this,
    Rev. 8:2, 6, 13; 9:14;
  (*d*) of a summons to John to the presence of God, Rev. 1:10; 4:1;
  (*e*) of the act of the Lord in raising from the dead the saints who have fallen asleep and changing the bodies of those who are living, at the Rapture of all to meet Him in the air, 1Cr 15:52, where "the last trump" is a military allusion, familiar to Greek readers, and has no connection with the series in Rev 8:6 to 11:15; there is a possible allusion to Num. 10:2–6, with reference to the same event, 1 Th. 4:16, "the (lit., a) trump of God" (the absence of the article suggests the meaning "a trumpet such as is used in God's service").

1. Matt. 24:31 KJV — "And he shall send his angels with a great sound of a **trumpet [salpigx]**, and they shall gather together his elect from the four winds, from one end of heaven to the other."

2. 1 Cor. 14:8 KJV — "For if the **trumpet [salpigx]** give an uncertain sound, who shall prepare himself to the battle?"

Why Shofars Wail in Scripture and Today—   By Mary A. Bruno, Ph.D.

286

3. **1 Cor. 15:52 KJV** — "In a moment, in the twinkling of an eye, at the last **trump [salpigx]**: for the trumpet shall sound, and the dead shall be raised incorruptible, and we shall be changed."

4. **1 Thess. 4:16 KJV** — "For the Lord himself shall descend from heaven with a shout, with the voice of the archangel, and with the **trump [salpigx]** of God: and the dead in Christ shall rise first:"

5. **Heb. 12:19 KJV** — "And the sound of a **trumpet [salpigx]**, and the voice of words; which [voice] they that heard intreated that the word should not be spoken to them any more:"

6. **Rev. 1:10 KJV** — "I was in the Spirit on the Lord's day, and heard behind me a great voice, as of a **trumpet [salpigx]**."

7. **Rev. 4:1 KJV** — "After this I looked, and, behold, a door [was] opened in heaven: and the first voice which I heard [was] as it were of a **trumpet [salpigx]** talking with me; which said, Come up hither, and I will shew thee things which must be hereafter."

8. **Rev. 8:2 KJV** — "And I saw the seven angels which stood before God; and to them were given seven **trumpets [salpigx]**."

9. **Rev. 8:6 KJV** — "And the seven angels which had the seven **trumpets [salpigx]** prepared themselves to sound."

10. **Rev. 8:13 KJV** — "And I beheld, and heard an angel flying through the midst of heaven, saying with a loud voice, Woe, woe, woe, to the inhabiters of the earth by reason of the other voices of the **trumpet [salpigx]** of the three angels, which

are yet to sound!"

11. **Rev. 9:14 KJV** — "Saying to the sixth angel which had the **trumpet [salpigx]**, Loose the four angels which are bound in the great river Euphrates."

Sound a Trumpet
Trumpet: Strong's G4537 –
Salpizō: (säl-pē'-zō) [125]

Strong's Number G4537 matches the Greek (*salpizō*). Salpizō occurs thirteen (13) times in twelve (12) verses in the Greek concordance of the KJV as follows: sound (ten times), sound of a trumpet (one time), and trumpet sounds (one time).See:
http://www.blueletterbible.org/lang/Lexicon/Lexicon.cfm?strongs=G4537&t=KJV&ss=0.

1. **Matt. 6:2 KJV** — "Therefore when thou **doest [salpizō]** [thine] alms, do **[salpizō]** not sound a trumpet before thee, as the hypocrites do in the synagogues and in the streets, that they may have glory of men. Verily I say unto you, They have their reward."

2. **1 Cor. 15:52 KJV** — "In a moment, in the twinkling of an eye, at the last trump: for the trumpet shall **sound [salpizō]**, and the dead shall be raised incorruptible, and we shall be changed."

3. **Rev. 8:6 KJV** — "And the seven angels which had the seven trumpets prepared themselves to **sound [salpizō]**."

[125] "G4537 - salpizō - Strong's Greek Lexicon (KJV)." Blue Letter Bible. Accessed 7 Jun, 2016. https://www.blueletterbible.org//lang/lexicon/lexicon.cfm?Strongs=G4537&t=KJV

Why Shofars Wail in Scripture and Today—   By Mary A. Bruno, Ph.D.

4. **Rev. 8:7 KJV** — "The first angel **sounded [salpizō]**, and there followed hail and fire mingled with blood, and they were cast upon the earth: and the third part of trees was burnt up, and all green grass was burnt up."

5. **Rev. 8:8 KJV** — "And the second angel **sounded [salpizō]**, and as it were a great mountain burning with fire was cast into the sea: and the third part of the sea became blood;"

6. **Rev 8:10 KJV** — "And the third angel **sounded [salpizō]**, and there fell a great star from heaven, burning as it were a lamp, and it fell upon the third part of the rivers, and upon the fountains of waters;"

7. **Rev. 8:12 KJV** — "And the fourth angel **sounded [salpizō]**, and the third part of the sun was smitten, and the third part of the moon, and the third part of the stars; so as the third part of them was darkened, and the day shone not for a third part of it, and the night likewise."

8. **Rev. 8:13 KJV** — "And I beheld, and heard an angel flying through the midst of heaven, saying with a loud voice, Woe, woe, woe, to the inhabiters of the earth by reason of the other voices of the trumpet of the three angels, which are yet to **sound [salpizō]**!"

9. **Rev. 9:1 KJV** — "And the fifth angel **sounded [salpizō]**, and I saw a star fall from heaven unto the earth: and to him was given the key of the bottomless pit."

10. **Rev. 9:13 KJV** — "And the sixth angel **sounded [salpizō]**, and I heard a voice from the four horns of the golden altar which is before God,"

11. **Rev. 10:7 KJV** — "But in the days of the voice of the seventh angel, when he shall begin to **sound [salpizō]**, the mystery of God should be finished, as he hath declared to his servants the prophets."

12. **Rev. 11:15 KJV** — "And the seventh angel **sounded [salpizō]**; and there were great voices in heaven, saying, The kingdoms of this world are become [the kingdoms] of our Lord, and of his Christ; and he shall reign for ever and ever."

Why Shofars Wail in Scripture and Today—   By Mary A. Bruno, Ph.D.

288

Glossary

A, B, C.

abode. Home, residence,

abominable. Repulsive or terrible

abstinence. Self-denial, self-restraint

adulterer. One who has sexual relations with another person's husband or wife

adversary. Opponent or enemy

alliance. Agreement, association

Almighty, LORD God Almighty. The True and Living God.

altar. The place of sacrifice

amassed. Accumulated, collected

amphitheater. In Exodus it was a large flat open area surrounded with natural walls in the wilderness

anguish. Suffering, agony, distress

anointed. Smeared, rubbed, massaged, oiled

apprentice. Trainee, student

Ark of the Covenant. A beautiful box-like reminder of God's Presence, salvation and mercy

annihilate. To destroy

armorbearer. One who carries a shield (and possibly weapons?) of war for a king

arrogance. Pride, over-confidence

artisan. Skilled crafts person

assassinated. Deliberately killed

assumed. Expected, presumed

assuredly. For sure, doubtless

attackees. The ones being attacked.

avenge. Punish, revenge, get even

baptize. To dip, immerse, or to saturate, as to dye a garment

battlefront. Military location where combat happens.

beget. To produce, to father

believers. People of the Old Testament who trusted in God; or persons in the New Testament and modern times, who believe and receive Jesus Christ (Yeshua, the Messiah) as Savior

Benjamite. A person from the Tribe of Benjamin

berserk. Crazy, nuts, or bonkers

bestowed. Gave, granted, imparted

billowing. Rising, curling, flowing upward

bleating. Moaning, whining, bellyaching

bonds. From Strong's H2784, *chartsub-bah,* which meant a bond or fetter, or pangs of grief. Captives wore fetters of brass and iron that restrained their feet.

bilingual. In two languages.

botched. Spoiled, ruined, bungled

breakthrough. Discovery, step forward

breastplate. Protective covering, body armor

brimstone. Sulfur

captives. Prisoners or hostages

censer. A covered incense burner

chaff. Seed coverings that fall off when the grain is threshed

chalice. A drinking cup

chamber. Bedroom

Cherethites. Foreign mercenary soldiers and executioners hired as bodyguards to the king

cherubim. Plural of cherub, hefty angelic beings who are *powerful guards* in God's kingdom.

circumcision. Implies to cut off; a Jewish rite performed on male infants

cobblestones. Paving stones

Commandments. Laws that God wrote on stone tablets at Mount Sinai (Exodus 20:1–17).

Why Shofars Wail in Scripture and Today— By Mary A. Bruno, Ph.D.

289

commend. Recommend, as worthy of confidence or notice

commission. A command, charge, assignment, order

conceived . To become pregnant, cause to begin

confirmation. To make firm or approve

conniving. Scheming, deceitful

conqueror. To gain, acquire, or overcome by force of arms

consecrate. To bless, sanctify, or dedicate

consequences. Penalties

contempt. Dislike, disrespect, hatred, scorn.

coronation. Ceremony to crown a king

counterfeit. Imitation, fake

covenant. Agreement, promise

covetous. Envious, jealous, greedy

coward. One who shows disgraceful fear

cringe. To wince, draw back in fear

crunch numbers. To do math

crying. Hebrew word used for their *crying,* in Judges 7:21, is *ruwa,* "to shout a war cry or alarm for battle."

cubit. Length from a man's elbow to tip of his middle finger, about 17"-21"

cymbals. Brass disks, that when struck produce a bright tone. Resonating cymbals were the noisy kind that kept on ringing

D, E, F.

dastardly. Mean or cowardly

dazed. Confused, shocked, surprised

death list. List of people who were scheduled to be killed

decade. A period of ten years

deception. The act of deceiving, trickery

defiant. Disobedient, insubordinate, rebellious

defied. Challenged, disobeyed, disregarded

degrading. Humiliating, debasing, shameful

delegate. To deputize or substitute

demise. Death, departure, end

demons. Evil spirit beings

desolation. Ruined barren wasteland

destiny. Previously determined course

devious. Tricky, deceitful, scheming

devour. Eat, wolf down, consume

disciples. In the Christian sense; disciplined ones who follow Jesus Christ (Yeshua, the Messiah) and His teachings

discomfited. From Strong's H2522, *chalash;* to be weak, prostrate, or disabled

disintegrated. Crumbled, collapsed

diversions. Distractions or deviations

divisive. Disruptive, conflict-ridden, bringing division

DNA. Genetic material, chromosomes

domain. Province, territory

dominion. Colony, region, domain

doomed. Hopeless, ruined

dynamic. Lively, energetic, forceful, vibrant, vigorous

dynamis. God's *dynamis power* in Acts 1:8, from Strong's G1411— *dynamis*—pronounced du-na-mes. It means, "strength, power, ability; power to perform miracles; power and influence, which belong to riches; and power consisting in or resting upon armies, forces, and hosts.[126]

Eagles' Wings. A Christian organization based in Clarence, NY, that has outreaches in the United States and Israel.

effeminate. A man with feminine qualities.

ROCK, http://www.liveattherock.com/pkb/authority/ (accessed May 04, 2016).

Why Shofars Wail in Scripture and Today—   By Mary A. Bruno, Ph.D.

290

Elohiym. The plural name for God,

ephah. A bushel (basket) that could contain 35 liters, about 5 gallons

ephod. A large linen apron worn by priests

eunuch. A castrated man who oversees a harem or other palace assignments

Euphrates. The longest river in Southwest Asia (over 1700 miles long), starts in Turkey, crosses Syria, and flows through Iraq.

euthanasia, The killing of sick or injured people or animals

falafel. A tasty fried ball made from garbanzo beans.

fasting. Going without food, or other things for spiritual, health, or other reasons

flaw. An imperfection

fornicators. People who have sexual relations with someone to whom they are not married.

fortress. A place that has been made strong

G, H, I.

garrison. A military post with troops

go viral. News that spreads quickly over the Internet

Green Berets. Special Forces of the US Army.

horns of the altar. People who were desperate for mercy grabbed hold of the horns of the altar.

idolatrous. Involving the worship of a physical object

idols. Objects of devotion

immorality. Sin or wickedness

imparting. Giving or granting

incited. Encouraged or prompted

iniquity. Evil, crime, wickedness, sin

insubordinate. Disobedient, defiant, rebellious, unruly

Intercede. To plead or ask on someone's behalf

interrogate. To question formally

J, K, L.

Lamb of God. Jesus Christ (Yeshua the Messiah) is called, The Lamb of God, because He gave His sinless life as the ultimate sacrifice that paid for the sins of all

Liberty Bell. A large metal bell in Philadelphia, PA, that represents liberty for the United States of America

M, N , O.

mediator. An arbitrator, go-between, or negotiator

meditate. To ponder, consider, contemplate

medium. A person who claims to be a communication channel between humans and the spirit world

midwives. Women who assist pregnant women during childbirth

mission statement. A description of duties or assignment

myrrh. Brown gum resin from a thorny plant, used for purification and embalming, etc.

new moon. First day of the Jewish month

P, Q, R.

pagan. Follower of more than one god, one who lives for pleasure and material goods

plagues. Evil calamity, disaster, or disease

potentate. A king, queen, monarch or ruler

priority. importance.

prophecy. A special message from God

prophet. Receives and speaks special messages from God

Why Shofars Wail in Scripture and Today—   By Mary A. Bruno, Ph.D.

291

Redeemer. Savior, rescuer, one who buys back

repentant, To show remorse and turn from sin

résumé. [res-oo-may] Outline or rundown (of one's job qualifications)

revile. To insult, despise, scorn, berate, abuse

revolt. Rebellion, uprising, mutiny, riot

S, T, U.

Sabbath. Saturday, the day of rest

salvation. Redemption, being saved from sin's penalty

sanctified. Set apart for God's use

sanctuary. Consecrated place, the most holy part of a place of worship

Scripture. Books of the Bible, sacred writings

sorcerers. Wizards, witches, magicians

sovereign. Supreme power, authority

sparring partner. Boxing partner

spewed. Vomited, ejected

strategy. Plan, scheme, line of attack

stronghold. Fortified place that is controlled by a particular power or group

sundial. A device that told time by the sun's shadow.

surmised. Guessed, assumed, presumed

swindlers. Cheats, crooks, tricksters

swoon. To faint or black out

symbolized. Represented, indicated, suggested

synagogue. Jewish house of worship

tangible. Real, solid, something that could be touched

taunts. Boos, hissing, mocking

tempered. Hardened, strengthened, toughened

Theology. The study of God

tithing. Giving a tenth of one's increase (profit) to God

transgressors. Law-breakers, criminals, evildoers, sinners

trespasses. To enter someone's territory, rights or property, to make a mistake or sin

tunic. A long slip-on garment, (knee-length or longer), with or without sleeves

type. Example or symbol

V, W, X.

unrighteous. Sinful, unholy, wicked, impure

usurp. To seize, hold, or take over a position without legal right

valiant. Courageous, heroic

valor. Brave, fearless, valiant, courageous

vengeance. Revenge, punishment

vermin. Bugs, mice, rats

vigor. Stamina, strength, energy

VIP. Very important person

virtue. Dynamic miracle power (dynamis) that flowed when a woman touched Jesus' garment; (God's power that flows from a believer who is filled with the Holy Spirit (Ruach Kodesh)).

vowed. Swore, promised, declared

vulnerable. Helpless, exposed

Y, Z.

wail. Howl, scream, cry, or screech

wanton. Cruel, vicious, excessive

winepress. Stone that squeezes out grape juice for wine

wrath. Anger, rage, fury

Yowbel. Jubilee, ram's horn, a shofar made from a ram's horn.

Zion. A synonym for Jerusalem, the city of God.

_____

Why Shofars Wail in Scripture and Today—   By Mary A. Bruno, Ph.D.

292

Bibliography

Resources consulted during research for this book include the following:

Books

The Amplified Bible. Grand Rapids: Zondervan, 1980.

Bivin, David and Roy Blizzard, Jr. *Understanding the Difficult Words of Jesus*. Austin: Center for Judaic-Christian Studies, 1984.

The Chicago Manual of Style, Sixteenth Edition. Chicago: The University of Chicago Press, 2010.

Dake, Finis Jennings. *Dake's Annotated Reference Bible.*   Lawrenceville, GA: Dake Bible Sales, Inc., 1991.

Dockery, David S., ed. *Holman Bible Handbook*. Nashville: Holman Bible Publishers, 1972.

Duffield, Guy P. and Nathaniel M. Van Cleave. *Foundations of Pentecostal Theology*, Los Angeles: L.I.F.E. Bible College, 1987.

Ellison. H. L., ed. *The Daily Study Bible (Old Testament), Exodus.* Philadelphia: The Westminster Press, 1982.

Fairbairn, Patrick. *The Typology of Scripture*. Grand Rapids: Zondervan, 1969.

Gaebelein, Frank E., ed. *The Expositor's Bible Commentary*, vol. 2 (Genesis - Numbers). Grand Rapids: Zondervan, 1990.

Gaebelein, Frank E., ed. *The Expositor's Bible Commentary*, vol. 3 (Deuteronomy - 2 Samuel). Grand Rapids: Zondervan, 1992.

Gaebelein, Frank E., ed. *The Expositor's Bible Commentary*, vol. 4 (1 Kings - Job). Grand Rapids: Zondervan, 1988.

Gaebelein, Frank E., ed. *The Expositor's Bible Commentary*, vol. 6 (Isaiah - Ezekiel). Grand Rapids: Zondervan, 1986.

Gaebelein, Frank E., ed. *The Expositor's Bible Commentary*, vol. 8 (Matthew - Luke). Grand Rapids: Zondervan, 1984.

Gower, Ralph. *The New Manners And Customs of Bible Times*. Chicago: Moody Press, 1987.

Habershon, Ada R. *The Study of the Types*. Grand Rapids: Kregel Publications, 1973.

Hayford, Jack W., ed. *Hayford's Bible Handbook*. Nashville: Thomas Nelson Publishers, 1995.

Holdcroft, L. Thomas. *The Historical Books*. Oakland: Western Book Company, 1970.

Holdcroft, L. Thomas. *The Pentateuch.* Oakland: Western Book Company, 1966.

Jenkins, Simon. *Nelson's 3-D Bible Mapbook*. Nashville: Thomas Nelson Publishers, 1984.

Knight. George A. F. *The Daily Study Bible (Old Testament), Leviticus.* Philadelphia: The Westminster Press, 1981.

MacDonald, William, ed. *Believer's Bible Commentary, Old Testament.* Nashville, TN: Thomas Nelson Publishers, 1992.

Why Shofars Wail in Scripture and Today—   By Mary A. Bruno, Ph.D.

293

McConville Esther, J. G.. ed. *The Daily Study Bible (Old Testament)*. Philadelphia: The Westminster Press, 1985.

Meyer, F.B. *Great Men of the Bible, Volume I*. Grand Rapids: Zondervan, 1981.

Parsons, John J. *A Year Through the Torah*. Scottsdale: Hebrew Heart Publications, 2008.

Radmacher, Earl D. *The Nelson Study Bible*, New King James version. Nashville: Thomas Nelson, 1997.

Simeon, Charles. *Expository Outlines on the Whole Bible, vol. 4 (1 Chronicles – Job)*. Grand Rapids: Baker Book House, 1988.

Spence, H. D. M. and Joseph S. Exell, editors. *The Pulpit Commentary, vol. 1, (Genesis – Exodus)*. Grand Rapids: Eerdmans, 1950.

Spence, H. D. M. and Joseph S. Exell, editors. *The Pulpit Commentary, vol. 2, (Leviticus - Numbers)*. Grand Rapids: Eerdmans, 1950.

Spence, H. D. M. and Joseph S. Exell, editors. *The Pulpit Commentary, vol. 3, (Deuteronomy - Judges)*. Grand Rapids: Eerdmans, 1950.

Spence, H. D. M. and Joseph S. Exell, editors. *The Pulpit Commentary, vol. 4, (Ruth – II Samuel)*. Grand Rapids: Eerdmans, 1950.

Stern, David H. *Complete Jewish Bible*. Clarksville, MD: Messianic Jewish Resources International, 1998.

Strong, James, LL.D., S.T.D. The New Strong's Exhaustive Concordance of the Bible Nashville, Thomas Nelson Publishers, 1990

Trepp, Leo. *The Complete Book of Jewish Observance*. New York: Behrman House, Inc. and Summit Books, 1980.

Vine. W. E. *Vine's Expository Dictionary of New Testament Words*. McLean, VA: Mac Donald Publishing Company, 1989.

Zimmerman, Martha. *Celebrate the Feasts of the Old Testament in Your Own Home or Church*. Minneapolis: Bethany House Publishers, 1981.

Websites Contacted

aJudaica.com. "Shofar Guide." http://www.ajudaica.com/guide_shofar.ph.

archiveofourown.org This Is The Way We End (Or Begin Again) - Chapter 1 .., http://archiveofourown.org/chapters/14524063?add_comment_reply_id=56002849&s

biblestudy.org. Search for: "How many pounds in an ephah of flour." http://www.biblestudy.org/beginner/bible-weights-and-measures.html

Arnoldussen, Peg. "Yemenite Shofar Kudu Horn." http://pinebaskets.tripod.com/shofar.html.

Becky. "Cleaning the Shofar." http://answers.yahoo.com/question/index?qid=20080528093839AAsrQpF.

bbcamerica.com. Personality Quiz: Which Beatle Are You? | Anglophenia .., http://www.bbcamerica.com/anglophenia/2014/01/personality-quiz-beatle/

BibleGateway.com. "1 Kings 1-2." http://www.biblegateway.com/passage/?search=i%20kings%20.

BibleGateway.com. "1 Kings 16." http://www.biblegateway.com/passage/?search=I+Kings+16&version=NASB.

Why Shofars Wail in Scripture and Today—   By Mary A. Bruno, Ph.D.

BibleGateway.com. "1 Kings 19."
http://www.biblegateway.com/passage
/?search=I+Kings+19&version=NASB.

BibleGateway.com. "2 Kings 9." http:
//www.biblegateway.com/passage/?se
arch=II+Kings+9&version=NASB.

BibleGateway.com. "2 Kings 10."
http://www.biblegateway.com/passage
/?search=II+Kings+10&version=NASB.

BibleGateway.com. "Jehu."
http://www.biblegateway.com/quickse
arch/?quicksearch=Jehu&qs_version=N
ASB.

BibleGateway.com. "Nathan."
https://www.biblegateway.com/quicks
earch/?quicksearch=Nathan&qs_versio
n=NIV.

BibleGateway.com. "Numbers 14."
http://www.biblegateway.com/passage
/?search=Numbers+14%3A14-
45&version =NASB.

BibleGateway.com. "Zadok." http://
www.biblegateway.com/quicksearch/?
quicksearch=Zadok&qs_version=NASB.

Bible.com. Joshua 5:13-15, New
International Version (NIV) Now when
..,
https://www.bible.com/bible/111/jos.
5.13-15.niv#!

Biblehub.com. 1 Samuel 31:6 So Saul
and his three sons and his armor ..,
http://biblehub.com/1_samuel/31-
6.htm

Biblehub.com. Isaiah 6:8 Then I heard
the voice of the Lord saying ..,
http://biblehub.com/isaiah/6-8.htm

Bible.org. he Ethiopian Eunuch (Acts
8:26-40) | Bible.org,
https://bible.org/seriespage/13-
ethiopian-eunuch-acts-826-40

Bible Study Daily. Judges 6-7 - Bible
Study Daily,
http://biblestudydaily.org/judges-6-7/

BlueLetterBible.org. "Abishai."
"KJV Search Results for "Abishai"." Blue
Letter Bible.
https://www.blueletterbible.org//searc
h/search.cfm?Criteria=Abishai&t=KJV#s
=s_primary_0_1

BlueLetterBible.org. "Absalom." "KJV
Search Results for "absalom"." Blue
Letter Bible.
https://www.blueletterbible.org//searc
h/search.cfm?Criteria=absalom&t=KJV#
s=s_primary_0_1

BlueLetterBible.org. "account" "G3056 -
logos - Strong's Greek Lexicon (KJV)."
Blue Letter Bible.
https://www.blueletterbible.org//lang/
Lexicon/Lexicon.cfm?Strongs=G3056&t
=KJV

BlueLetterBible.org. "Amalek." "KJV
Search Results for "amalek"." Blue
Letter Bible.
https://www.blueletterbible.org//searc
h/search.cfm?Criteria=amalek&t=KJV#s
=s_primary_0_1

BlueLetterBible.org. "Arabia" "H6152 -
`Arab - Strong's Hebrew Lexicon (KJV)."
Blue Letter Bible. Accessed 19 Jun,
2016.
https://www.blueletterbible.org//lang/
Lexicon/Lexicon.cfm?Strongs=H6152&t
=KJV

BlueLetterBible.org. "ark." "KJV Search
Results for "ark"." Blue Letter Bible.
https://www.blueletterbible.org//searc
h/search.cfm?Criteria=ark&t=KJV#s=s_
primary_0_1

BlueLetterBible.org. "ark" (Strong's
H727 arown). "H727 - 'arown - Strong's
Hebrew Lexicon (KJV)." Blue Letter
Bible.
https://www.blueletterbible.org//lang/

Why Shofars Wail in Scripture and Today—   By Mary A. Bruno, Ph.D.

lexicon/lexicon.cfm?Strongs=H727&t=K
JV

BlueLetterBible.org. "Atonement"
(Strong's H3722). "KJV Search Results
for "atonement"." Blue Letter Bible.
https://www.blueletterbible.org//searc
h/search.cfm?Criteria=atonement&t=KJ
V#s=s_primary_0_1

BlueLetterBible.org. "Atonement"
(Strong's H3725). "H3725 - kippur -
Strong's Hebrew Lexicon (KJV)." Blue
Letter Bible.
https://www.blueletterbible.org//lang/
Lexicon/Lexicon.cfm?Strongs=H3725&t
=KJV

BlueLetterBible.org. "Be strong and of
good courage." "KJV Search Results for
"be" AND "strong" AND "and" AND "of"
AND "good" AND "courage"." Blue Letter
Bible.
https://www.blueletterbible.org//searc
h/search.cfm?Criteria=be+strong+and+
of+good+courage&t=KJV#s=s_primary_
0_1

BlueLetterBible.org. "Cherethites" "KJV
Search Results for "cherethites"." Blue
Letter Bible.
https://www.blueletterbible.org//searc
h/search.cfm?Criteria=cherethites&t=KJ
V#s=s_primary_0_1

BlueLetterBible.org. "Cherubim"
(Strong's H3742). "KJV Search Results
for "cherubims"." Blue Letter Bible.
https://www.blueletterbible.org//searc
h/search.cfm?Criteria=cherubims&t=KJ
V#s=s_primary_0_1

BlueLetterBible.org. "Cornet." "KJV
Search Results for "cornet"." Blue Letter
Bible.
https://www.blueletterbible.org//searc
h/search.cfm?Criteria=cornet&t=KJV#s
=s_primary_0_1

BlueLetterBible.org. "Blast." 1 "KJV
Search Results for "blast"." Blue Letter
Bible.
https://www.blueletterbible.org//searc
h/search.cfm?Criteria=blast&t=KJV#s=s
_primary_0_1

BlueLetterBible.org. "Blast" (Strong's
H4900 – mashak) "H4900 - mashak -
Strong's Hebrew Lexicon (KJV)." Blue
Letter Bible.
https://www.blueletterbible.org//lang/
lexicon/lexicon.cfm?Strongs=H4900&t=
KJV

BlueLetterBible.org. "Blow" (Strong's
H8628 taqa) "H8628 - taqa` - Strong's
Hebrew Lexicon (KJV)." Blue Letter
Bible.
https://www.blueletterbible.org//lang/
lexicon/lexicon.cfm?Strongs=H8628&t=
KJV

BlueLetterBible.org. "Clap" (Strong's
H8628). "H8628 - taqa` - Strong's
Hebrew Lexicon (KJV)." Blue Letter
Bible.
https://www.blueletterbible.org//lang/
lexicon/lexicon.cfm?Strongs=H8628&t=
KJV

BlueLetterBible.org. "Cornet" (Strong's
H7782). "KJV Search Results for
"cornet"." Blue Letter Bible.
https://www.blueletterbible.org//searc
h/search.cfm?Criteria=cornet&t=KJV#s
=s_primary_0_1

BlueLetterBible.org. "Cornet" Strong's
H7162. "H7162 - qeren (Aramaic) -
Strong's Hebrew Lexicon (KJV)." Blue
Letter Bible.
https://www.blueletterbible.org//lang/
Lexicon/Lexicon.cfm?Strongs=H7162&t
=KJV

BlueLetterBible.org. "Courage"
(Strong's H553). "KJV Search Results
for "courage"." Blue Letter Bible.
https://www.blueletterbible.org//searc
h/search.cfm?Criteria=courage&t=KJV#
s=s_primary_0_1

Why Shofars Wail in Scripture and Today—   By Mary A. Bruno, Ph.D.

296

BlueLetterBible.org. "David anointed king." "KJV Search Results for "David" AND "anointed" AND "king"." Blue Letter Bible. https://www.blueletterbible.org//search/search.cfm?Criteria=David+anointed+king&t=KJV#s=s_primary_0_1

BlueLetterBible.org. "Discomfited." H2522, H3807, H2000, H2729, H4522. "KJV Search Results for "discomfited"."

Blue Letter Bible. https://www.blueletterbible.org//search/search.cfm?Criteria=discomfited&t=KJV#s=s_primary_0_1

BlueLetterBible.org. "Elijah" (Strong's H452). "KJV Search Results for "Elijah"." Blue Letter Bible. Accessed 4 Jun, 2016. https://www.blueletterbible.org//search/search.cfm?Criteria=Elijah&t=KJV#s=s_primary_0_1

BlueLetterBible.org. "Fountain gate" (Strong's H5869). "KJV Search Results for "Fountain" AND "gate"." Blue Letter Bible. https://www.blueletterbible.org//search/search.cfm?Criteria=Fountain+gate&t=KJV#s=s_primary_0_1

BlueLetterBible.org. "Gihon" (Strong's H1521). "KJV Search Results for "Gihon"." Blue Letter Bible. https://www.blueletterbible.org//search/search.cfm?Criteria=Gihon&t=KJV#s=s_primary_0_1

BlueLetterBible.org. "God" (Strong's H410). "KJV Search Results for "Gihon"." Blue Letter Bible. https://www.blueletterbible.org//search/search.cfm?Criteria=Gihon&t=KJV#s=s_primary_0_1

BlueLetterBible.org. "God" (Strong's H426). "H426 - 'elahh (Aramaic) - Strong's Hebrew Lexicon (KJV)." Blue Letter Bible. https://www.blueletterbible.org//lang/lexicon/lexicon.cfm?Strongs=H426&t=KJV

BlueLetterBible.org. "God" (Strong's H433). "H433 - 'elowahh - Strong's Hebrew Lexicon (KJV)." Blue Letter Bible. https://www.blueletterbible.org//lang/lexicon/lexicon.cfm?Strongs=H433&t=KJV

BlueLetterBible.org. "God" (Strong's H3068). "H3068 - Yĕhovah - Strong's Hebrew Lexicon (KJV)." Blue Letter Bible. https://www.blueletterbible.org//lang/lexicon/lexicon.cfm?Strongs=H3068&t=KJV

BlueLetterBible.org. God" (Strong's G2316). "H3068 - Yĕhovah - Strong's Hebrew Lexicon (KJV)." Blue Letter Bible. https://www.blueletterbible.org//lang/lexicon/lexicon.cfm?Strongs=H3068&t=KJV

BlueLetterBible.org. "God" (Strong's G2304). "G2304 - theios - Strong's Greek Lexicon (KJV)." Blue Letter Bible. https://www.blueletterbible.org//lang/lexicon/lexicon.cfm?Strongs=G2304&t=KJV

BlueLetterBible.org. "God" (Strong's G2305). "G2305 - theiotēs - Strong's Greek Lexicon (KJV)." Blue Letter Bible. https://www.blueletterbible.org//lang/lexicon/lexicon.cfm?Strongs=G2305&t=KJV

BlueLetterBible.org. "God" (Strong's H6697). "H6697 - tsuwr - Strong's Hebrew Lexicon (KJV)." Blue Letter Bible. https://www.blueletterbible.org//lang/lexicon/lexicon.cfm?Strongs=H6697&t=KJV

BlueLetterBible.org. "God" (Strong's H3069). "H3069 - Yĕhovih - Strong's

Why Shofars Wail in Scripture and Today—   By Mary A. Bruno, Ph.D.

Hebrew Lexicon (KJV)." Blue Letter Bible. https://www.b

BlueLetterBible.org. "Hallow" (Strong's H6942). "H6942 - qadash - Strong's Hebrew Lexicon (KJV)." Blue Letter Bible. https://www.blueletterbible.org//lang/lexicon/lexicon.cfm?Strongs=H6942&t=KJV

BlueLetterBible.org. "Hazael" (Strong's H2371). "H2371 - Chaza'el - Strong's Hebrew Lexicon (KJV)." Blue Letter Bible. https://www.blueletterbible.org//lang/lexicon/lexicon.cfm?Strongs=H2371&t=KJV

BlueLetterBible.org. "Horn." "KJV Search Results for "horn"." Blue Letter Bible. https://www.blueletterbible.org//search/search.cfm?Criteria=horn&t=KJV#s=s_primary_0_1

BlueLetterBible.org. "Horn" (Strong's H7161 queren). "H7161 - qeren - Strong's Hebrew Lexicon (KJV)." Blue Letter Bible. https://www.blueletterbible.org//lang/lexicon/lexicon.cfm?Strongs=H7161&t=KJV

BlueLetterBible.org. "Horns" (Strong's H7161 queren). "H7161 - qeren - Strong's Hebrew Lexicon (KJV)." Blue Letter Bible. https://www.blueletterbible.org//lang/lexicon/lexicon.cfm?Strongs=H7161&t=KJV

BlueLetterBible.org. "idle" (argos) "G692 - argos - Strong's Greek Lexicon (KJV)." Blue Letter Bible. https://www.blueletterbible.org//lang/Lexicon/Lexicon.cfm?Strongs=G692&t=KJV

BlueLetterBible.org. "Jehovah" (Strong's H3068). "H3068 - Yĕhovah - Strong's Hebrew Lexicon (KJV)." Blue Letter Bible.

https://www.blueletterbible.org//lang/lexicon/lexicon.cfm?Strongs=H3068&t=KJV

BlueLetterBible.org. "Jehovahjireh" (Strong's H3070). "H3070 - Yĕhovah yireh - Strong's Hebrew Lexicon (KJV)." Blue Letter Bible. https://www.blueletterbible.org//lang/lexicon/lexicon.cfm?Strongs=H3070&t=KJV

BlueLetterBible.org. "Jehovahnissi" (Strong's H3071). "H3071 - Yĕhovah nicciy - Strong's Hebrew Lexicon (KJV)." Blue Letter Bible. https://www.blueletterbible.org//lang/lexicon/lexicon.cfm?Strongs=H3071&t=KJV

BlueLetterBible.org. "Jehu" (Strong's H3058). "H3058 - Yehuw' - Strong's Hebrew Lexicon (KJV)." Blue Letter Bible. https://www.blueletterbible.org//lang/lexicon/lexicon.cfm?Strongs=H3058&t=KJV

BlueLetterBible.org. "Joshua" (Strong's H3091). "H3091 - Yĕhowshuwa` - Strong's Hebrew Lexicon (KJV)." Blue Letter Bible. https://www.blueletterbible.org//lang/lexicon/lexicon.cfm?Strongs=H3091&t=KJV

BlueLetterBible.org. "Joshua." "Joshua 1 (KJV) - Now after the death of." Blue Letter Bible. https://www.blueletterbible.org//kjv/jos/1/1/ss1/s_188001

BlueLetterBible.org. "Joyful" (Strong's H7321). "H7321 - ruwa` - Strong's Hebrew Lexicon (KJV)." Blue Letter Bible. https://www.blueletterbible.org//lang/lexicon/lexicon.cfm?Strongs=H7321&t=KJV

Why Shofars Wail in Scripture and Today—   By Mary A. Bruno, Ph.D.

298

BlueLetterBible.org. "Jubile." "KJV Search Results for "Jubile"." Blue Letter Bible.
https://www.blueletterbible.org//search/search.cfm?Criteria=Jubile&t=KJV#s=s_primary_0_1

BlueLetterBible.org. "Jubilee" (Strong's H8643 teruwah). "H8643 - tĕruw`ah - Strong's Hebrew Lexicon (KJV)." Blue Letter Bible.
https://www.blueletterbible.org//lang/lexicon/lexicon.cfm?Strongs=H8643&t=KJV

BlueLetterBible.org. "Judges 3." "Judges 3 (KJV) - Now these are the nations." Blue Letter Bible.
https://www.blueletterbible.org//kjv/jdg/3/1/ss1/s_214001

BlueLetterBible.org. "Lord" (Strong's H113). "H113 - 'adown - Strong's Hebrew Lexicon (KJV)." Blue Letter Bible.
https://www.blueletterbible.org//lang/lexicon/lexicon.cfm?Strongs=H113&t=KJV

BlueLetterBible.org. "Lord" (Strong's H135). "H135 - 'Addan - Strong's Hebrew Lexicon (KJV)." Blue Letter Bible.
https://www.blueletterbible.org//lang/lexicon/lexicon.cfm?Strongs=H135&t=KJV

BlueLetterBible.org. "Lord" Strong's H3050). "H3050 - Yahh - Strong's Hebrew Lexicon (KJV)." Blue Letter Bible.
https://www.blueletterbible.org//lang/lexicon/lexicon.cfm?Strongs=H3050&t=KJV

BlueLetterBible.org. "Lord" (Strong's H1376). "H1376 - gĕbiyr - Strong's Hebrew Lexicon (KJV)." Blue Letter Bible.
https://www.blueletterbible.org//lang/lexicon/lexicon.cfm?Strongs=H1376&t=KJV

BlueLetterBible.org. "Lord" (Strong's G1203). G1203 - despotēs - Strong's Greek Lexicon (KJV)." Blue Letter Bible.
https://www.blueletterbible.org//lang/lexicon/lexicon.cfm?Strongs=G1203&t=KJV

BlueLetterBible.org. "Lord" (Strong's G2962). "G2962 - kyrios - Strong's Greek Lexicon (KJV)." Blue Letter Bible.
https://www.blueletterbible.org//lang/lexicon/lexicon.cfm?Strongs=G2962&t=KJV

BlueLetterBible.org. "Mercy seat." "KJV Search Results for "Mercy" AND "seat"." Blue Letter Bible.
https://www.blueletterbible.org//search/search.cfm?Criteria=Mercy+seat&t=KJV#s=s_primary_0_1

BlueLetterBible.org. "Moses minister." "KJV Search Results for "Moses" AND "minister"." Blue Letter Bible.
https://www.blueletterbible.org//search/search.cfm?Criteria=Moses%27+minister&t=KJV#s=s_primary_0_1

BlueLetterBible.org. "Nathan." "KJV Search Results for "Nathan"." Blue Letter Bible.
https://www.blueletterbible.org//search/search.cfm?Criteria=Nathan&t=KJV#s=s_primary_0_1

BlueLetterBible.org. "Nehemiah 3:1-32 KJV." "Nehemiah 3 (KJV) - Then Eliashib the high priest." Blue Letter Bible.
https://www.blueletterbible.org//kjv/neh/3/1/ss1/s_416001

BlueLetterBible.org. "Oshea" (Strong's H1954). "H1954 - Howshea` - Strong's Hebrew Lexicon (KJV)." Blue Letter Bible.
https://www.blueletterbible.org//lang/lexicon/lexicon.cfm?Strongs=H1954&t=KJV

Why Shofars Wail in Scripture and Today—   By Mary A. Bruno, Ph.D.

BlueLetterBible.org. "Pelethites" (Strong's H6432). "H6432 - Pĕlethiy - Strong's Hebrew Lexicon (KJV)." Blue Letter Bible. https://www.blueletterbible.org//lang/lexicon/lexicon.cfm?Strongs=H6432&t=KJV

BlueLetterBible.org. "Pitch" (Strong's H3724). "KJV Search Results for "Pitch"." Blue Letter Bible. https://www.blueletterbible.org//search/search.cfm?Criteria=Pitch&t=KJV#s=s_primary_0_1

BlueLetterBible.org. "Plagued" (Strong's H6062). "KJV Search Results for "plagued"." Blue Letter Bible. https://www.blueletterbible.org//search/search.cfm?Criteria=plagued&t=KJV#s=s_primary_0_1

BlueLetterBible.org. "Qeren" (Aramaic - Strong's H7162) "H7162 - qeren (Aramaic) - Strong's Hebrew Lexicon (KJV)." Blue Letter Bible. https://www.blueletterbible.org//lang/lexicon/lexicon.cfm?Strongs=H7162&t=KJV

BlueLetterBible.org. "Was rent"(Strong's G4977) in Matthew 27:51. "KJV Search Results for "Was" AND "rent"." Blue Letter Bible. https://www.blueletterbible.org//search/search.cfm?Criteria=Was+rent&t=KJV#s=s_primary_0_1

BlueLetterBible.org. "rhēma" "G4487 - rhēma - Strong's Greek Lexicon (KJV)." Blue Letter Bible. Accessed 9 Jun, 2016. https://www.blueletterbible.org//lang/Lexicon/Lexicon.cfm?Strongs=G4487&t=KJV

BlueLetterBible.org. "Saul." "KJV Search Results for "Saul"." Blue Letter Bible. https://www.blueletterbible.org//search/search.cfm?Criteria=Saul&t=KJV#s=s_primary_0_1

BlueLetterBible.org. "Shophar" (Strong's 7782) "H7782 - showphar - Strong's Hebrew Lexicon (KJV)." Blue Letter Bible. https://www.blueletterbible.org//lang/lexicon/lexicon.cfm?Strongs=H7782&t=KJV

BlueLetterBible.org. "Sing"(Strong's H7442). "KJV Search Results for "Sing"." Blue Letter Bible. https://www.blueletterbible.org//search/search.cfm?Criteria=Sing&t=KJV#s=s_primary_0_1

BlueLetterBible.org. "speak" [1] "G2980 - laleō - Strong's Greek Lexicon (KJV)." Blue Letter Bible. https://www.blueletterbible.org//lang/Lexicon/Lexicon.cfm?Strongs=G2980&t=KJV

BlueLetterBible.org. "Trumpet" "G4537 - salpizō - Strong's Greek Lexicon (KJV)." Blue Letter Bible. https://www.blueletterbible.org//lang/lexicon/lexicon.cfm?Strongs=G4537&t=KJV

BlueLetterBible.org. "Visit" (Strong's H6485) in Ex. 32:34. "KJV Search Results for "Visit"." Blue Letter Bible. https://www.blueletterbible.org//search/search.cfm?Criteria=Visit&t=KJV#s=s_primary_0_1

BlueLetterBible.org. "Water gate" (Strong's H4325). "H4325 - mayim - Strong's Hebrew Lexicon (KJV)." Blue Letter Bible. https://www.blueletterbible.org//lang/lexicon/lexicon.cfm?Strongs=H4325&t=KJV

BlueLetterBible.org. "word" "G2980 - laleō - Strong's Greek Lexicon (KJV)." Blue Letter Bible. https://www.blueletterbible.org//lang/Lexicon/Lexicon.cfm?Strongs=G2980&t=KJV

Why Shofars Wail in Scripture and Today—   By Mary A. Bruno, Ph.D.

300

BlueLetterBible.org. "Yowbel" (Strong's H3104). "H3104 - yowbel - Strong's Hebrew Lexicon (KJV)." Blue Letter Bible. https://www.blueletterbible.org//lang/lexicon/lexicon.cfm?Strongs=H3104&t=KJV

Brix, Shawn. "The Final Sacrifice." Today 61, no. 2, March/April 2011 (Palos Heights, Illinois: ReFrame Media, a division of Back to God Ministries International). http://today.reframemedia.com/archives/the-final-sacrifice-2011-04-22. Used by permission.

Conservapedia.com. "Shofar." www.conservapedia.com/Shofar.

Camp Leroy. News From Camp Leroy, http://campleroy.blogspot.com/

ccmonte.com. Jesus - ccmonte.com, http://www.ccmonte.com/believe/jesus/

chrisreimersblog.com. LET NOT YOUR HEART BE TROUBLED; NEITHER LET IT BE AFRAID .., http://chrisreimersblog.com/2010/04/29/let-not-your-heart-be-troubled-neither-le

codoh.com. Codoh.com | Notebook, http://codoh.com/library/document/3709/

Collin, Stuart. Colin's Corner, http://colinstuart.blogspot.com/

Crivoice.org. "Hebrew Calendar of the Old Testament." http://www.crivoice.org/calendar.html.

Crocket, Kent. Jonah 1 Unwelcome Assignments By Kent Crockett www .., http://storage.cloversites.com/makinglifecountministriesinc/documents/Jonah%201

Deadheroesdontsave.com. Why the Cross? | Dead Heroes Don't Save, http://deadheroesdontsave.com/2013/03/27/why-the-cross/

Ecatholic2000. WHAT TO DO ABOUT TEMPTATION - e-Catholic 2000, http://www.ecatholic2000.com/cts/untitled-704.shtml

fanfiction.net. A Plate of Cookies Chapter 1: Silence is Golden, an .., https://www.fanfiction.net/s/5681123/1/A-Plate-of-Cookies

Gaon, Saadia. "Decoding the Shofar." http://www.myjewishlearning.com/article/decoding-the-shofar/.

Gordon, Iain and Brett Wilton. "Nehemiah's Chapter 3: The gates of spiritual progression." http://jesusplusnothing.com/studies/online/nehem3.htm.

Hilah Cooking. Herbed Compound Butter - Hilah Cooking, http://hilahcooking.com/herbed-compound-butter/

Holy Bible Easy-to-Read Version. Proverbs 7:13-22, Holy Bible: Easy-to-Read Version (ERV .., https://www.bible.com/bible/406/pro.7.13-22.erv#!

Hubpages.com. In Florida how many lies does it take to make a Conspiracy?, http://hubpages.com/politics/In-Florida-how-many-lies-does-it-take-to-make-a-Con

I grandi condottieri (1965) - IMDb, http://www.imdb.com/title/tt0060570/

In Touch. Cease Striving - In Touch, https://www.intouch.org/read/magazine/daily-devotions/cease-striving

ISC Netherlands. PRAYERS FOR THE LORD'S MERCY - ISC Netherlands,

Why Shofars Wail in Scripture and Today—   By Mary A. Bruno, Ph.D.

301

http://www.iscnetherlands.nl/downloads/prayer.doc

jashow.org. How to Become a Christian - how to have eternal life .., https://www.jashow.org/how-to-become-a-christian

Kavanaugh, Ellen. "Yom Teruah: Day of The Shofar Blast." http://www.lightofmashiach.org/yomteruah.html.

Kay, Glenn. "Jewish Wedding Customs and the Bride of Messiah." http://messianicfellowship.50webs.com/wedding.html.

Kim the Career Coach. How to Defeat Your Goliath | Kim the Career Coach, http://kimthecareercoach.com/2013/09/25/how-to-defeat-your-goliath/

lbctruthforlife.org. JOSHUA Joshua s life Before the Conquest - lbctruthforlife.org, http://www.lbctruthforlife.org/wp-content/uploads/2015/06/TRUTH-FOR-LIFE-Joshua

ldsperfectday.blogspot.com. The Perfect Day: Alignment, Part 1 of 6: Face To Dirt, http://ldsperfectday.blogspot.com/2015/09/alignment-part-1-of-3-face-to-dirt.htm

Leroe, Robert. Aaron & Hur sermon, Aaron & Hur sermon by Robert Leroe ..,http://www.sermoncentral.com/sermons/aaron--hur-robert-leroe-sermon-on-encourage

Life From Brooklyn. Live from Brooklyn - blogspot.com, http://buriednova.blogspot.com/

lowpc.org. Restoration of Davidic Praise: 7 Hebrew Words for Praise .., http://lowpc.org/files/media/newsong/2014/4-27 14%20Hebrew%20Words%20for%20Prais

Mirror Match. mirror match - @arcaneadagio, http://arcaneadagio.tumblr.com/

Orthodox Union. "How to Blow the Shofar." http://www.ou.org/news/article/how_to_blow_the_shofar.

Quia. "Rosh Hashanah – The Sounds of the Shofar." http://www.quia.com/cz/14175.html.

Our Daily Bread. Life After Miracles | Our Daily Bread, http://odb.org/2003/02/20/life-after-miracles/

pbs.org. Why Did Christianity Succeed? - Audio Excerpt | From Jesus .., http://www.pbs.org/wgbh/pages/frontline/shows/religion/first/audio.html

PBS. PRESSURES WITHIN AND WITHOUT SERIES: THE MESSAGE OF NEHEMIAH, https://www.pbc.org/system/message_files/7758/4615.pdf

Reluctantentrtainer.com. Making Peach Upside Down Cake for Dinner Guests, http://reluctantentertainer.com/making-peach-upside-down-cake-for-dinner-guests/

Richman, Chaim. "The Meaning Behind the Sounding of the Shofar." http://www.lttn.org/R3_Article2_MeaningOfShofar.htm.

Rjones. "12 Gates of Jerusalem (Part I)." http://www.talkjesus.com/threads/12-gates-of-jerusalem-part-i.17945/.

Rjones, "12 Gates of Jerusalem (Part II)." http://talkjesus.com/devotionals/17951-12-gates-jerusalem-part-ii-html.

Rjones. "12 Gates of Jerusalem (Part III)." http://www.talkjesus.com/threads/12-gates-of-jerusalem-part-iii.17960/.

Why Shofars Wail in Scripture and Today—   By Mary A. Bruno, Ph.D.

302

Rjonehttp://www.talkjesus.com/devotionals/17945-12-gates-jerusalem.html.

R. Jones' articles at http://www.talkjesus.com/devotionals/17945-12-gates-jerusalem.html.

Rejoice Marriage Ministries. YOU WOULD NOT BELIEVE! - Rejoice Marriage Ministries, Inc, https://www.rejoiceministries.org/charlyne-cares-daily-devotional/2010/11/09/you

www.salon.com. "The definition of insanity" is the most overused cliché .., http://www.salon.com/2013/08/06/the definition of insanity is the most ove rused

seekinggodslove.com. FullArticle - Seeking God's Love, http://www.seekinggodslove.com/Articles/FullArticle/

sermoncentral.com. Avoiding the Mistake of Materialism sermon page 2 .., http://www.sermoncentral.com/sermons/avoiding-the-mistake-of-materialism-david-o

sermoncentral.com. Seeing God's Glory sermon page 2, Seeing God's Glory .., http://www.sermoncentral.com/sermons/seeing-gods-glory-david-elvery-sermon-on-go

sermonoutlines.org. Praise Him, Praise Him - SERMON OUTLINES, http://www.sermonoutlines.org/Owen%20Sermons/Psalms/(OT%2019)%20Psalm%20100%20-%

Shofar Be Tzion Ministries. "Learn the Shofar." http://www.shofarbetzion.com/learn_ofar.htm. Send mail to diane.chester@sbcglobal.net with questions or comments about this website

Shofar Be Tzion Ministries. "Shofar Scriptures." Send mail to diane. chester@sbcglobal.net with questions or comments about this website (http://www.shofarbetzion.com/).

Shofar.co. "Shofar News/Articles." http://www.shofar.co/?item=90&section=170.Shofar-Sounders.com.

"Frequently Asked Questions." http://www.shofarsounders.com/sh_scents2.html.

Shulman, Mark. "Blasts from the Past, Present and Future: Many Horns, One Voice." http://beitsimcha.org/demoSite/s_ser/Mark-Blasts.asp.

Smith, Rev. Greg. Love the Word: When Jesus Stopped By for a Bier, http://revgregsmith.blogspot.com/2010/06/when-jesus-stopped-by-for-bier.html

Studylight.org. NLV - Joshua 5:13 - When Joshua was by Jericho, he looked .., https://www.studylight.org/bible/nlv/joshua/5-13.html

The New York Times. Voting Machines - Elections - Ballots - Politics - The New .., http://www.nytimes.com/2008/01/06/magazine/06Vote-t.html

Thepostgame.com. U.S. Men's And Women's Soccer Teams Are Fighting, And .., http://www.thepostgame.com/daily-take/201604/americas-mens-and-womens-soccer-tea

The Rain. APPENDIX 59. THE TWELVE GATES OF JERUSALEM (NEH. CHS. 3 .., http://www.therain.org/appendixes/app59.html

Truth Seekers Ministries - The Potter's House: A lesson on .., http://www.truthseekersministries.org

Why Shofars Wail in Scripture and Today—   By Mary A. Bruno, Ph.D.

/index.php/8-general-articles/49-the-potter
ucg.org.

Examining Ourselves Before the Passover - ucg.org,
http://www.ucg.org/sermons/examining-ourselves-before-the-passover

W., Lisa. "Feast of Trumpets," blog entry, September 2, 2007.
http://followingtheancientpaths.wordpress.com/2007/09/02/yomteruah-2007/.

White Estate.
Patriarchs and Prophets - White ® Estate,http://www.whiteestate.org/books/pp/pp45.html

Wikihow.com. "How to Blow a Shofar." http://www.wikihow.com/Blow-a-Shofar.

Wikipedia. "Liberty Bell." http://en.wikipedia.org/wiki/Liberty_Bell.

Wikipedia. Va'eira - Wikipedia, the free encyclopedia,
https://en.wikipedia.org/wiki/Va%27eira

Wikipedia. "Shofar." http://en.wikipedia.org/wiki/shofar.

Williams, Kevin. "The Call of the Shofar." http://www.pneumafoundation.org/article.jsp?article=article_kw02.xml.

Wordpress.com. Evangelicals in the Episcopal Church | Refreshing ..,
https://barnabasproject.wordpress.com

Wordpress.com. when Joshua was first mentioned in Bible « THE CHURCH OF ..,https://churchofphiladelphia.wordpress.com/tag/when-joshua-was-first-mentioned-i

Wordpress.com. The Word Made Flesh: Real Life Meets Real Truth | Just ..,
https://twmf.wordpress.com/

van Zuijlekom, Denijs. "The Twelve Gates of Jerusalem." http://www.levendwater.org/companion/append59.html.

Yahoo Answers. Do u think the world wil end by 2012? | Yahoo Answers,
https://answers.yahoo.com/question/index?qid=20100216085324AAJkDrn

Yahoo Answers. Those who dont believe in God? | Yahoo Answers,
https://answers.yahoo.com/question/index?qid=20080903210724AAqpe5b

Yahoo Answers. Those who dont believe in God? | Yahoo Answers,
https://answers.yahoo.com/question/index?qid=20080903210724AAqpe5b

Why Shofars Wail in Scripture and Today—   By Mary A. Bruno, Ph.D.

304

Index

Why Shofars Wail in Scripture and Today—   By Mary A. Bruno, Ph.D.

Why Shofars Wail in Scripture and Today—   By Mary A. Bruno, Ph.D.

306

F

G

Why Shofars Wail in Scripture and Today—   By Mary A. Bruno, Ph.D.

307

Why Shofars Wail in Scripture and Today—   By Mary A. Bruno, Ph.D.

Why Shofars Wail in Scripture and Today—   By Mary A. Bruno, Ph.D.

310

Why Shofars Wail in Scripture and Today—   By Mary A. Bruno, Ph.D.

Why Shofars Wail in Scripture and Today—   By Mary A. Bruno, Ph.D.

Why Shofars Wail in Scripture and Today—   By Mary A. Bruno, Ph.D.

313

Y

Z

Why Shofars Wail in Scripture and Today—   By Mary A. Bruno, Ph.D.

314

Dare to Write a Review!

May God bless you for reading *Why Shofars Wail in Scripture and Today—The Exciting Stories and Miracles!* by Mary A. Bruno, Ph.D. If you have enjoyed this book, she would like to see your review on www.Amazon.com, and on ministrylit.com. She reads every one.

As Barbara Anne Waite,[127] author of *Elsie's Mountain*, once mentioned, "Many people are unaware of the enormous boost that even a few words from a reader can mean for an author. Every review helps, no matter how brief."

Your notes will not only bless Dr. Bruno and others, but may help to boost sales. Your review could even help someone to find peace with God, and to lift up his or her voice as a shofar.

How To Write A Review—It's Easy!

1. Type, www.amazon.com on your browser.
2. Type, *Mary A. Bruno*, Ph.D., on Amazon's search bar, and then click on the magnifying glass.
3. Click on the book's title: *Why Shofars Wail in Scripture and Today—The Exciting Stories and Miracles!*
4. Click on the *customer reviews*, (blue writing), by the yellow rating stars (next to a picture of the book).
5. Read a few of the reviews to get an idea of what goes into one.
6. Click on the (gray) *Write A Customer Review* box, and then complete the *Sign In* box that pops up.
7. Dare to wax eloquent and compose your review with your unique observations and style.

For a writer, knowing that a reader has taken the time to compose a brief comment is equal to having received an extremely generous tip. Thank you!

---

[127] www.barbaraannewaite.com

Why Shofars Wail in Scripture and Today—   By Mary A. Bruno, Ph.D.

315

And you shall consecrate the fiftieth year, and proclaim liberty throughout *all* the land to all its inhabitants. It shall be a Jubilee for you; and each of you shall return to his possession, and each of you shall return to his family.

— Leviticus 25:10

Color photos: Photos from this book (and those not printed) are viewable online at www.ministrylit.com.

Why Shofars Wail in Scripture and Today—   By Mary A. Bruno, Ph.D.

316

How to Order This Book

Order *Why Shofars Wail in Scripture and Today—The Exciting Stories and Miracles!* Authored by Mary A. Bruno, Ph.D.

See Dr. Bruno's writings, at <u>www.ministrylit.com</u>. Her books are also available at <u>www.amazon.com</u>.

Or write: **Dr. Mary A. Bruno**
P.O. Box 2107
Vista, CA 92085-2107 United States of America

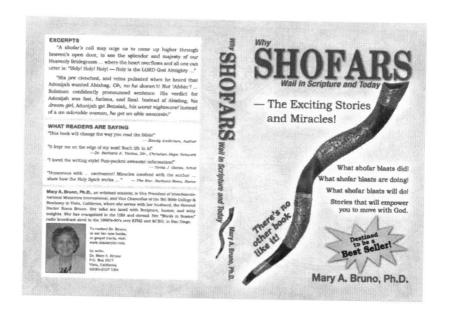

ISBN: 9781533383020

This book is printed on 322 pages of 6"x 9" white paper.

Also available in LARGE PRINT, and eBook/Kindle. The Audio Version is coming soon.

Why Shofars Wail in Scripture and Today— By Mary A. Bruno, Ph.D.

How to Order This LARGE PRINT Book

Order Why Shofars Wail in Scripture and Today **(LARGE PRINT)** —The Exciting Stories and Miracles! By Mary A. Bruno, Ph.D.

See Dr. Bruno's writings, at **www.ministrylit.com**. Her books are also available at **www.amazon.com**.

Or write: **Dr. Mary A. Bruno**
P.O. Box 2107
Vista, CA 92085-2107 United States of America

ISBN: 978-1539406891
This book is printed on 630 pages of 8 ½" x 11" white paper.

Easy-to-read print with lots of white space between the lines! (Sample of print)

Why Shofars Wail in Scripture and Today— By Mary A. Bruno, Ph.D.

How to Order The Study Guide/Journal

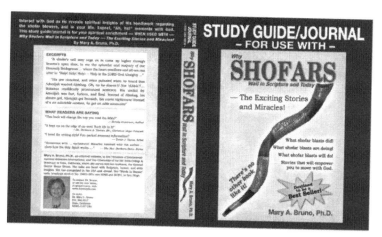

Want to learn more from your shofar study?

Discover God's long-range plans for the shofar blowers and people affected by their ministry. Learn how God prepared, helped and guided them, and led you to where you are today.

If new to guided study and journaling, this is a good place to start. God will remind you of places in His Word that will flood your soul with truth that begs to go in your notes. Those sacred *nuggets*/Journal entries will become your love gifts from God and a treasure of Scripture and wisdom for reflection and teaching.

God intends more for you regarding these books, than a few hours of reading enjoyment. You may never be the same!

This Study Guide/Journal is Ideal for group study and/or personal spiritual enrichment! Enjoy jotting down what God teaches you—on 320 8"x10" white pages—with spacious lines that are ready to document your answers, insights, comments, lessons learned, prayer requests/potential miracles, and notes.

Order Today: *STUDY GUIDE/JOURNAL—FOR USE WITH— Why Shofars Wail in Scripture and Today—The Exciting Stories and Miracles!* ISBN: 9781535012584 .
www.ministrylit.com and www.amazon.com. Also available as: eBook/Kindle.

Why Shofars Wail in Scripture and Today—   By Mary A. Bruno, Ph.D.

Why Shofars Wail in Scripture and Today—   By Mary A. Bruno, Ph.D.

320

For Speaking Engagements

Visit the website at www.ministrylit.com.
Email: drmaryabruno@ministrylit.com
Or write:

Dr. Mary A. Bruno
P.O. Box 2107
Vista, CA 92085-2107 USA

More by Dr. Mary A. Bruno:

1. *STUDY GUIDE/JOURNAL*—FOR USE WITH—*Why Shofars Wail in Scripture and Today—The Exciting Stories and Miracles!*
2. *What to Consider When Making Important Decisions (A Workbook for Making Wholesome Choices).* Coming Soon!

Watch for Dr. Bruno's new books and other ministry materials at, www.ministrylit.com and www.amazon.com.

Personal Evangelism Tracts:

Keep a stack of Dr. Bruno's uplifting tracts on hand to share. They may become God's Words in season for a cashier, food server, person at a bus stop or waiting room. Someone may be in crisis or just need to hear an encouraging word from God.

"Is My Heart Right With God?" (How to have peace with God)
"The Shofar Calls" (What they mean. How to have shofar impact.)
"Remember Me" (Faith strengtheners for crisis times)
"When Pressures Seem Unbearable" (Victory at a breaking point)

Why Shofars Wail in Scripture and Today—   By Mary A. Bruno, Ph.D.

321

V119-123016

Why Shofars Wail in Scripture and Today—   By Mary A. Bruno, Ph.D.

Made in the USA
Middletown, DE
30 December 2016